GOETHE:

Wisdom and Experience

GOETHE:

Wisdom and Experience

Selections by
LUDWIG CURTIUS

Translated and edited,
with an introduction, by
HERMANN J. WEIGAND

FREDERICK UNGAR PUBLISHING CO.
NEW YORK

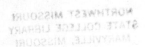

Printed in the United States of America

Library of Congress Catalog Card No. 64-25551

338
N41g

Contents

CONTENTS

CONTENTS

CONTENTS

INTRODUCTION

GOETHE is the man of most commanding stature ever to have issued from the German people. He has been hailed, not by Germans alone, as the most universally gifted individual ever to be born into this world. Few men have that sweep of perspective and that intimate knowledge of the subject which warrant authoritative pronouncements of so general a nature. A more modest judgment stands on rather firm ground, however, in saying at least this: No comparably gifted individual has striven like Goethe to make all his talents tell; no man has been conscious to a like degree of feeling himself to be an epitome of civilized mankind; no other man has left so full and detailed a record of a career keyed to the aim of universality. Napoleon may have caught something of this essence of Goethe's spirit when he remarked in the course of that famous interview: "Voilà un homme!"

To say the same thing in another way: Goethe's life exhibits two dominating aspects—genius and responsibility. Goethe's youth is one incredible, uninterrupted exhibition of genius, prodigal in its effusions, profligate in its unconcern for their fate. The maturing process brings responsibility to the fore. Genius has not evaporated, but it is bridled by a sense of responsibility. There is a close interpenetration between the two. Aware of his inexhaustible fund of giftedness, Goethe comes to think of his gifts as a trust to be developed. No item of his endowment must be lost or neglected; each is to be cultivated, rather, to the ultimate limit of its potentialities. As he conceived

7

the demigod Prometheus taking the clay in his hands and fashioning out of it the image of man, so he focuses upon the individual aptitudes he has discovered in himself; he takes them in hand to form them and bring to fulfillment the latent promise of each. For this exacting task and aim Goethe has the word *Bildung*. Simultaneous, not excessive development is his concern. The whole is to be an organism exhibiting all its functioning members in harmonious balance. But there is a second consideration which encroaches upon the free play of genius: social responsibility. Rather despite himself Goethe is made aware of his individual self in relation to the community with which his lot has been cast. By a turn of fate rather than as the result of personal ambition, Goethe found himself in a position of authority, power and influence. The bonds were not of his choosing, but the implications could not be ignored.

The acquaintance of young Goethe's genius can be made in a very delightful way by reading *Dichtung und Wahrheit,* the autobiography, which takes the whole story somewhat beyond the end of his twenty-sixth year to the point where the ducal carriage is waiting to take him to Weimar on a visit destined to expand into lifetime residence. It includes the great events of his childhood and adolescence, the occupation of his native Frankfurt by the French during the Seven Years' War involving the billeting of the King's deputy upon the Goethe household, and a few years later the coronation of Joseph the Second as head of the Holy Roman Empire of the German Nation with all the pomp that the Free City of Frankfurt, proud of its long tradition as the site of such august festivities, could muster. It includes the account of his three years at the University of Leipzig in an atmosphere of rococo culture and the year at the University of Strassburg, where Herder transmitted to him the new naturalistic anticonventional outlook fathered by Rousseau and destined to revolutionize the intellectual and emotional climate of successive generations. It includes the famous Sesenheim idyll as it does the sojourn at Wetzlar that was to supply the material for *Werther* which gave Goethe the status of a European celebrity and involved a sensational success never again equaled during his literary life. It includes several intervals spent at home with more entanglements of the heart, a trip down the Rhine and another to Switzerland. And it includes a full account of the writing of his *Götz,* and of a host of other works in the making. Some of them, like *Prometheus,* never got beyond the second act, while *Faust* occupied Goethe intermittently over sixty years.

In this autobiography the genius of young Goethe is omnipresent, but it is not his genius in the raw; it is filtered through the medium of a mind that has moved three and a half decades beyond the end point of that glorious and turbulent epoch of free adventure. There is a perspective about the biography which was not a part of that life as it was lived, a perspective which shows a great awareness of responsibility toward his own self and toward his fellows. If we want to get the impact of his genius in the raw there is no way but to read that documentary collection of his youthful works and letters which fills the six volumes of *Der Junge Goethe,* and if we have the patience to begin with his *Juvenilia* and look at the samples of calligraphy submitted by the seven-and-a-half-year-old Wolfgang in a prize contest and pore over his schoolboy exercises in Latin and Greek and follow these up with his early letters which present a fantastic medley of prose and verse in German, English, French, Italian, and even Yiddish, we find ourselves on the threshold of an astounding wealth of imaginative production. And we must not overlook the abundant testimony contained in letters by a host of bosom friends and more casual acquaintances to the effect that they were as we would say "crazy about Goethe," that they saw in him a unique human phenomenon, a prodigy and a marvel. There was no catching up with his lightning-like changes of mood. He knew of this faculty and repeatedly spoke of himself as a chameleon. They were captivated as well as bewildered, men and women alike. Only Herder's irritable humor rebelled against this volatility and tried to disparage it when he said that Goethe had the brain of a sparrow. Fritz Jacobi had a lively pique against Goethe for circulating a cruel skit about him and his brother. But the moment he laid eyes on Goethe—in July 1774—his grudge melted away; he retracted the warning he had addressed to Wieland and wrote:

> The more I think it over, the more impossible it becomes to convey to one who has not seen Goethe or heard Goethe, any comprehensible idea of this extraordinary creature of God. To quote Heinse, Goethe is genius from top to toe. He is possessed: there is hardly a situation in which he is free to act at will. Spending an hour with him is enough to make it seem ridiculous in the highest degree to expect of him that he should think and act in a manner different from what he does.

A year and a half later, it was Wieland's turn to duplicate this experience, despite more serious provocation, and to express it in verse that revolved about the idea: Never in God's world have we seen a son of man to match him—

> *So hat sich nie in Gottes Welt*
> *Ein Menschensohn uns dargestellt.*

In 1780 Goethe himself could write to Frau von Stein:

> The greatest gift for which I thank the gods is that the speed and variety of my thoughts allows me to

split up such a serene day into a million parts and turn it into an eternity in miniature.

To take a long jump, it is fitting to recall some lines to the same effect dictated by Goethe to his friend Zelter during the last year of his life; but to the versatility of youth there is superadded a sense of majesty and mass that warrants his contemplating of his inner world as another solar system:

> You see things are taking their accustomed course with me. Of the hundred-odd matters that interest me one always constitutes itself in the focus as the major planet. Meanwhile the remaining what-have-you of my life keeps rotating like so many moons showing as many phases, until one or the other succeeds in its turn in moving into full focus.

(This image involves a doubling of the personality—the vital energy, the *entelechy*, as the source of light in the center, and consciousness as a lone eye somewhere outside the system.)

The marriage of genius and responsibility was not achieved without friction. By and large, to be sure, Goethe viewed all of nature, both its inorganic and its organic manifestations, as governed by law. It simply did not make sense to him to think of tampering with the continuity of natural processes in any way. In this he saw eye to eye with Spinoza, who confirmed his view that God and Nature are one and that nothing can be conceived as not emanating from the one divine source. And this necessary evolution of the present out of the past included, of course, the unfolding of his own personality from moment to moment. The idea of repudiating any feature of his own past was thus constitutionally alien to him. There was no room for recrimination or remorse in his philosophy. On the other hand the extreme high points of youthful ecstatic intensity were not subject to recapture by the memory at will. The mature man was able to experience a sense of identity with his youth in only a limited way. Thus the Titanism of the divinely glorious *Wanderers Sturmlied* no longer throbbed in his pulse when he wrote the *Autobiography*. Half-nonsense, *Halbunsinn*, he apologetically called it. In setting it for print he broke up one of its lines into three and ruined a rhythmical unit of superb momentum. And in the case of another great hymn of this period, *An Schwager Kronos*, he jettisoned the very spirit of the poem by substituting a tame and modest conclusion for the original climax of self-conscious princely triumph.

There can be no doubt about it: Goethe was embarrassed by this and similar effusions of his youth. As a mature man he had come to realize his limits; he had redefined his conception of greatness in a way to exclude the noisy and tempestuous, the abrupt and erratic—in nature and in art as well. He felt called upon, moreover, to guide a succeeding literary generation partly by teaching, more by his own example, in the direction he was now espousing. Now the indiscretions of his youth were coming home to roost. Like the Cumaean Sibyl who wrote down her prophecies on loose leaves to be whirled about by the winds, Goethe had been prodigal with autograph copies of his youthful productions. They passed, repeatedly copied, from hand to hand, they even found their way into print without his authorization. Thus the dramatic monologue of his *Prometheus* made its first public appearance without mention of Goethe in a book of Fritz Jacobi's more than a decade after Goethe had abandoned the *Prometheus* theme. In Jacobi's book the poem was assigned a key role in a religious controversy. Goethe found the idea distasteful that his poem should be made to serve as a weapon in an ideological battle. Such use involved a

sharp distortion of the spirit that it expressed. The poem
breathed a mood of defiance to supernatural authority; it
contained transparent avowals of the fact that it was the
projection of one of Goethe's own moods. But in this setting the fact was lost sight of that it was essentially the
mood of Prometheus, the traditional arch rebel challeng-
ing the Olympian gods. When Goethe included the poem
in his collected works he placed it next to his *Ganymed*—
those verses that throb with an equally ecstatic abandon
to all-loving Nature and are climaxed by a mystic merg-
ing of his person with the all-loving Father. He was
right in pairing the two; for these moods by no means ex-
cluded one another. They existed in him side by side, they
did not feature successive epochs of his development.
They are rather two equally valid aspects of a personality of sufficient amplitude to harbor both states at once.
They are representative of a set of vital contradictions in
which Goethe's life abounds. (Many instances of this will
confront the reader in the present volume.) As polar opposites they are in a sense identical twin creations. In
their juxtaposition they exemplify that sense of continuity
so peculiar to Goethe. Most unlike Nietzsche, he never
recoiled against his own past. As he was instinctively
averse to violence and revolution in human society, he re-
pudiated them as primary agencies in evolving nature
and in the microcosm of his own self. He might err and
flounder, he was constantly finding himself entangled in
situations that by their momentum carried him in directions far from the path he had envisaged. He was convinced none the less that his vital inner drive and the
world of circumstance were coöperating to a good end.
That law of life which the Lord so confidently formulates
as he contemplates Faust—

> *Ein guter Mensch in seinem dunklen Drange*
> *Ist sich des rechten Weges wohl bewusst . . .*

(A good man, darkly groping, has an inner sense of direction to guide him), is in reality an article of faith with application to his own person. Even more vigorous is this affirmation in such lines as

> *Jeder Weg zum rechten Zwecke*
> *Ist auch recht in jeder Strecke . . .*

(Every road to a right end is right too in its every stretch.) Just as in nature everything is necessarily conditioned at any given moment, so in his own development every thought and act is seen to be functioning as part of an integrated pattern, promoting his development, his *Bildung,* via polarity and *Steigerung.*

In view of this highly developed sense of continuity it comes as a great surprise that Goethe was forever revising and altering the productions of an earlier stage of his career. They had been right and necessary as they issued forth, but curiously enough Goethe felt the urge to harmonize them with the progress and insight meanwhile achieved. Theoretically he knew and expressed the fact that a work of genius cannot be improved by subsequent fussing and emendation after the original creative impulse has spent itself. Yet he recast his *Götz* and his *Werther,* to mention only two of a host of conspicuous instances, many years after they had appeared in print and stamped themselves upon the public mind. (The slow growth of works like *Egmont* and *Tasso,* the growth of *Faust* by lifelong accretion, the multiple revisions of *Iphigenie* before publication, and the fresh start that transformed Wilhelm Meister's *Mission* (as regards the theater) into the *Apprenticeship* are in a different class: here the creative impulse, inhibited and dormant over long stretches of time, had not run its full course.) It would seem that Goethe's hereditary *Anlage* (disposition) was the principal factor to account for his need to keep fussing over works long since cast off. In his youth those features of his personality were the first to develop which can be correlated with his mother's exuberant temperament, while as he grew older the disposition inherited from his father, his pedantic sense of order, his collector's drive, his finickiness, came more and more to the fore.

As to the time when Goethe's sense of responsibility began to encroach on the free expression of his genius it is not possible to be too precise. His thirtieth birthday is an impressive date line, to be sure. On that day Carl August, Duke of Weimar, conferred upon him the title of Privy Counsellor, *Geheimer Rat,* an honor usually reserved for a much more advanced stage of a man's career. Goethe was deeply impressed. He wrote of the event rather solemnly to Frau von Stein:

> It amazes me to think of it. It is like a dream, finding myself elevated at the age of thirty to the highest honor that can fall to the lot of a commoner in Germany.

This was somewhat less than four years after his arrival in Weimar. He had come as an invited guest for an indeterminate stay, under unpredictable conditions. Carl August, eighteen years old, had just been handed the reins of government by the Regent-Mother, Anna Amalia, then only thirty-six herself. She had first arranged his marriage to a suitable princess without there being any real attachment between the couple. Beside the fact of a new, untried régime, the life of the court had a provisional aspect. A fire had destroyed the ducal residence, and the ducal household, which included a younger prince, was dispersed in various temporary quarters. There was no common center of interest holding the members of the ducal family together. Each formed a circle of his own, and Goethe found himself in a cross fire of conflicting interests. Goethe was there as the young Duke's favorite. It was natural for many of the others to look upon him as an adventurer and an interloper. But he had the unbounded confidence and admiration of Carl August who hoped to sow his wild oats in company with the outstanding celebrity of the Storm and Stress age. Goethe's presence in Weimar was a magnet that drew a variety of his friends to the scene, Lenz and Klinger among them. He began to realize that his relation to the impressionable and talented but wayward young ruler presented him with a task.

Here was an opportunity to make his influence count. Goethe worked to make the young ruler take his position seriously, in line with the enlightened absolutism of the age which had its most shining exemplar in Frederick the Great. He began to interest himself in the functions of government, and before he knew it he was initiated into the branches of the administration one by one. When the Duke assigned him a seat in his Privy Council a crisis was precipitated threatening the resignation of the Council's president, von Fritsch. It is notorious, Fritsch wrote to the Duke, that Dr. Goethe is unfitted for any responsibility. He soon proved the contrary. In a short time he was administering the department of public works, including construction, highway building, the fire department and mining. This last was his pet hobby. Despite great efforts lavished upon it by Goethe in the form of consultations, reports and inspection trips it proved impossible to put the Ilmenau mines into profitable operation again. But he had no reason to regret the time thus spent. This activity aroused his interest in rocks and minerals, in earth features and the forces that govern their formation. It taught him to observe natural phenomena with detachment and to correlate and interpret his various observations. It laid the foundation for his lifelong interest in the infant science of historical geology.

In addition to all his administrative duties—they included diplomatic missions too, for Saxe-Weimar, though tiny, was a sovereign state and Carl August was not without political and military ambition—Goethe was expected to function as *maître de plaisir,* to direct amateur performances acted by the members of the court, to establish a regular theater and take charge of all its affairs, to devise masks and pageants, and to write operettas. The burden of his many obligations, all of which he took seriously, made him mature more rapidly than would have been the case had he been free to follow his own devices. The poem *Ilmenau,* written in 1783, marks a milestone in his coming of age. Addressed to his Duke, it is a grave recapitulation of their nearly eight years of intimate association. It draws a truthful and unflattering portrait of the young ruler's unmanageable temperament; it records how Goethe watched and worried over him, and how he was alarmed and dismayed to find his message of courage and unconventionality distorted into a vindication of license. Reproach mingles with self-justification when he says:

> *Ich brachte reines Feuer vom Altare,*
> *Was ich entzündet, ist nicht reine Flamme . . .*

(I brought pure fire from the altar. But the flame that I kindled is not pure.) And the poem culminates in an exhortation to the Duke to practice self-restraint and to employ his high privilege in the service of his people. In a similar way the *Zueignung* (Dedication), a year later, adds up the balance sheet of his own career: the erstwhile *Übermensch* who fancied the truth to be his individual monopoly has learned the sobering lesson of his limitations; his perspective has altered; all he wants now is to be a man among men, and use his talents in brotherly coöperation with like-minded friends.

All in all, the first eleven years of Goethe's life in Weimar, ending with his abrupt and secret departure for Italy, represent a period of accumulating strain and self-discipline without a counterpart in Goethe's life. Judged by standards of high resolve and idealistic fervor this was the noblest epoch of his career. Never before or after did he strive with comparable zeal for self-purification. *Iphigenie,* the purest exemplar of ideal humanity among Goethe's creations, is the shining symbol of this period. And it is the period of the most ideally attuned love relationship in Goethe's life, a love in part heavenly bliss and in part the cleansing fire of purgatory.

As everyone knows, immediately on his arrival in Weimar Goethe fell in love with Charlotte von Stein, mother of seven children and nearly eight years his senior. He had completed his twenty-sixth year, she was nearly thirty-four. To Goethe's eyes, she was surrounded by an ethereal aura. Decorous and calm, she was deeply distrustful of the life of the senses, in sharp contrast to his own excess of vitality. No doubt this aloofness added to her fascination for a man accustomed to regard himself as irresistible. Goethe attached himself to her with a steadfastness that belied his early reputation as a heartbreaker, and after years of the most zealous and ardent wooing—his "novitiate" he significantly calls them—he succeeded in breaking through her defenses. During those eleven years he wrote her thousands of notes and letters—in large part simple unstudied improvisations of a few lines that are almost inexhaustible in the variations with which a caress is put into words. In a manner and to a degree defying analysis her temperament compensated his. He confided his every thought to her. He derived inspiration from her existence, and he projected her idealized image into all the major works he conceived while under her influence. Being so sedulous in his attentions, he ended up by making himself indispensable to her. In due time Goethe dimly came to realize by degrees that he had set a pattern that was bound to exert an ever increasing strain on his constitution. He had nurtured a demand that assumed an ominous cast the moment he felt a slackening of spontaneity. The affair was pitched in so high a key that the strain was eventually bound to exhaust the active party in the relation. The remarkable thing is not that the bond finally snapped but rather that it held for so long. A sense of impending total nervous collapse, felt but scarcely admitted to himself, caused Goethe to make secret preparation for his flight. When he was gone and a gap of many weeks ensued without letters, she felt bereft and her heart contracted. When Goethe realized what had happened, he made himself wretched, grieving and weeping and imploring her to restore her heart to him. This self-torment was the inevitable price he had to pay for his liberation. But thanks to the fund of his vitality Goethe experienced a "rebirth" in Italy. He made his adjustment to a new life. When he returned after two years' absence it was for him not a case of re-establishing the old relationship but of trying to salvage a part of it and put it on a new and sounder basis that would not again threaten the integrity of his personality. Having no corresponding resources, Charlotte was unable to make a similar readjustment. While Goethe never uttered a disparaging word about her to anyone— this was to his credit, but it was no more than an obligation of chivalry—she wore herself out in recrimination and spiteful rancor. To take her to task for this, as some biographers have done, to spread out the record of her human-all-too-human resentment against her one-time lover, to gloat over the contrast between the alleged former mask of the woman and her petty and spiteful real self, is to show a most ungenerous lack of imagination.

The cynic's approach moreover reflects no credit on Goethe if we are to think of him as a fool who could be hoodwinked so long by an ordinary goose posing as an Egeria. We take satisfaction, rather, in the fact that after some years of complete estrangement the two came to be on speaking terms again and that Goethe's kindness and long-suffering patience eventually succeeded in effecting a genuine reconciliation. Charlotte's last letter to Goethe, a birthday greeting dated August 28, 1826, written by the almost mummified old lady of eighty-four, reads as follows:

> Happiness and blessings a thousandfold on this day. May the guardian spirits assembled in heavenly parliament ordain that everything lovable and good continue to be yours, beloved friend, with all hope for the future and absence of fear. But as for me, my honored friend, I solicit your liberal good will for the short remaining span of my life's journey.

The stilted and sclerotic phrasing parallels the aloofness of Goethe's own late epistolary style, but the quaver of the voice reflects a genuine courtesy of the heart. He replied the next day with some general verses of acknowledgment to which he added this personal postscript:

> By rights, my dearest, the enclosed poem should end as follows: To see sympathy and love of those living in close neighborly contact endure over such a protracted span of time is the highest boon vouchsafed to man.

Goethe came back from Italy a changed man. The resolute act of his carefully prepared, secret departure from Germany had cured him of the creeping anxiety neurosis that was poisoning his life. His affair with Frau von Stein had been carried on with the most punctilious

regard for her reputation, an exhausting feat in the lime-
light of the court in a small town of 6,500 people rife with
gossip. He came back determined to put the responsibility he owed to himself above all other considerations.
He was resolved to live a healthy life as a son of the earth
in quiet disregard of convention. He was not going to reform the world, but on his part he wanted to be let alone.
Within a few weeks after his return he took up with a
simple, almost illiterate girl of twenty-two, Christiane
Vulpius, and the following year when she was pregnant
with a child of his, he took her into his household. His
son August, the only child of Goethe to survive to manhood, was born on Christmas day 1789, but it was not
until 1806 that Goethe legalized their union, their marriage of conscience, *Gewissensehe*, as he called it. He did
not want to challenge society, he simply wanted to ignore
it. In the nature of things society was outraged, and the
friends whom Goethe saw in his house took absolutely
no notice of Christiane's existence. Difficult as the situation was for all parties, Goethe felt compensated by what
the relation offered him. He had drifted into it without
plan and he was content to let it develop without plan.
He loved Christiane with a sensuous animal passion,
totally different from that inspired by Frau von Stein.
Charlotte von Stein had been a living exemplar of the
"Beautiful Soul" as characterized by Schiller in his essay
on *Grace and Dignity*. She had personified that grace
which in everyone of its unconscious movements reflects
a morality that had become second nature. Whereas
beauty is a natural phenomenon, grace lies outside of nature's competence, Schiller had maintained; an animal
can be beautiful but never graceful because grace is
moral freedom translated into visible terms and moral
freedom is a prerogative of man. Schiller's treatise, his
first great act of assimilation of Kant's moral philosophy,

21

appeared a few years after Goethe had formed his tie with Christiane. How Goethe flushed with resentment at the disparagement of nature involved in this essay! Was not Christiane an animal, a soft, warm, purring, caressable kitten? For concepts like moral freedom she would have had only a blank stare. She was artless and untutored; she had had precious little of moral or any other education. But that she was graceful in the individual movements of her warm sensuous curves Goethe would have maintained against a world of philosophers. To the world she was a common woman of rather gross tastes, as evidenced by her figure in later years, but for Goethe her temperament had that indefinable quality which spelled relaxation to his mind. She continued somehow to have this appeal for him to her death, in 1816. Some of Goethe's tenderest lyrics like *Gefunden* (Ich ging im Walde so für mich hin) and *Frühling übers Jahr* owe their existence to Christiane. And, remarkable to note, they date from the last years of Christiane's life. *Gefunden* was written in 1813, and *Frühling übers Jahr,* in praise of his beloved's charms which turn all the seasons of the year into one glorious springtime, dates from a few months before her death. Goethe's sense of bereavement at her death is attested by the simplicity of the closing lines of a letter to his friend, the musician Zelter:

> When I announce to you, staunch tried son of earth, that my dear little wife has left us these days you know what it means. June 8, 1816.

Zelter knew indeed; for their friendship had suddenly swung into the orbit of closest intimacy, on Goethe's initiative, four years earlier after Zelter had informed Goethe of his beloved stepson's suicide.

In the early years of his association with Christiane Goethe lived close to earth. He was beginning to feel himself a man of substance in every sense of the word. His economy expanded, he took on weight. He relished creature comforts in a new way. His manner had become resolute and virile. In his poetry he celebrated the pleasures of sex love in frankly pagan style without recourse to innuendo—not love as sentiment, but love as recreation. The classical form of the distich in which he cast his *Römische Elegien* underlined the absence of anything suggestive of romantic longing. (The title Elegy is used in the classical sense as a designation of form, not of content.) In those of the Elegies which Goethe released to the public, Eros is the god who holds sway. In those which he circulated among a few intimates, Priapus is accorded a place of honor. In this his most un-Christian period, Goethe consolidates his status as a creature of sense in a world of substantial, finite values.

This period coincides with the outbreak of the French Revolution, setting off an era of turmoil and confusion in the political world that lasted more than fifteen years and saw the rise and fall of Napoleon and the awakening of German nationalism. Goethe was not insensitive to the abuses of the old order at home and abroad. In his own confined sphere the poverty of the underprivileged mass had drawn from him expressions of deep concern, even of despair—*die Verdammnis dass wir des Landes Mark verzehren, lässt keinen Segen der Behaglichkeit grünen.* All hope of improvement seems an illusion. We do nothing but tinker with what is beyond curing—*wenn man denn einmal die Sache mit offnen Augen sieht, und sieht das Unheilbare, und wie doch immer gepfuscht wird!!*—Thus he had written in 1782 to Frau von Stein. But Goethe's deep aversion to violence and confusion made him see only the destructive aspect of the Revolution. He hated it, and so he hailed Napoleon as the political genius whose mission it was to bring order out of chaos and eventually consolidate the whole European continent. He wept no tears over the demise of the Holy Roman Empire. The collapse of Prussia in 1806, which drew its little ally Saxe-Weimar in the wake of its ruin and involved the pillaging of Weimar itself by French troops, did not arouse him to patriotic indignation. And even the ground swell of political German nationalism which rose to a great tidal wave in the Wars of Liberation did not engulf him. To the last he clung to the conviction that Napoleon's overshadowing greatness would triumph over any coalition of adversaries. Even after Napoleon's star had set it remained for Goethe a star of the first magnitude—the supreme example of what in later years he termed the daemonic personality. The fact that despite this Goethe was culturally German to the core need not be labored, and his admiration for the genius of the strong man of Europe never involved a wavering of his instinctive awareness of the fundamentally alien character of Gallic tradition and its cultural incompatibility with what was native German. (It is noteworthy that except for two sojourns in Italy Goethe spent all his life in the Rhineland, Switzerland, Thuringia, Bohemia—a very confined geographical area even judged by eighteenth-century standards. Once in his early Weimar years he spent a few days in Berlin, on duty, but he felt the atmosphere of the Prussian capital so alien that he could never be induced to repeat his visit. His only first-hand experience of French life and customs he obtained during the military campaign of 1792. And even in Italy he associated almost exclusively with German artists.) In his political thought, however, Goethe was definitely out of step with his time. He had grown up in an era which knew the German Empire only as an impotent frame harboring numerous sovereign members. His personality, set in this mold, was strong enough to withstand the impact of the new na-

tionalism which proved to be the dominating current of
the nineteenth century all over Europe. Ingrained habit
and superior wisdom both contributed in such equal proportion to his aloofness that to call Goethe a political re-
actionary or a political prophet is an idle game of affixing
meaningless labels. His roots were solidly anchored in the
German soil, but the mighty canopy borne by the stately
trunk kept extending its reach without regard to national
frontiers. To be a German was Goethe's fate; it was his
destiny to become a citizen of the world.

Amid the distractions of an era of wars and revolutions
Goethe turned more and more to pursuits of a timeless
character. When he accompanied his Duke on the ill-
fated invasion of revolutionary France on the part of the
allied Prussian and Austrian armies in 1792 it was as a
dispassionate observer who viewed the maneuvering of
embattled armies as just one other natural phenomenon.
He was interested in everything that went on, in the behavior of men divorced from the safeguards and re-
straints of civilization, in his own psychological reactions
when under fire, but equally so in certain color phenomena that confirmed his observations on the nature of light.
As a poet he was interested in the specific transitory phenomenon as such, but Goethe was not only a poet, not
even always primarily a poet. He was also a philosopher-scientist, concerned with the eternal processes of
nature in their typical manifestations. And the singular
thing is that this interest also bore fruit in contributions
of a lasting character.

The writings of Goethe that deal with natural science
fill thirteen volumes of the Weimar Edition. This is
enough to make us realize that he devoted a substantial
portion of his long life to these pursuits. And he took
pains to stress the fact that in science fruitful new leads—
aperçus he called them—presuppose a steady and patient

cultivation of the subject of study. Goethe's aptitude as a philosopher-scientist rests on two considerations: he had a phenomenal faculty of first-hand observation, and his interest always embraced a whole related set of natural manifestations rather than one special aspect. What he learned about nature he owed to his clear steady eye, trained by lifelong practice with the delineating pencil, rather than to books. He rarely read a book from cover to cover. He was impatient of mere factual information as such. "You know that I never learn anything except by irradiation," he wrote to Frau von Stein in 1781; "only nature and the greatest masters can steer me toward comprehension of anything. To grasp something by half or in isolation is utterly impossible for me."

Whatever the eye can encompass by direct observation became for Goethe an object of systematic study. His observation and interpretation of earth features has already been mentioned. This, of course, led him to mineralogy. He published a magnum opus on the phenomena of color in all their aspects. He studied cloud formations. He collected meteorological data day after day for months at a time. But it was on plant and animal life that he brought his intuitive powers to bear most remarkably. Under expert guidance he became intimately familiar with the characteristics of a great variety of plants. Linné's invention of the binomial nomenclature was an enormously useful device for inventorying all the plants on earth, but it answered no fundamental questions. It gave no insight into any genetic pattern, whereas Goethe was groping all the time for a natural system of classification that would range plants in a biologically related series. To this end he studied the life process of the plant. He followed it from germination to fruition. He observed that variation of the environmental factors involved a most far-reaching modification and adaptation of the plant's vital organs.

Grasping the basic implications, he arrived at the point of view that all the plant's organs of growth and reproduction from the cotyledons through the leaves to the calyx, the corolla, the stamens and pistil, though utterly dissimilar in appearance, are without exception modifications of one single organ of growth. He set this forth in a now famous little treatise entitled: *Metamorphosis of Plants* (1790). The remarkable thing about it was the point of view repudiating the older pre-formation theory and emphasizing the infinite plastic powers inherent in the living organism.

Goethe's intuitive philosophizing had one curious feature: he was convinced at this time that somewhere in nature there must be a discoverable archetypal plant, an *Urpflanze* that would exhibit the basic organ of growth in unmodified form but endowed with the potentiality of infinite modification—a sort of *Ding an sich* existing as a numerical adjunct to the infinite series of the thing's aspects. When Goethe discussed his "experience" of the archetypal plant with Schiller in 1794 and even took paper and pencil in an effort to trace its outline, Schiller protested that the *Urpflanze* was not an "experience" but an idea. Goethe took offense at this, he stuck to his point and left in something of a huff. But this argument turned out to be of inestimable benefit to both men. That meeting breached the barrier that had stood between Goethe and Schiller up to this point. Thanks to Schiller's intelligence and astuteness mingled with a dose of suave flattery, Goethe soon came to discover that his own mind and Schiller's were a most remarkable pair of complementary opposites. For ten years after that, up to Schiller's death, they carried on the most fruitful interchange of ideas involving a mutual *Steigerung* of their creative powers. At every turn Schiller's keen, analytical intellectualism proved a foil for Goethe's rich but less articulate fund of sensuous experience, and although Goethe never came to move with ease in the abstract realm of Kantian philosophy, he learned that intuitions like that of the *Urpflanze* are "ideas" and incommensurable as such with the finite data of sense experience.

As for zoölogy, Goethe had had an early introduction to this subject, first through his association with medical students at the university, and a few years later through his collaboration in Lavater's *Physiognomik* to which he contributed drawings of characteristic facial features as the visible counterpart of the individual's psychological make-up. That there is an expressive correspondence between inner and outer formation in every living organism was an axiom of Goethe's approach to life. In his early Weimar years he devoted a great deal of time to comparative anatomy, especially to the skull formation of the mammals including man. He executed any number of meticulously accurate drawings in order to demonstrate how skulls of the most diverse species are built up out of the identical number of bones however thoroughly disguised in the course of the plastic process that fashioned each species. It was an axiomatic idea of his, an idea on which hinged the very meaning of comparative anatomy, that all mammals, all animals, in fact, constituted a continuous series without a break. Each animal organism was just another modification of creative nature's fundamental pattern. This conviction led him in 1784 to the rediscovery of the pre-maxillary bone in man in which the upper incisors are lodged. The anatomists of his day claimed that the absence of such a bone in man distinguished him from his nearest relations in the animal kingdom. They were extremely reluctant to be converted by Goethe's demonstration and provoked him to many bitter reflections on the prejudices obscuring the vision of the practitioners of science.

On all his studies dealing with organic life Goethe brought to bear one inclusive guiding idea: There is no rigidity about nature. All forms spawned in the inexhaustible abundance of her creative invention derive from a common principle of design at bottom. By essentially identical processes of development they undergo infinite modifications and adaptations in the course of producing the types which we label species. There is nothing capricious about these types, they all manifest the workings of identical forces. For the study of organic life from this point of view Goethe coined the term "morphology" and he published his studies serially in a periodical which bore this title.

Whether Goethe was an evolutionist in the nineteenth-century sense is a moot question. There is no unambiguous evidence to show that Goethe necessarily thought of all forms of organic life as genetically derived from one original vital plasm. His view would accord equally well with the idea that creative nature simultaneously spawned a host of variations of the same model at the beginning of time, leaving room for multiple subsequent variation by crossing, and both views came no nearer to solving the essential mystery of life. The fundamental difference between Goethe and Darwin is that the latter set forth a clearly defined hypothesis which aimed to account for the infinitude of specific variations and which is subject to the check of exact observation and experiment within certain narrow limits. No similar claim can be made for Goethe. It is just as important to stress, on the other hand, that Goethe contemplated life in terms of an unbroken fluid development. And of equal importance is the fact that he viewed nature in every one of her organic manifestations as an end in itself, as functionally self-sufficient, in contrast to the eighteenth-century teleological view which interpreted nature's forms in terms of purposes correlated with the specific needs of man:

> *Natur hat weder Kern noch Schale,*
> *Alles ist sie mit einem Male.*

(Nature allows no distinction between kernel and shell; she is both in one.)

> During the development of classical biology in the nineteenth century, there arose two great generalizations: 1) the theory of evolution, and 2) the cell theory. The theory of evolution proclaims the relatedness of all living things, the cell theory sets forth a universal principle of construction for them. Both these generalizations unified biology and distinguished it from the study of the inorganic world.

This statement by Max Delbrück in the November 1948 issue of the *Scientific American* admirably serves to point up Goethe's close affinity to biological science as it developed during the half-century after his death. Goethe was one of the first to stress the relatedness of all living organisms. And Goethe's insistence on nature's use of the identical means in arriving at her myriad forms assumes an archetypal structural pattern. He would have been certain to espouse the cell theory as a vindication of his view. Did he not point out that the higher plant, like the rose and the oak, constitutes in reality a collective society, and not, as we commonly regard it, an individual?

Goethe's interest in human affairs and his concern with the problems of natural science did not move in separate compartments of his brain. The wholeness of Goethe shows up signally in the fluid intermingling of both pursuits. There was a constant cross fertilization between the ideas of the scientist and those of the moralist—this term taken in the sense of the French as denoting a philosophical study of the varieties of human behavior. All of Goethe's literary works show evidence of this. The most remarkable case of such cross fertilization is the novel which startled his contemporaries by its enigmatic title *Elective Affinities* (1809). Here Goethe used the behavior of substances in the chemical laboratory, their spontaneous disposition to enter into stable and volatile combinations, to exchange partners and regroup at will, as a profound symbol of the mysterious irrational attractions that prevail between the sexes in human life. The human material is admirably selected to illustrate the central problem. The novel presents a variety of human groupings and an interplay of varying cross currents of attraction, ranging from the casual to the compulsive, from the frivolous to the tragic. With a scientist's detachment Goethe plots the field of force as it bears on the various couples. In consequence he has been both denounced as lax and immoral and upheld as an advocate of the inviolable sanctity of the marriage bond. In the case of Ottilie the combination of personality and circumstance results in tragedy of a poignancy that is unique in Goethe's writings. Normally Goethe was averse to situations that present a strictly tragic dilemma. His nature tended toward conciliation and compromise; it would break him, he said, to write a real tragedy. His dramas illustrate the point. In the case of Götz, we have tragedy of a very mitigated sort: the hero, succumbing to overwhelming outward force, remains stalwart to the last. Egmont faces the executioner with a consciousness of ultimate victory which is even translated for the audience into strains of a triumphal symphony. Tasso's uncontrollable temperament heads by rights for a total inner collapse, but Goethe sidesteps the inner logic of the situation to conclude on a half-hearted note of compromise. The Faust of the chapbook, launched on a hell-bent career, becomes with Goethe a symbol of stirring and erring mankind and is adjudged worthy of salvation despite his compromise with the powers of evil. But as for Ottilie, her tragedy is inwardly conditioned to an extent that puts it beyond the reach of any softening manipulation. A single moment of inadvertence has sufficed to upset the infinitely delicate balance of her moral adjustment. The past stands as an impassable gulf between the present and any conceivable future. Goethe was wont to say that no individual can be expected to embrace a point of view which denies to him the indispensable conditions of his specific existence. Just that is Ottilie's case. Her death by voluntary starvation is the precise symbolic counterpart of the fact that the will to live has suffered a mortal lesion. Without a trace of outward violence tragedy takes its inexorable course.

Goethe was always the philosopher-scientist. It was always his method to see the special problem in its total framework. He inveighed against blind induction that attempts to dispense with the guidance of general ideas. In his view the study of the parts must proceed from a living experience of the whole. There was danger, of course, in laying too exclusive a stress on *a priori* intuitions of a general nature. Some of Goethe's pronouncements sound as though they issued straight forth from the inner sanctum of nature, as when he tells us that nature never could have created a horned lion because her economy operates with a given limited amount of material, and when she expends what is available on a full set of teeth there is none left over for fashioning such excrescences. Since excavation has brought to light its thousands of extinct species designed along lines that failed of adaptation to fundamental changes of the environment, we have become more wary of setting forth propositions that carry the claim of self-evident truth. Having learned so much more of nature's economy we are more distrustful of prediction in a field replete with improbabilities.

Another limitation of Goethe as a scientist involves his disparagement of mathematics. In his extraordinary endowment the gift of operating with abstract numbers had been omitted. This led to his feud with Newton and his followers over the theory of light and to his opinionated attempt to make the limits of his peculiar endowment the measure of all things. There was a tendency in other fields too to overstress the constitution of his temperament and to think of the conditions of his own specific habitat as a norm permitting trustworthy generalizations for the world as a whole. This tendency made it impossible for him to keep step with the new theories regarding the formation of the earth's surface. Catastrophism, repugnant to Goethe in human life, was repugnant to him also in connection with nature. To be asked to embrace its assumptions amounted to a personal insult. He was a man of peace, accustomed to look at progress in terms of quiet, unspectacular development. To be told now of evidence pointing to the formation of block mountains and faulting on an enormous scale, of lateral thrusts producing folds and overlaps in the form of colossal mountain ranges, of a succession of inundations of the continents by the sea and their repeated re-emergence was tantamount to being asked to throw overboard the thought patterns of a lifetime. In true pragmatist fashion he airs his indignation over such an importunity in a letter to Zelter written a few months before his death:

> That the Himalaya mountains should have pushed out of the earth to a height of 25,000 feet and that in spite of this lift they should tower as proud and rigid as though nothing had happened, is something that my brain cannot conceive. It belongs in those somber regions where notions like transubstantiation dwell. My whole cerebral system would have to undergo reorganization (which would surely be a pity) to make room for the harboring of such miracles.

If it is the normal course of life to age and to become set in its ways, the amazing thing about Goethe is rather his faculty of repeated rejuvenation. Time and again when the fund of his creative fertility seemed largely spent, a new current of vitality made him take hold of the plastic stuff of the world with the intensity and the freshness of a brand new experience. In his late thirties he underwent a rebirth in Italy. In his middle forties the association with Schiller gave a powerful spurt to his intellectual faculties. In his middle sixties a new spring of lyricism gushed forth to expand into the limpid current of his *Divan*. And in the last years of his life his powers of language underwent another mutation to achieve the completion of his *Faust*. The superb blending of lyric genius with inner drama of the utmost intensity in the final act of *Faust* is an incomparable achievement. And is there anything in the world's literature to match the sublime orchestration of its conclusion?

When all is said and done, the continuing vitality of the phenomenon Goethe rests largely upon his stature as a lyric poet. Goethe excels in the concentrated expression of passionate intimate experience. This is not to disparage the great treasure of Goethe's philosophical poems, but as statements of general truth they are impersonal in formulation and more removed from the core of the lyric self. In a peculiar sense modern German lyric poetry begins with Goethe. The epoch preceding him is not only more distant in time but remote in its appeal. The songs of young Goethe, on the other hand, discarding the provincial conventionalism of the baroque age, have a glow that has not tarnished with the passage of time. Goethe's love poetry is grafted on the stock of the folk song. It translates the simple artlessness of folk song into a higher medium. It is not pointed and epigrammatic; it does not revel in subtle conceits. It has a freshness and a pulsating

34

movement that never allows a static emotional situation to develop. The mood has an unerring way of fashioning its own right rhythmical counterpart. Goethe has an astonishing wealth of simple metrical forms. Even if they are not new inventions they have in each of his outstanding songs the effect of having been employed for the first time and created for the specific occasion. Thus a poem like *Auf dem See,* a mere twenty lines in all, has three distinct moods expressed in three rhythmical units of extremely diverse character which nevertheless form a perfect, rounded whole. In all periods of Goethe's life, but especially in his youth and again in his last decades, we find poems that have this spontaneity. In much of his later verse, to be sure, it is overlaid or even replaced by measures of a more formal character. But the *Marienbader Elegie,* to mention a supreme example, suffers no inhibition of spontaneity from the formal iambic pentameter of the six-line stanza. Despite its length, this poem dispenses with anything suggestive of logical organization: it is from first to last a weaving of moods around a single emotional center; though forever returning to the basic poignant theme of bereavement, it is new in every line and inexhaustible in the devices it employs to snatch at consolation. We continue to marvel at Goethe's faculty of being swept off his feet by passionate experience time after time as if it had been a wholly new element in his life. In line with this is the fact that he remained incorrigibly impulsive and unselfconscious in his surrender to inspiration. He could claim on occasion that poetry is distinct from all the arts in its lack of any technique that can be transmitted from master to pupil—an astounding statement as such, even more so coming from a man to whom the writing of verse was second nature during all his adult life. He was not referring to verse, of course, but to poetry, and he was not thinking of that more modern phenomenon, the poetic specialist whose life is equated with his poetic production. He was thinking of himself rather as a man alive to a thousand human interests and engaged in a hundred pursuits, a man who was among other things also a poet.

Even though Weimar was but a small spot on the political map of Germany, it became with Goethe the nerve center of European culture. There was no provincialism about Goethe as regards the life of the spirit. It is amazing to see how this one man had his finger on the pulse of the intellectual and literary life of all Europe. He translated Diderot and Voltaire; he wrote a sheaf of essays about the Italian Manzoni; he followed Lord Byron's career with admiration and apprehension and incorporated a poignant memorial to him in *Faust*. The extent to which he assimilated the cultural heritage of the Western World, beginning of course with the Bible, makes of his writings an epitome reflecting two thousand years of civilization. Homer, Pindar, the Greek tragedians, the Roman poets of the Augustan age, left their mark on his poetry as though they had been contemporaries. Even Dante's thorny greatness was not entirely passed up. Petrarch and the Renaissance poets came to life anew in his sonnets. Overshadowing them all, however, in the intensity and duration of the impulse transmitted, stood Shakespeare. Young Goethe responded to him with an enthusiasm that knew no bounds. In the brashness of his youth he apostrophized Shakespeare in fraternizing terms. In his *Götz* he submitted to Shakespeare's influence without reservation. In his *Wilhelm Meister* the tragedy of *Hamlet* became the ideal center around which a large part of the action revolved. By then Goethe was no longer comparing himself with Shakespeare. He had come to regard the world of Shakespeare's creation as incommensurable, as dwarfing everything that challenged comparison. In his old age he warned young poets against the folly of trying to match their talents against his genius.

The world we live in is no longer Goethe's world. A mind of his cast, in harmony with the silent working of nature's eternal laws, would find no room to develop in the world in which we live. The present generation finds itself thrust from infancy into a world of technical marvels that allows no sense of natural continuity to develop. Man has become both larger and smaller since Goethe's day. Goethe still clung to the idea that man represents a summation of all of nature's creative impulses; we have come to think of the human race as a highly specialized development with a rather precarious prospect of survival. The reader may well ask, therefore, what this book of Goethe's wisdom and experience adds up to in terms of our own situation. The answer is this:

Two attitudes toward life are characteristic of modern man. Either he flounders in skepticism or he clutches at the straw of made-to-order ideologies from which he does not dare to deviate by a hair's breadth lest he lose his last hold on certainty. By contrast, Goethe, subscribing to no creed and no ideology, felt himself borne along by the current of life in its wholeness. Although the unknowable loomed large in the field of his contemplation, he showed an essential trust in life, a faith in what is hidden from the eye. With this faith he responded to the summons of the day. Something of that same pragmatic faith may come to us through these pages.

EDITOR'S NOTE

THIS SELECTION is limited to Goethe's prose. It includes not one of his lyrics. It includes no lines from his poetic dramas, his elegies, his narrative poems and the vast body of his epigrammatic and gnomic verse. The reason for this omission is simple. True poetry essentially defies translation. Its spirit cannot be detached from its form; soul and body are indissolubly one. The life of a poem resides in its rhythm, in its melody, in that complex structure of human speech as sound that has meaning and beauty only within the phonetic framework of the language in which the poem was conceived. Translators, the best of them, are craftsmen who attempt to fit the spirit of a poem into a new body with sensuous values of its own. Theirs is inevitably an art of compromise between form and meaning. In only the rarest of instances the resultant product can be called a poem in its own right, without apologies, and it is then a new poem. Most translations of Goethe, however carefully done, make him sound like a third-rate Victorian. Inasmuch as this book does not present the German and the English side by side, it would be rendering a disservice to Goethe—the least known of great foreign poets in the Anglo-Saxon world—to include here either respectable translations or travesties of his verse. For those who want to take the measure of Goethe's stature as a poet, there is no recourse but to read him in German.

The present translation is a new and independent version of the passages chosen. Whatever its shortcomings—and there are many—it was made on the basis of careful consideration of each passage in its context. It was often desirable, even necessary, to take liberties with the form. As regards the substance, the unswerving aim has been the faithful retaining of Goethe's meaning. It is a question how much an English translation can preserve of the flavor of Goethe's prose—how much of this flavor it should aim to preserve. Goethe's prose—leaving out of account the vast difference between the style of his youth and that of his mature years—is precise and loose, terse and redundant, natural and stilted, disciplined and willful. Despite his expressed preference for Greek, much of his late prose sounds as though translated from Latin. Occasionally it is so highly personal in its sentence structure that it is difficult to recognize as German. All of it is marked by a pronounced rhythmical swing and a great predilection for synonyms and double terms serving rhythmical ends. Goethe's terminology bristles with difficulties. Terms like *Bildung* and *Humanität* have no one recognizable counterpart in English. They have often been left, sometimes followed by an English approximation in brackets, sometimes to negotiate their way unaided within their setting. Words like *steigern* and *Steigerung*—always denoting a progressive dynamic increase, a qualitative mutation, never a mere quantitative expansion—had to be rendered by many devious circumlocutions in as many contexts. For *Folge,* another pivotal term of Goethe's vocabulary, I borrowed a term of the golf course: Follow-Through. Despite Goethe's aversion to sport, skating excepted, this might have won his approval, in view of his great admiration for the English and their way of taking life in their stride.

The passages included in this volume are drawn from

39

Goethe's works, both literary and scientific, published during his lifetime and posthumously. They also include portions of his diaries, of his letters, and of his oral utterances as reported by disciples, collaborators, friends, and casual visitors. The selection is heavily weighted in favor of the older Goethe, in part because experience and wisdom are attributes of maturity. Another reason, however, is the fact that the young Goethe's effusive, oracular, inspirational style stresses expression at the expense of communication. Many of his most personal and colorful utterances are unintelligible when detached from their context.

The captions that subdivide the chapters aim—without being systematic—to introduce an element of order into the great diversity of material covered. Two other helps to clarify the picture should be noted.

The arrangement of the passages under each caption is chronological, and the items are dated. Thus the presentation moves the reader from Goethe's literary beginnings down to the end of his career a great many times in the course of each chapter.

Every item not only quotes the exact title (including often a series of very characteristic subheadings) of the work in question, a novel, treatise, essay, or review, as the case may be, but it also ends with an exact reference enabling the reader to find it quickly in its context. As for the dating, a word of caution is in order. The items covering letters, diary entries, and (for the most part) conversations are, in the nature of things, exactly dated. The dating of the works, on the other hand, called for some arbitrary decisions. As every student of Goethe knows, many of his works took shape over a period of years. Some, like the *Autobiography*, were published piecemeal in 1811, 1812, 1814 and posthumously, respectively. Some, like the *Italian Journey*, the *Campaign in France*, the

40

Annals, are full of dated passages referring to the time of the events reported, but in many instances touched up and revised years, even decades, later. In many instances of this kind a double date has been appended. In many cases the date represents only an approximation. Thus *Wilhelm Meister's Journeyings,* radically recast in its second edition, is always given here as 1829.

Symbols to identify the references have been used as follows:

Diary entries are listed as *Diary,* followed by a date.

Letters are listed as *To* . . . . followed by a date.

Conversations are listed by the name of the *reporter* (with date), followed by *Biedermann* and a number, e.g. *Eckermann,* Sept. 1, 1819. *Biedermann* 2731. All conversations are quoted on the basis of *Goethes Gespräche,* Gesamtausgabe, neu herausgegeben von Flodoard Freiherr von Biedermann, 5 Bände, Leipzig, 1909 f.

The works, in the great majority of cases, are quoted, for the sake of convenience, according to the scholarly and widely used *Jubiläumsausgabe* in 40 volumes (Cotta, 1902 f.). This source is indicated wherever a title is followed by two numbers, designating volume and page.

The *Maxims and Reflections,* distributed among various volumes in the older editions, are quoted according to the numbering and dating given them in Max Hecker's edition representing volume 21 of the *Schriften der Goethe Gesellschaft,* 1907. Hecker's numbering and dating has been adopted as the standard by some recent editions, such as that of the Bibliographisches Institut, *Festausgabe* 1926.

Those relatively few passages from Goethe's writings which are not to be found in the *Jubiläumsausgabe* are quoted on the basis of the monumental but cumbersome and not widely available *Sophienausgabe* (Weimarer Ausgabe), 1887 f. Such references are designated by

Religion

RELIGION IN GENERAL

The only religion that can be of use must be simple and warm. The only true religion is no concern of ours. Who will presume to determine the true relation of the soul to God other than God himself?

Two Important as Yet Undiscussed Biblical Questions
(1773); 36, 97

We owe a great debt of gratitude to nature for having provided the existence of every living being with sufficient curative power to enable it to patch itself together after having got torn at one end or the other. And what are the thousand-odd religions other than a thousand manifestations of this curative power? You may find my plaster inefficacious; I yours. In my father's dramshop are many recipes. *To Lavater,* Oct. 4, 1782

Men continue to be creative in poetry and art only so long as they are religious. After that they merely imitate and repeat, as is our case with regard to antiquity. All the monuments of the ancients were created as matters of faith, and we imitate them to indulge and gratify nothing but our fancy. *Riemer,* July, 1810. *Biedermann* 1314

I for my part, drawn in many directions as I am, cannot content myself with one way of thinking. As poet and artist I am a polytheist; in my nature studies I am a pantheist—both in a very determined way. When I require one god for my personality, as an ethical being, this is provided for also. The things of heaven and earth con-

45

tain such a wealth of value that only the organs of all beings jointly can encompass it.

To F. Jacobi, Jan. 6, 1813

The faculty of ennobling every object of sense and of infusing the life of the spirit into dead matter is the surest guarantee of our more than earthly origin. However much we are attracted and fascinated by the myriad phenomena of this earth, an inner longing compels us again and again to turn our eye heavenward because an inexplicable deep feeling convinces us that we are citizens of those worlds that mysteriously shine above us and that we shall some-day return thither. It is the function of religion to establish a peace between the laws of that spiritual realm and the sensuous nature of man. Morality tried to bring this about, but it lost its force with the attempt to reduce it to a theory of calculated happiness.

Caroline von Egloffstein, April 29, 1818. *Biedermann* 1837

Unflinching faith and resignation are the true basis of all the better religions—the subordination of the self to a higher will directing events, a will that we do not comprehend, because it surpasses reason and understanding. The religion of Islam and that of the Reformed Church resemble each other most closely in this.

von Müller, March 28, 1819. *Biedermann* 1869

All that has reference to what is eternal, all that in our earthly life by way of image or parable suggests what is imperishable, should rightly not be made the subject of debate, difficult though such exclusion may be. For, in so far as we translate our ways of thinking and feeling into terms of outward circumstance, in so far as we form a society about us or join such a one, something belonging to the inner world becomes externalized. What is thus established, whether received with favor or disfavor, must be maintained and defended. And so, despite ourselves, we have made a retreat from the realm of the spiritual to that of the secular, from the celestial to the earthly, and from the eternal and immutable to what is subject to the laws of time and change.

> *Prefatory Observation*, the first fascicle of the second volume On Natural Science in General (1823); W. A. Werke, Zweite Abteilung, 13, 405

A man, born to and trained in the so-called exact sciences and fully matured in his powers of reason, will not find it easy to understand that there is such a thing, too, as an exact sensuous imagination—a faculty without which art would not be conceivable. The same point at issue makes the quarrel between the adherents of a religion of feeling and one of reason. If the latter refuse to concede that religion originates as a feeling, the former do not want to admit that it must find fulfillment in reason.

> *Ernst Stiedenroth: Psychology, Part I* (Review; 1824); 39, 374

To have a positive religion is not necessary. To be in harmony with oneself and the whole is what counts, and this is possible without positive and specific formulation in words.

> *Riemer's Diaries*, Dec. 24, 1824. Jahrbuch der Sammlung Kippenberg 1924

No religion that is based on fear is respected among us.

> *Wilhelm Meister's Journeyings* II, 1 (1829); 19, 182

Only with reluctance does man resolve upon an attitude of reverence. But in truth this is never a resolve on his part. It must be bestowed upon him as a higher sense. Only in the case of singularly favored individuals does it develop from within, and such individuals have at all times had the status of saints and gods. Here lies the dignity, the concern of all true religions, of which there are only three in accordance with the objects to which they turn their devotion.

Wilhelm Meister's Journeyings II, 1 (1829); 19, 181-182

Continue to make the demands of the day your immediate concern, and take occasion to test the purity of your hearts and the steadfastness of your spirits. When you then take a deep breath and rise above the cares of this world in an hour of leisure, you will surely win the proper frame of mind to face devoutly what is above us, with reverence, seeing in all events the manifestation of a higher guidance.

Wilhelm Meister's Journeyings III, 13 (1829); 20, 187

There are only two genuine religions: the one that acknowledges and adores what is sacred in and about us without recourse to any form; the other, which does so in the most beautiful form. All that lies between is idolatry.

Maxims and Reflections 667 (1829)

No man is likely to be without a stirring of religious feeling. But unable to cope with it individually, he seeks fellow-believers or tries to make converts.

The latter is not my way, whereas my life gives evidence enough of the former. Of all the creeds since the dawn of creation I did not happen on one that I could have embraced without reservations. But now a sect, known as the Hypsistarians, has come to my notice. These folk, squeezed between heathens, Jews, and Christians, announced that they would esteem, admire, and revere whatever appealed to them as good and perfect to a supreme degree and that they would worship it as something closely related to the divine. Here all at once I perceived a happy ray beamed upon me from a dark age; for I felt that I had been striving all my life to qualify as a Hypsistarian. But that is no small effort; for how can one, with the limitations of one's individuality, press forward to the perception of what is most perfect?

To S. Boisserée, March 22, 1831

Art is based on a kind of religious sense, on a deep and firmly fixed earnestness; hence its tendency to join forces with religion. Religion is in need of no aesthetic sense for support. Self-contained in its earnestness, it awakens no aesthetic response and has nothing to do with the cultivation of taste.

Maxims and Reflections 1107 (posthumous)

As students of nature we are pantheists, as poets polytheists, as moral beings monotheists.

Maxims and Reflections 807 (posthumous)

CHRISTIANITY

You think in terms of supreme reality, but this is the basis of Spinoza's system on which everything rests, the source from which everything flows! He does not prove the existence of God; existence *is* God! And if others on this account brand him an *Atheus*, I should like to label and praise him as *Theissimus*, indeed *Christianissimus*.

To F. Jacobi, June 9, 1785

Christianity is so deeply founded upon human nature and its needs that in this respect, too, it can be justly said: The word of the Lord endureth forever.

C. F. John, May 2, 1812. Biedermann 1468

The Christian religion deserves the highest praise. Proof of its pure and noble origin is forthcoming ever anew in the fact that no matter what deformations the

49

blind impulse of man has forced it to undergo, it always reverts to its original lovely character of a mission, a household sodality and brotherhood, in response to ethical need.

Divan. Notes. Mahmud of Gasna (1819); 5, 175-6

What is it that has caused the Christian religion to win out over all others? What has made it mistress of the world, and deservedly? What else but the fact that it incorporated the truths of natural religion into itself! Where is there a conflict between the two? They are identical in substance.

von Müller, June 8, 1821. *Biedermann* 1945

But now we must speak of the third religion, founded on reverence for that which is below us. We call it the Christian, as representing the most perfect embodiment of this attitude. It is one of the ultimate attainments on man's destined path. Consider what it meant, not only to rise above the earth and to proclaim the conviction of man's higher origin, but also to acknowledge poverty, scorn and contempt, wretchedness and misery, suffering and death as divine; even more, not to look upon sin and crime as obstacles, but to reverence and love them as positive agents of sanctification. Traces of such an attitude we find, of course, during all epochs, but traces are not the goal. Since this has once been reached mankind cannot regress. It is safe to say that the Christian religion, having once made its appearance, cannot disappear again; since the divine has once experienced embodiment in it, it cannot again be dissolved.

Wilhelm Meister's Journeyings II, 1 (1829); 19, 182-3

Already this adherence [to the three religions] is voiced by a large part of the world, but unconsciously. "How and where?" Wilhelm asked. "In the Apostles'

Creed," they shouted; "for the first article is ethnic and belongs to all peoples; the second is Christian, for those who wrestle with suffering and are glorified in suffering; the third, finally, teaches an enthusiastic communion of saints, that is to say of those good and wise in the highest degree. Should not then the three divine persons, under whose symbol and name such convictions and promises are uttered, rightly be looked upon as the highest unity?"

Wilhelm Meister's Journeyings II, 1 (1829); 19, 183-4

The life of this divine man [Christ] was not involved in the historical events of his time. His was a private life; his teaching addressed itself to individuals. What happens to nations and their component members on the stage of public life belongs to world history and is the province of that religion which we call the first. But that which the individual experiences in his bosom belongs to the second religion, the religion of the sages. Such a one was the religion that Christ taught and practiced during his sojourn on earth. In indication of this division the outer gallery ends here, and I now introduce you to the inner apartments.

A door opened, and they entered a similar gallery, hung with pictures which Wilhelm at once recognized as subjects taken from the second division of Holy Writ. They seemed to be painted by a different hand. Everything was more delicate—figures, movements, settings, light, and color.

Having passed some of the pictures in review, the companion said: Here you see neither deeds nor events, but miracles and parables. It is a new world, with a new exterior, different from the previous one, and an inner quality that was entirely missing there. Through miracles and parables a new world is opened up. The former make what is common extraordinary; the latter, what is extraordinary common. You will have the kindness, said Wilhelm, to elucidate these few words, for I am at a loss to do so myself. They carry a straightforward meaning, though a deep one, he replied. Examples are the quickest way to make it explicit. There is nothing more ordinary and common than eating and drinking; it is extraordinary, on the other hand, to turn water into wine, to multiply a quantity of food to make it suffice for a multitude. There is nothing commoner than disease and bodily ailment, but to remove these or mitigate them through spiritual or quasi-spiritual means is extraordinary; for this is the miraculous feature of miracle, that the ordinary and the extraordinary, the possible and the impossible become one. In the case of the parable we have the reverse of this process: Here the sense, the insight, the concept are what is high, extraordinary, out of reach. When this becomes incorporated in a common, ordinary image that may be grasped, so that it faces us as a living, present reality, so that we assimilate it, seize it, and hold it fast, and move in its company as with our own likes, then a second kind of miracle confronts us, to be fairly ranged alongside the first, even to be preferred to it in fact. Here the living doctrine is uttered, the doctrine that does not lead to disputation. It is not an opinion concerning what is right or wrong. It *is* right or wrong, barring contradiction.

Wilhelm Meister's Journeyings II, 2 (1829); 19, 188-9

Like Hegel, Schubarth drags the Christian religion into philosophy, where it has no business. The Christian religion is a mighty essence in its own right. It has helped humanity, sunk low and suffering, to rise from its degradation time and again. When one concedes this effect to Christianity, it is superior to all philosophy and does not require it for support.

Eckermann, Feb. 4, 1829. *Biedermann* 2652

You know how I esteem Christianity, or perhaps you do not. And who in the world is a Christian nowadays, such as Christ wanted? I alone perhaps. even though you look upon me as a heathen.

von Müller, April 7, 1830. *Biedermann* 2815

The Creed of a Man of Rational Faith Goethe did not disapprove of, but he termed it a melancholy sign of the times, based on straddling of issues and makeshift accommodation. One should either cling to traditional faith without getting involved with criticism, or, pursuing the latter course, abandon that faith. There is no third way. For me Christ remains a highly significant though problematic being, he added.

Now that people have begun to realize what a lot of nonsense is involved in the traditional make-up of the apostles and saints; now that they have begun to believe that they were fellows of the same stuff as Klopstock, Lessing, and the rest of us poor sons-of-bitches, it is small wonder that the wires get crossed in their heads!

von Müller, June 8, 1830. *Biedermann* 2838

This genuinely Christian tendency was innate in Schiller. He would touch nothing common without ennobling it. His inner trend led him to that.

To Zelter, Nov. 9, 1830

There are two ways of looking at Biblical matters. There is the standpoint which assumes a kind of fundamental religion at the beginning of things, the standpoint of pure nature and reason. This standpoint, divine in origin, will forever remain the same, and its validity will endure as long as there are beings endowed with God's gifts. But this standpoint is only for the chosen few. It is much too high and noble to become general. Then there is the standpoint of the Church, running more along human lines. It is imperfect, changeable, and in process of change, and it, too, will endure, though forever changing, as long as weak human beings continue to exist. The light of undimmed experience of the divine is much too pure and radiant to fit the capacities of poor weak men. Here the Church enters as a beneficent mediator, to soften and moderate, in order that all may be helped and many may feel at their ease. The Church is a very great power, owing to the belief that by virtue of its succession to Christ it can free man from his burden of sin. And to maintain this power and this authority, and thus to safeguard the edifice of the Church, is the foremost aim of the Christian priesthood.

It is therefore of minor concern to it to ask whether this or that Biblical book may serve to bring about a marked enlightenment of the spirit, or whether it contain doctrines of high ethical quality or present noble exemplars of humanity. It is concerned rather with putting emphasis in the Pentateuch upon the story of the fall of man and the origin of the craving for a savior. In the prophets, it is the repeated reference to him, the awaited one; and in the Gospels it must emphasize his actual appearance in the flesh and his death on the cross in atonement for our human sins. Granting such aims and purposes, you see that, weighed by such standards, neither the noble Tobit nor the Wisdom of Solomon nor the Proverbs of Sirach can command any particular weight. . . .

But if you ask whether I feel an urge to extend to Christ the reverence of worship, I say: By all means! I bow down before him as the divine revelation of the highest principle of morality. If you were to ask me whether I feel an urge to revere the sun, again I say: By all means. For it is likewise a revelation of the All-Highest, the mightiest in fact, that is given to us mortals to grasp. In the sun I worship the light and the creative energy of God by which we live and have our being and all plants and animals along with us.

Eckermann, March 11, 1832. *Biedermann* 3055

PROTESTANTISM · CATHOLICISM

What a lovely invention the Mother of God is you can begin to feel only in Catholic surroundings. A *Vergine* with the son on her arm; *Santissima Vergine,* because she has given birth to a son. It is an object to fix your senses and make your mind reel. It has a certain inner poetic grace, so pleasurable to behold and so incapable of inducing thought that it seems expressly made for religious contemplation.   *Diary of the Italian Journey,* Oct. 9, 1786

On the difference between the Catholic and the Protestant religion. It is important that man should be constantly reminded of his three ideal postulates, God, immortality, virtue, and be assured of them as much as possible. Protestantism concentrates on the moral development of the individual; virtue is the first and last of its concerns, hence it also is a factor in our social lives. God recedes into the background; heaven remains empty; and immortality is reduced to an object of speculation.

Catholicism puts prime emphasis on guaranteeing to man his immortality—a state of bliss for the good. To the orthodox believer it is assured with absolute certainty. And because of certain differences of degree Catholicism assumes an intermediary existence, purgatory, which we can influence from on earth by good and pious actions. The God of the Catholics also remains in the background, but rather as a resplendent circle of equal, similar, and subordinate gods, so that their heaven is very rich and well stocked. Since ethical self-development is out of the picture, or rather, since former cruder ages did not believe in its possibility, the confessional was instituted in its place. By this arrangement no one needs to tussle with his own inner man. Instead of being under pressure to resolve and harmonize inner conflicts by his own efforts, he puts the matter up to a professional adviser.

Diary, Sept. 7, 1807

In moral and religious matters, just as in his physical life and in civil affairs, man does not like to act impromptu. He requires a sequence that leads to habits. What he is to love and to perform he cannot conceive individually, in piecemeal terms; and to repeat a thing with pleasure presupposes an abiding sense of familiarity. Taken as a whole, the Protestant ritual lacks richness. If we examine particular aspects we find the Protestant has not enough sacraments; he has only one, in fact, in which he actively participates, that of communion. As to baptism, he sees it performed only on others, and it does not make his being expand. The sacraments are the highest feature of religion—the sensuous symbol of an extraordinary divine grace and favor. In holy communion the earthly lips are to receive a divine essence embodied in matter and partake of a heavenly sustenance in earthly form. This is its meaning in all Christian churches, regardless of the degree of mystical exaltation experienced in its celebration, or the degree of accommodation to a rational interpretation. It always remains a sacred solemn rite which achieves a fusion of reality with the possible and the impossible, with that which man can neither grasp nor relinquish. But such a sacrament cannot afford to stand alone. No Christian can feel true joy in partaking of it unless a feeling for symbol and sacrament has been nurtured within him, unless he has been brought up to regard the inner religion of the heart and that of the visible Church as absolutely one, as the great universal sacrament that branches out into a variety of particular sacraments and endows all these parts with its own sacred, indestructible, and eternal character.

Here a youthful pair joins hands, not for the dance or by way of a casual greeting; the priest pronounces his blessing, and the bond becomes indissoluble. Soon husband and wife bring an offspring in their image to the threshold of the altar. It is cleansed with holy water and taken into the fold of the Church so securely that it can forfeit this benefit only by the most blatant apostasy. Its earthly environment gradually opens up by way of experience; in heavenly matters the child requires instruction. When this process has been completed and attested by catechization, the child is now taken into the pale of the Church as a full-fledged citizen, as a genuine adherent by a free act of will, and this achievement is also duly solemnized. Only now he has become a Christian in the full sense of the word, only now he knows the benefits conferred and also the duties involved. But meanwhile the individual has undergone many singular experiences. By teaching and punishment he has come to realize the precarious nature of his inner constitution. Teachings and transgressions will continue as topics throughout his life, but he has advanced beyond the stage of punishment. Now, in the infinite tangle of confusion induced by the conflict of natural with religious demands, a capital means is provided for unburdening himself regarding his deeds and misdeeds, his failings and doubts, in the person of a worthy man expressly appointed for this purpose—a man who can comfort, warn, and strengthen him, one who can castigate him by symbolical penance, one who can eventually wipe the slate of his guilt absolutely clean and restore it to him in its pristine unspotted purity. Thus, prepared, pacified, and quieted by various sacramental rites, each of which on closer inspection breaks up into several sacramental performances, he kneels down to receive the host; and, to add a further touch to this sublime mystery, he sees the chalice only at a distance: this is no ordinary eating and drinking; it is a heavenly food that makes him athirst for heavenly drink.

But let not the youth believe that with this all is settled, and let not the man believe it either! In the affairs of our earthly life we gradually learn, indeed, to rely upon ourselves, and even here knowledge, intelligence, character, fail us at times. In matters of heaven, on the other hand, we never graduate from the stage of the learner. The higher feeling in us, which is often ill at ease in the domicile of the heart, finds itself beset by so many outward things, moreover, that our own resources scarcely suffice to offer us all that is necessary in the way of counsel, comfort, and help. But for this contingency that solace is provided for the duration of our whole life, and there is always available a pious man, schooled in insight, to direct the straying and to lighten the burdens of tortured souls.

But what has been a stay during the whole course of life is destined to prove its efficacy tenfold in the hour of death. In line with habits that have become familiar and dear since childhood, the dying fervently embraces these symbolic assurances charged with tangible meaning. Where every earthly guarantee fails, a heavenly guarantee assures to him a life of bliss through all eternity. He is definitely persuaded that neither a hostile element nor a malevolent spirit can prevent him from being arrayed in a transfigured body, destined to dwell in the immediate precincts of Godhead and to participate in the immeasurable ecstasies that emanate from it.

At the last, in order that the whole man be sanctified, the feet too are anointed and consecrated. Even in case that he should recover, they are to touch this hard, impenetrable matter of earth only with reluctance. They are to be endowed with a marvelous elasticity, causing them to repel the clod that attracted them heretofore. And thus the cradle and the grave, however wide a span may chance to separate them, are linked by a shining circle, punctuated by sacred rites of equal dignity and of a beauty that we have briefly tried to suggest.

But unlike other fruits, all these spiritual miracles do not spring from the natural soil; there they can neither be sown nor be planted. They must be invoked from another region, and this is not in everyone's power, nor at all times. Here we encounter the highest of these symbols transmitted by old, pious tradition. We hear that one man can be favored from above, blessed and sanctified above the rest. But in order that it may not have the semblance of a gift of nature, this distinction, bound up with a heavy duty, must be transmitted from one authorized individual to another. This greatest boon, in no man's power to achieve by an act of will, must be preserved on earth through the ages by spiritual inheritance. Indeed, the consecration of the priest contains the totality of elements that gives efficacy to those sacred rites performed for the benefit of the multitude, without anything being required on its part other than faith and implicit confidence. Thus the priest, a link in the series of his predecessors and successors, in the circle of his co-anointed, is all the grander to behold as it is not he whom we revere, but his office; not his nod at which we bow our knee, but the blessing which he dispenses—a blessing which now seems all the more sacred and directly heaven-sent, as the earthly vessel has not the power to weaken, let alone invalidate it by personal sin or outright vice.

And now, look at Protestantism by contrast. How fragmented is not this truly spiritual pattern, where some of the above-mentioned symbols are branded apocryphal and only a few of them pass muster as canonical! How can the indifferent quality of the former prepare us for the dignity of the latter!

The Autobiography II, 7 (1812); 23, 90-4

Let me say a word regarding your plan to write a cantata for the [tercentenary] celebration of the Reformation. Something after the manner of Händel's *Messiah*, which you have studied with so much insight, would probably be most fitting.

The fundamental character of Lutheranism affords a fine opportunity for poetic treatment as well as musical execution. It is based on the decided conflict of the Law and the Gospels and on the mediation of these extreme opposites. If we take a higher stand and substitute Necessity and Freedom with their synonyms in place of those two terms, we are obviously moving in a sphere that embraces everything of interest to man.

Thus Luther sees in the Old and the New Testaments the symbol of the great ever-repeated rhythm of life. There the Law, tending in the direction of Love; here Love, with a counter-swing in the direction of Law and fulfilling the Law, not by virtue of human strength, however, but by virtue of faith; specifically by exclusive faith in the Messiah, all-proclaimed and all-availing. This sketch is enough to convince one that Lutheranism, while fundamentally at odds with Popery, is not opposed to pure reason, provided that reason is willing to look upon the Bible as a mirror of the world—a not very difficult adjustment for it to make.

To express these conceptions in a singable poem I should begin with the thunder of Mount Sinai—*Thou shalt*—and close with the resurrection of Christ—*Thou wilt*.

Perhaps I may fittingly add a word about Catholicism. Soon after it came into being and spread out, Christianity began to suffer from heresies—some profound, some nonsensical; it lost its original purity. But when it was called upon eventually to tame and rule both crude and degenerate races, drastic means had to be employed. Not doctrine but the 'service of ritual was needed. The only mediator between the highest God and man on earth did not suffice, as we all know, and thus a sort of pagan Judaism arose and is alive and flourishing to this day. All this had to be overturned in human hearts; that is why Lutheranism takes solely the Bible as its foundation. Luther's procedure is no secret. And now that we are asked to celebrate his memory we can do so fittingly only by recognizing his merit and by portraying what he achieved for his contemporaries and their descendants. This festival should be so arranged that every broad-minded Catholic could take part in it with us.

To Zelter, Nov. 14, 1816

Let us compare the difference between a Protestant and a Catholic beggar and suppliant. The former calmly expresses the wish that God may reward you for your gifts without his undertaking to contribute to this end; and thus giver and receiver each goes his own way for good. The latter says he will pray for you, he will importune God and his saints with supplications until they shower you with worldly and spiritual gifts. There is something touching about this situation: An individual unable by means of prayer and contact with the deity to achieve a tolerable condition for himself, yet convinced of the value of his patronage as he appears before God, surrounded by many clients!

The German Gil Blas (Review; 1821); 37, 199

When there is a genuine desire for a great reform present among a people, God is on its side and it succeeds. God was visibly on the side of Christ and his adherents, because the manifestation of the new religion of love was in answer to a universal craving. He was just as visibly on the side of Luther, for the purification of doctrine from priestly adulteration was no less a crying need.

Eckermann, Jan. 4, 1824. *Biedermann* 2214

A poet born and raised a Catholic is in a position to make a vastly more effective use of the beliefs and practices of his Church than an outsider. We others labor to project ourselves into that sphere by the power of imagination, but we never really come to feel at home in it.

Goethe's Interest in Manzoni (Preface; 1827)
W. A. Werke, 42 (I), 138

We do not realize how much we owe to Luther and the Reformation in general. We have slipped off the fetters that cramped our spirits. Thanks to our developing culture, we have learned to return to the source and take Christianity pure. We again have the courage to plant our feet firmly upon God's earth and to glory in our divinely endowed human nature. Let intellectual culture progress indefinitely, let the natural sciences expand and deepen as they may, let the range of man's spirit seek wider and wider horizons—it will not overtake the loftiness and ethical culture of Christianity, as we see it shine and glow in the Gospels. But the more vigorously we Protestants advance in noble development, the more quickly will the Catholics follow. As soon as they feel caught up by the rapidly expanding great enlightenment of the age, they must follow suit regardless of inhibitions, and the day will come when unity will have been re-established.

Also that odious Protestant sectarianism will come to an end, and father and son, brother and sister will no longer eye each other askance. For as soon as the true message and the love of Christ has been grasped in its essence and become a part of life, man will feel great and free and no longer attach any particular importance to divergent outward forms of worship.

And by and by we shall all progress more and more from a Christianity of profession and creed to a Christianity of sentiment and practice.

Eckermann, March 10, 1832. *Biedermann* 3055

There is an esoteric element in philosophy and in religion. There is no sense in exhibiting this to the public, and it is downright mischievous to force such topics upon the attention of the people. Epicurus says somewhere: This is right, because it is offensive to the views of the average man. What deplorable aberrations of the spirit have not followed in the wake of the Reformation by its exposure of the mysteries of religion to the manhandling touch of the multitude, leaving them the defenseless prey of every one-sided exercise of wit; and the end is not in sight.

The range of the average understanding is surely not great enough to have such a vast task entrusted to it, to function as an umpire in such matters. The mysteries, especially the dogmas of the Christian religion, are properly the objects of the deepest philosophy, and it is only their positive formulation that distinguishes them from the truths of speculation. For that reason, depending upon the point of view, theology is often termed a metaphysics gone astray, and vice versa metaphysics a Platonic theology gone astray. Both of them stand too high for the ordinary understanding to flatter itself with being able to snatch their jewel. . . .

Indeed, if Protestantism would only discriminate more carefully between what is to be loved, lived, and taught;

if the mysteries could be accepted in reverent silence, instead of being forced upon people in one-sided, presumptuous, distorted, dogmatic formulation or, worse, being desecrated and endangered by untimely scoffing and frivolous mockery in the public forum—then I would be the first to attend the church of my co-religionists with an honest heart and subordinate myself with genuine edification to the general practical confession of a faith anchored to action. *Falk* (undated). *Biedermann* 3095

OLD AND NEW TESTAMENT

If there is to be a connecting thread for us between the old world and the new, we must think in the main of three forces that enjoyed a great, a decisive, at times, in fact, an exclusive influence: the Bible, Plato, and Aristotle.

The high esteem in which the Bible has been held by many nations over many generations derives from its inner worth. It is not simply a national monument; it is the book of nations, because it exhibits the story of one people as a symbol of all the others, linking its history with the origin of the world and carrying it through a series of material and spiritual developments, of necessary and fortuitous events, to the remotest reaches of eternity. . . .

We cannot go into particulars here. It is universally recognized, however, how in both divisions of this important monument the narration of historical events is intimately bound up with the development of doctrine in such a way that the one sustains and supplements the other more consistently, perhaps, than is the case in any other book. As for the content, little would need to be added to make it extend down to our times. If one were to add to the Old Testament a digest from Josephus carrying

Jewish history down to the destruction of Jerusalem; if one were to supplement the Acts of the Apostles by a concise sketch of the spread of Christianity and the dispersion of Jewry throughout the world, continuing down to the last zealous missions of apostolic figures and the most recent barter and credit manipulations of the descendants of Abraham; if, finally, one were to insert before the Book of Revelation a compendium of pure, Christian, New Testament doctrine to disentangle and clarify the doctrinal method of the Epistles—then this monument would straightway deserve to reassert its old rank and to figure henceforth not only as a universal book but as a universal library of the nations. Then, with the increase of culture throughout the centuries, it could come to serve more and more as the basis in part and in part the tool of education as administered not by men of clever conceit but by men of wisdom.

> *On Theory of Color.* Historical Division. Part Three.
> Tradition (1810); 40, 152-4

I for my part love and cherish the Bible. My moral education I owed almost exclusively to it, and its stories, doctrines, symbols, parables—all had made a deep impression upon me and influenced me in one way or another.

> *The Autobiography* II, 7 (1812); 23, 72-3

Sacred writings suffer no harm, any more than any other tradition, by a critical approach which discovers inner contradictions and makes us aware how an original better version has often been obscured and distorted by later additions, interpolations, and attempts to gloss over difficulties. The inner, basic, original value of the passage is brought out all the more visibly by this procedure. And it is this value that everyone, consciously or unconsciously, envisages and tries to grasp for his edification, throwing away the rest or letting it take care of itself.

> *Divan.* Notes. Israel in the Desert (1819); 5, 267

We cannot ignore the cultivation that we owe to the Bible, a collection of significant documents which exerts its vital influence to this day despite its being as remote in time and as foreign in its setting as any other relic of antiquity. That we feel it closer to us is due to the fact that it focuses upon faith and highest ethical aspirations whereas other literary works are concerned only with taste and the median range of human pursuits.

Classicists and Romanticists in Italy (1820); 37, 121

Of prime advantage, the oldest replied, is the splendid collection of their [the Jews'] sacred writings. They are so felicitously arranged that the most diverse elements blend into the semblance of a homogeneous whole. They are complete enough to satisfy, fragmentary enough to challenge, delicate enough to assuage the mind. And what other contrary qualities could not be mentioned in praise of these books—of this book!

Wilhelm Meister's Journeyings II, 2 (1829); 19, 186

I am convinced that the Bible becomes more and more beautiful the better we understand it—the more we come to realize, that is, that every word that we accept in a general sense and apply to ourselves in particular originally had a special altogether individual meaning qualified by circumstances prevailing in a given time and locality.

Maxims and Reflections 672 (1829)

One might as well drink of the ocean, said Goethe, as get involved in a historical and critical investigation of the Gospels. It is much better to stick without further ado to what is given and to appropriate to oneself what one can use for one's ethical development and support.

Eckermann, Feb. 2, 1831. *Biedermann* 2914

Genuine or spurious is a strange question in matters of the Bible. What is genuine except what is superlatively good and harmonizes with purest nature and reason and continues to promote our highest development to this day? And what is spurious other than what is absurd, hollow, and stupid, what bears no fruit, at least no good fruit? If the genuineness of a Biblical book were to hinge on the question whether it is factually reliable in all respects, then in a few matters even the authenticity of the Gospels might be questioned, inasmuch as Mark and Luke did not write from direct observation and experience but relied on late oral tradition, while the last Gospel was not written by John, the disciple, until he was very old. Despite this, I regard all four Gospels as altogether genuine. They have caught the reflection of a grandeur that emanated from the person of Christ, a grandeur as divine as divinity has ever assumed upon earth.   *Eckermann,* March 11, 1832. *Biedermann* 3055

SUPERSTITION

Astrological superstition is based on a vague feeling of the world as a vast totality. Experience tells us that the heavenly bodies closest to the earth exert a definite influence on the weather, vegetation, etc. One needs only to continue upward along this line, and there is no telling where such influence stops. The astronomer finds evidence of mutual interference among the stars everywhere. The philosopher is inclined—forced, I should say —to attribute to every effect a scope extending to the outermost reaches of the universe. Thus man needs only to feel his way forward one step more and to extend this influence to the moral sphere and to fortune and misfortune. This and similar delusions I hesitate even to label as superstition. It is bound up with human nature, with as many features pointing pro and con, as any faith.

To Schiller, Dec. 8, 1798

[In his youth, Riemer reports, Goethe was extremely attached to a young friend. He died. At his funeral Goethe tossed his left glove onto the lowered coffin. This caused great excitement among those present, each one censuring or excusing this impulsive gesture in his own way.]

What is called superstition is rooted in a much deeper and more sensitive layer of the psyche than skepticism.

Riemer, Dec. 12, 1806. *Biedermann* 926

[Mittler says,] Now, on top of all, comes superstition, which I regard as the most noxious thing that can lodge in a human breast. We play with predictions, divinations, and dreams in an effort to make humdrum daily life significant. But when life itself becomes significant, when everything about us becomes significant and stirs and seethes, then those specters simply add to the fury of the storm that breaks over our heads.

Elective Affinities I, 18 (1809); 21, 140

The only trouble with superstition is that it resorts to false means to satisfy a real need. It neither deserves the abuse that is heaped upon it, nor is it as uncommon as one would think in enlightened ages and among enlightened people.

For who can claim that his way of satisfying his indispensable needs is always pure, true, blameless, and complete? Where do we find so high a seriousness of purpose, backed by faith and hope, as to be without its admixture of superstition and delusion, frivolity and prejudice? . . .

It has often rightly been said that skepticism is superstition in reverse, and this would seem to be pre-eminently an ailment of our own age: A noble deed must have its mainspring in selfishness, a heroic action in vanity; a great poem is reduced to terms of feverish excitement; and what is even stranger, the most significant phenomena are refused credence as long as there is a shred of a possibility of maintaining a negative attitude.

This insanity of our own age is certainly worse than that which prevailed when men perforce acknowledged extraordinary phenomena as existent and then attributed them to the devil. Superstition is a heritage of energetic, progressive personalities who are active on a large scale; skepticism is the mark of weak, petty-minded, regressive, and egocentric men. The former love to marvel, because this stirs the sense of the sublime of which their souls are capable; and since this is always accompanied by a certain shudder of apprehension, the suggestion of an evil principle is close at hand. An impotent generation, on the other hand, feels the sublime as a menace to its existence; and since no one can be expected to submit willingly to his destruction, these people are perfectly right in refusing to acknowledge what is great and colossal when they meet it as part of the contemporary scene. They wait to modify their views until it has passed into history and presents a more tolerable aspect, its brilliance subdued by a sufficient distance from the observer.

On Theory of Color. Historical Division. Roger Bacon
(1810); 40, 165-9

Goethe was agreed that our regard for superstition should be limited to a sense of reverence for the mysterious power surrounding us in all things. He regarded this as a basis of true wisdom.

S. Boisserée, Oct. 5, 1815. *Biedermann* 1723

Since such incidents [transcending the range of verifiable experience] can be adduced by the dozen, it is necessary to remark that from a practical point of view belief in their authenticity and skepticism are on a par. It would seem reasonable, therefore, not to dwell in these questionable regions too long, but rather to use such incidents in a symbolic and parabolic way as designed to awaken the moral sense. It would seem that equal damage might be wrought by ignoring the inscrutable aspect of life altogether, as by presuming to get involved with it too deeply.

The German Gil Blas (Review; 1821); 37, 199

Superstition is the poetry of life. Both invent imaginary beings. Both sense the strangest connections between real, tangible elements—an interplay of sympathies and antipathies. Poetry, having put on these shackles of its free accord, strips them off readily enough, time and again. Superstition, on the other hand, can be compared to magic fetters that draw tighter and tighter the more one struggles. Even the most enlightened epoch is not proof against superstition. But when it asserts itself in dark ages man's clouded mind at once reaches out for the impossible; it tries to exert power on the realm of spirits, across the distance, and upon the course of future events. Thus a wonderfully rich world takes shape, surrounded by an aura of fog. . . . Superstition does no harm to the poet, because he can turn his half-delusions to advantage in a variety of ways. *Justus Möser* (1823); 37, 253-4

FAITH

Therefore, dear brother, there is nothing for which I thank God more than the assurance of my faith. For I shall die in the faith that I have no happiness here and expect no bliss beyond, other than that imparted to me by the eternal love of God that mingled with the wretchedness of the world and became wretched in order that the wretchedness of the world should be glorified along with it.

Letter of the Pastor of xxx to the new Pastor of xxx
(1773); 36, 84-5

What is faith? To hold the account of an event to be true—how can that help me? I need to be able to appropriate to myself its effects, its consequences. This appropriating faith must be a peculiar state of mind unfamiliar to natural man. . . . In this way my soul approached him who had donned human form and died on the cross, and in that moment I knew the meaning of faith.

That is faith, I said to myself, as I leapt up startled. I now endeavored to become assured of what I felt and what I saw within. And in a short time I became convinced that my spirit had acquired a faculty of uplift that was quite new to it.

Wilhelm Meister's Apprenticeship VI. *Confessions of a*
Beautiful Soul (1795); 18, 137

As soon as we proceed from the principle that knowledge and faith are not designed to cancel each other out but rather to supplement each other, we are on the right path pointing to just solutions.

Falk, Jan. 25, 1813. *Biedermann* 1490

In the Gospels, Goethe said, we find particular emphasis on the categorical imperative of faith; and Mohammed carried this idea even further.

Eckermann, Feb. 13, 1813. *Biedermann* 2914

Concerning faith, I maintained [in my adolescent sophistication], the paramount issue is *that* you believe; *what* you believe is of no account whatever. Faith is a great feeling of security for the present and the future,

71

and this security derives from trust in an inscrutable being that is supremely great and powerful. Everything depends on the unshakable quality of this trust, whereas how we picture this being to ourselves will depend on all other faculties and on circumstances and is of no importance anyway. Faith is a sacred vessel in which each individual is prepared to sacrifice his feeling, his reason, his imagination, to the best of his ability. In the case of knowledge exactly the opposite holds true, I said. Not that one knows but what one knows, how well and how much one knows, is what counts. That is why knowledge is a subject for argument, inasmuch as it may be corrected, expanded, and concealed. Knowledge begins with isolated facts; it is endless and formless, and we can at most dream of grasping it as a totality. Hence it is diametrically opposed to faith.

Such half-truths and the mazes they lead us into may be exciting and entertaining in poetic presentation; in life, however, they disturb and confuse the conversation.

The Autobiography III, 14 (1814); 24, 202

The deepest, the only theme of human history, compared to which all others are of subordinate importance, is the conflict of skepticism with faith. All epochs that are ruled by faith, in whatever form, are glorious, elevating, and fruitful in themselves and for posterity. All epochs, on the other hand, in which skepticism in whatever form maintains a precarious triumph, even should they boast for a moment of a borrowed splendor, lose their meaning for posterity, because no one can take pleasure in wrestling with the study of what is essentially sterile.

Divan. Notes. Israel in the Desert (1819); 5, 247-8

Faith is a hidden household capital. Whereas public savings and mutual aid associations dispense funds to the

individual in times of need, here the believer draws the
interest himself in the quiet of his own heart.

Maxims and Reflections 163 (1821)

Christ walking on the sea. This is one of the most
beautiful legends, dear to me above others. It voices the
lofty teaching that by dint of faith and fresh courage man
will win out in the most difficult undertakings, whereas
if he doubt and falter ever so slightly he is instantly lost.

Eckermann, Feb. 12, 1831. *Biedermann* 2913

Faith is love of the invisible, trust in the impossible, in
the improbable.

Maxims and Reflections 815 (posthumous)

GOD AND NATURE

Forgive me for preferring to keep silent when you talk
of a divine being. I discern such a one only in and by
means of the *res singulares*. To the closer and deeper
study of these no one has a happier faculty of leading
than Spinoza himself, despite the fact that under his gaze
all individual things seem to disappear.

Here I am on and among mountains, seeking the divine
in *herbis et lapidibus*. *To F. Jacobi*, June 9, 1785

The division between mind and matter, soul and body,
God and the universe had come about. Both moral philosophy and religion found it to their advantage. For, in
trying to maintain his freedom man must set himself in
opposition to Nature; in striving to rise to God he must
leave Nature behind him. In both cases he cannot be
blamed for taking as disparaging a view of Nature as possible and regarding her as a hostile and oppressive agency. This led to the persecution of such men as endeavored

to reunite the separated entities. With the abandonment of the teleological principle of interpretation Nature was divested of understanding [*Verstand*]. Men lacked the courage to attribute to her the faculty of reason [*Vernunft*], and she was left to lie devoid of spirit. Nature was supposed to render technical, mechanical services. And the attempt to come to terms with her was finally limited to just this one aspect.

On Theory of Color. Historical Part. Robert Boyle (1810); 40, 221

Jacobi's book *On Divine Matters* made me feel ill at ease. Dearly beloved friend that he was, how could I welcome the development of the thesis that Nature conceals God? My own pure, deep, innate and schooled view of things had taught me without fail to see God in Nature, Nature in God, and this view was the foundation of my very existence. How then could so curious, one-sided, and narrow a dictum help but estrange my spirit forever from this high-minded friend whose heart I revered and loved?

Annals (1811); 30, 265

Jacobi . . . He handles dear Nature rather too unceremoniously for my liking, but I bear him no grudge for that. In keeping with the direction of his development, his God must detach himself from the world more and more, whereas mine becomes more and more intertwined with it. Both points of view are valid. The idea of humankind involves all kinds of tensions. There is room, too, for antinomies of conviction.

To Schlichtegroll, Jan. 31, 1812

That it should and must come to this pass with Jacobi I have long foreseen, and the combination of his narrow outlook with a ceaselessly active disposition has caused me, personally, plenty of suffering. He who cannot get it into his head that mind and matter, soul and body, thought and extension, or—to use the happy terms of a modern Frenchman—will and movement are the necessary co-ingredients of the universe, demanding equal recognition and capable on this account of standing for God in their union—he who cannot rise to this conception should long ago have given up thought as his preoccupation and turned to the vulgar traffic of the world.

To von Knebel, April 8, 1812

Nature is so constituted that the Trinity could not have fashioned it better. It is an organ on which the Lord plays the keys, and the devil works the bellows.

S. Boisserée, Sept. 8, 1815. *Biedermann* 1701

As we contemplate the edifice of the universe, in its vastest extension, in its minutest divisibility, we cannot resist the notion that an idea underlies the whole, according to which God and Nature creatively interact forever and ever. Intuition, contemplation, reflection give us an approach to these mysteries. We are emboldened to venture upon ideas; in a more modest mood we fashion concepts that might bear some analogy to those primal beginnings. *Doubts and Resignation* (1820); 39, 34-5

In the mind of man and in the universe as well there is no above or below; everything has equal claim upon a common center that manifests its invisible presence by the very harmony of all the parts with reference to it. All the quarrels of older and newer schools down to our own day spring from our separating of that which God brought forth as a unity in his creation of nature.

Ernst Stiedenroth: Psychology (Review; 1824); 39, 373

The power of Godhead permeates what is living, not what is dead; it is present in that which is in process of becoming and that which transforms itself, not in that which has become and has congealed in its form. Hence reason, in its affinity with the divine principle, is concerned only with what is evolving and living, whereas the understanding deals with what has become formed and congealed, in order to put it to use.

Eckermann, Feb. 13, 1829. *Biedermann* 2657

The simple archetype I hit on long ago. No organic being wholly corresponds to the underlying idea. The higher idea lurks behind each. That is my God; that is the God we all seek and hope to set our countenance upon; but we can only divine him, not see him.

von Müller, May 7, 1830. *Biedermann* 2823

They had brought me a nest of young linnets and one of the parent birds caught in a snare. How I marveled to see how the bird not only continued to feed its brood in the room, but even returned when released through the window. Such parental love transcending danger and captivity moved me deeply, and today I expressed my astonishment to Goethe over this fact. "Foolish fellow," he answered with a significant smile, "if you believed in God you would not be surprised. . . . If God had not implanted this all-powerful urge toward its brood into the bird, if the like of this did not permeate everything living in the domain of nature, the world could not exist! But it so happens that the power of God is diffused through all things, and eternal love is everywhere at work."

Goethe made a similar remark some time ago when a young sculptor sent him a model of Myron's Cow with the Suckling Calf. Here, he said, we have one of the noblest themes. Here, in a lovely parable, is set forth the principle that sustains and nourishes the world as we see it throughout nature. This and similar images are what I call the true symbols of God's omnipotence.

Eckermann, May 29, 1831. Biedermann 2965

Critical reason has disposed of the teleological proof of the existence of God. We concede it, but, giving up the argument, we cling to our feeling. . . . Who would forbid our sensing in lightning, thunder, and storm the proximity of an overwhelming power, and in the scent of blossoms and the warm fanning of the breeze the loving approach of a higher being?

Maxims and Reflections 808 (posthumous)

"Nature conceals God!" But not to every eye!

Maxims and Reflections 811 (posthumous)

Nature is always Jehovah. What she is, what she was, and what she ever shall be.

Maxims and Reflections 1304 (posthumous)

GOD AND THE WORLD

. . . then let me set forth my general confession of faith:

a) Nature contains everything that is contained in the subject,

y) Plus something more;

b) The subject contains everything that is contained in nature,

z) Plus something more.

b can come to know *a;* but of *y, z* can have no more than an intimation. This constitutes the balance of the world and the sphere of life assigned to us. The being which could span all four aspects with maximum clarity has at all times been given the name of God by all peoples.

To Schlosser, Feb. 19-May 5, 1815

At this moment the voice of a departed friend [*Hamann*] is heard seconding our conviction: If the operation of chance is assumed in small matters the world ceases to be good, or for that matter to exist. But if trifling effects have their source in eternal laws, just as a world age is automatically made up of an infinity of days, then it is really Providence operating in the tiniest parts which makes of the whole something that is good.

The German Gil Blas (Review; 1821); 37, 200

It would not be worth one's while to live to the age of seventy, if all the wisdom of the world were folly in the sight of God. *Maxims and Reflections* 618 (1829)

The apostles of utility would think they were losing their God if they should not pray to him who gave the ox his horns in order that he defend himself. May I on my part be permitted to adore him who was so great in the lavishness of his creation as to make a plant, after a thousand others, in which they are all contained, and after animals of a thousand varieties a being that contains them all: man.

Let them continue to adore him who gives the animals their pasture, and man food and drink according to his desire. But I pray to him who endowed the world with so productive an energy that if only the millionth part of it comes to life, the world teems with creatures, so that war, pestilence, water, and fire cannot destroy it. That is *my* God. *Eckermann,* Feb. 20, 1831. *Biedermann* 2921

God has by no means settled down to rest after the well-known fabled six days of creation. He is, rather, continuously active as on the first day. To put this clumsy world together out of simple elements and let it revolve year in, year out, in the rays of the sun would certainly not have diverted him if he had not had the plan to fashion, on this material basis, a nursery for a world of spirits. Thus he is now ceaselessly active in minds of higher endowment, in order to develop those of more limited range.

Eckermann, March 11, 1832. *Biedermann* 3055

To the mathematician everything appears tangible, comprehensible, and mechanical, and he comes under suspicion of being secretly an atheist, inasmuch as he fancies himself as comprehending in his scheme the most immeasurable essence which we call God, and thereby seems to renounce his specific or pre-eminent existence.

Maxims and Reflections 1286 (posthumous)

GOD AND MAN

I feel . . . borne along in the glorious, infinitely holy ocean of our Father whom though our arms cannot grasp we nevertheless can touch.

To Graf zu Stolberg, Oct. 26, 1775

Once we conceive it as possible [the uncle remarked] that the creator of the world should have taken on the guise of his creation and dwelt in the world for a time, subject to its conditions of existence, then this creature of his must appear endowed with infinite perfection to have permitted such intimate union with it on his part. There cannot then be any innate contradiction between the idea of man and that of Godhead; and even though we often sense ourselves as dissimilar to and removed from the Deity, we are under obligation all the more not to play the devil's advocate all the time and concentrate upon the frailties of our flesh, but rather to look for the marks of perfection by which we can confirm our claim to being constituted in the likeness of God's image.

Wilhelm Meister's Apprenticeship VI (1795); 18, 149

That factor which eludes human calculations and which is most conspicuously effective in those operations which are planned to show climactic moments of human greatness—after the event men call it chance—that is none other than God's omnipotence starkly emerging and glorifying itself by the most trifling means.

Riemer, Nov. 25, 1807. *Biedermann* 1050

A teacher who succeeds in awakening a response by his presentation of even a single good deed, a single good poem, does more than one who transmits to us by description and name whole series of subordinate natural formations; for the upshot of the latter's labors merely demonstrates what we know in advance, to wit: The human form is pre-eminently and uniquely fashioned in the likeness of God's image.

Elective Affinities II, 7 (Ottilie's Diary) (1809); 21, 213

For the individual, too, can give practical effect to his kinship with God only by submission and worship.

The Autobiography I, 5 (1811); 22, 239

Our condition, though it may seem to draw us down and oppress us, nevertheless affords us the opportunity and, in fact, imposes on us the duty to rise up and fulfill the designs of the Deity by a rhythmic pulsation of compensating activities: while we are compelled on the one hand to strive for self-realization, we must not neglect on the other to divest ourselves of our ego.

The Autobiography II, 8 (1812); 23, 167

On the text *In Te Domine Speravi* I could tell you a long story, how, harassed by inner and outer troubles, I revolved it in my Bohemian retreat, without rhythm and melody, as a four-person, not to say a four-part, song, consumed by the wish to hear these beautiful words set to music by you.

To Zelter, Feb. 23, 1814

This antinomy in our way of conceiving is why we men never arrive at entering a clean column of knowledge in our ledger, but keep formulating old truths and old errors in ever new ways. That is why we never succeed in expressing ourselves quite intelligibly on many things, and I often have to fall back on saying to myself: On this and that feature, in the way nature is constituted, I can talk only with God; what business is it of the world? It either grasps my way of conceiving or else it does not, and in the latter case men cannot help me. So, concerning many things I can talk only with God.

S. Boisserée, Aug. 2, 1815. *Biedermann* 1684

God, the good God. To them who daily use the expression, especially the clergy, it becomes a phrase, a mere name used without thinking. If they were imbued with a sense of his greatness, they would turn mute and not be able to utter the name for reverence.

Eckermann, Dec. 31, 1823. *Biedermann* 2212

As soon as we concede free will to man the omniscience of God falls by the boards; for as soon as God knows what I am going to do, I am compelled to act in conformity with his knowledge.

I simply mention this as an instance of how little we know and how hazardous it is to tamper with divine mysteries. *Eckermann,* Oct. 15, 1825. *Biedermann* 2364

[Fatalism of the Mohammedans.] I will not try to figure out what is true or false, useful or harmful about this doctrine; but at bottom we all share this belief in some manner even without its having been taught us. The bullet on which my name is not inscribed will not hit me, says the soldier in battle, and without this faith how could he keep up his courage and serenity in the thick of danger? The Christian doctrine, according to which not a sparrow falls to the ground without the will of the heavenly Father, springs from the same source and points to his Providence, which watches over the most infinitesimal trifles and without whose will and sanction nothing can happen.

Eckermann, April 11, 1827. *Biedermann* 2484

All productivity of the highest type, every significant *aperçu,* every invention, every great thought that brings fruit and has success, is subject to no one's bidding and transcends all human power. All such things man has to regard as unexpected gifts from above, as pure children of God to be received and revered with joyful gratitude. Such things are akin to the daemonic and its irresistible sway to which man surrenders unconsciously while he fancies that he is acting spontaneously. In such cases man is often to be regarded as the instrument of a higher ruling power, as a vessel found worthy of harboring the divine influence. I say this in the realization that often a single thought has altered the shape of whole centuries, and that individuals have sometimes impressed their whole age with a personal stamp still discernible to succeeding generations and continuing in its beneficent effect.

Eckermann, March 11, 1828. *Biedermann* 2578

And what cannot be resolved by any manner of means we leave to God as the all-conditioning and all-liberating being.

Wilhelm Meister's Journeyings I, 7 (1829); 19, 95

Putting it briefly, I [Wilhelm] would say: Great thoughts and a pure heart, that is what we should implore God to give us.

Wilhelm Meister's Journeyings I, 10 (1829); 19, 136

I do not ask whether this highest being has understanding and reason. I feel, it *is* understanding, it *is* reason. All creatures are permeated with it, and man has a sufficiently large share of it to let him discern the All-Highest in part.

Eckermann, Feb. 23, 1831. Biedermann 2924

[Faust II.] Its conclusion is in harmony with our religious conviction according to which we do not attain to salvation merely through our own strength but require the aid of divine grace as well.

Eckermann, June 6, 1831. Biedermann 2969

I believe in a God—this is a fine, praiseworthy thing to say. But to acknowledge God wherever and however he manifests himself, that in truth is heavenly bliss on earth.

Maxims and Reflections 809 (posthumous)

Kepler said: The God whom I find everywhere in the universe about me—to become aware of him in like measure within myself, that is my highest wish. This noble individual was not conscious of the fact that at that very moment the divine within him and the divine of the universe were most intimately united.

Maxims and Reflections 812 (posthumous)

If our horizon is wide, God is all; if our horizon is narrow, God is a supplement of our wretchedness.

Maxims and Reflections 813 (posthumous)

Question: What is predestination?
Answer: God is mightier and wiser than we and therefore does with us according to his pleasure.

Maxims and Reflections 817 (posthumous)

Nature

THE CREATIVE PROCESS

Even though I for my part adhere more or less to the doctrine of Lucretius and limit my aspirations to the sphere of this life, I always take pleasure and comfort in observing that Nature's motherly solicitude has delicate overtones in the modulations of her harmonies for tender souls and allows finite man to glimpse the eternal and the infinite in a variety of ways.

To Graf zu Stolberg, Feb. 2, 1789

Man is accustomed to value things only in the measure of their usefulness to himself; and since by virtue of his nature and position he is bound to regard himself as the last achievement of creation, it is only natural for him to think of himself also as its final aim. Why should not his vanity inveigle him into this little fallacy? . . . If he believes that everything exists for his sake, as a tool and aid for his own existence, he will naturally be led to the conclusion that Nature has gone to work in as intentional and purposive a way to provide him with aids as is his own practice. . . . A natural scientist will have to rise above this trivial view of things. . . . To say, for instance, that the fish exists for the water seems to me a much less meaningful way of puttings things than to say: The fish exists in the water and by means of the water; for this second formulation expresses much more clearly the idea, only vaguely suggested by the first, that the existence of a creature that we call a fish is possible only on condition that there be an element that we call water, not only as

the conditioning medium of its being but also of its be-
coming.
Essay on Comparative Biology (about 1790)
W. A. Werke, Zweite Abteilung, 7, 218-21

Our comparative study of the skull of the mammals
suggests an idea which we must grasp in its strictest application and never tire of repeating: Not only does Nature fashion this dominant part of the animal structure
according to one and the self-same model, but she also
accomplishes her aim in all cases by the identical means.
The great variety of bone formations in the skulls of all
mammals proceeds from an identical *Anlage*, and in all
instances they develop at bottom in an identical way, despite the greatest variety of modifications. . . . [Since
some parts tend to escape detection] a careful search for
these is indicated, and because we are convinced that
they must turn up we must not relax our efforts until they
have been found and their form and relation to the other
parts have been exactly defined.
Essay on the Gestalt of Animals (Fragment; 1790)
W. A. Werke, Zweite Abteilung, 8, 272-3

In studying the mystery of reproduction, the comparison of the two sexes brings us to the verge of sensuous-
intuitive corroboration of our supreme concept—that Nature is able to modify and transform identical organs in
such a manner as not only to make them seem totally un-
related in form and function but actually, in a sense, to
set them in opposition to one another.
Introduction to Comparative Anatomy (1796); 39, 170

The organic parts of the plant—leaves and flowers,
stamens and pistils, the great variety of covering tissues
and whatever else strikes the senses—they are all identical organs which a succession of vegetative operations
modifies and transforms beyond recognition.

The same organ can fan out into a compound leaf of the utmost complexity and contract to form the simplest stalk. Depending on circumstances, the same organ can develop into a flower bud or into an infertile twig. The calyx, forcing its development, can become a corolla; and the corolla can undergo a regression in the direction of the calyx.

Introduction to Comparative Anatomy (1796); 39, 173

The real truth is, however, that most people, being formless themselves and being unable to attain to any *Gestalt*, strive to deprive objects of their *Gestalt* and reduce everything to chaotic matter, in which category they themselves belong. They reduce everything to its so-called effect. Everything is relative in their sight; so they relativize everything except nonsense and triteness, which hold absolute sway, as is to be expected.

Wilhelm Meister's Apprenticeship VIII, 8 (1796); 18, 352

When Nature abhors she is loud in her protest. The creature that violates the laws of being cannot take shape. The creature that lives in violation of Nature's law is quickly destroyed. Sterility, a stunted existence, early disintegration—these are her curses, the marks of her rigor. She punishes only by way of direct consequences. Look about you, and you will readily see what is forbidden, what is accursed. In the stillness of the cloister and in the tumult of the world a thousand acts that enjoy the sanction of religion and convention fall under her ban. She looks with troubled eye upon easy indolence and overexertion, on indulgence and luxury no less than on dearth and want. Moderation is her counsel. All her relationships are true, and all her effects are accomplished without fanfare. *Wilhelm Meister's Apprenticeship* VIII, 9 (1796); 18, 364

At everything she wants to make Nature arrives only in

a sequence. She could not make a horse, for example, without that whole series of animals having gone before on which she climbs, as on a ladder, to the structure of a horse. Thus in all things the individual exists for the whole and vice versa, because the individual is at the same time the whole. Nature, however diverse her manifestations, is always one—a unity; and thus for each particular manifestation all the rest must serve as a basis and each in turn must fit into the context of all the rest.

Riemer, March 19, 1807. *Biedermann* 971

The skeletons of some marine animals show plainly that, even while designing these, Nature was already feeling her way toward the higher idea of land animals. . . . I would call them marvelous, these transitions in nature, if in nature the marvelous did not happen to be the universally common. . . . You can imagine Nature standing at a gaming-counter, as it were, constantly shouting "Double" and continuing to play with her winnings in all her domains with unfailing luck *ad infinitum.* The stone, the animal, the plant—after a number of such lucky throws they are all put at stake again; and who knows but that man himself is not in his turn just another throw for higher winnings?

Falk, June 14, 1809. *Biedermann* 1185

Plant chemistry—applying terms of lower organization symbolically to the higher. The time will come when intelligent students will have discarded mechanistic and atomistic conceptions altogether in favor of viewing all phenomena in terms of dynamic and chemical processes, thus making the divine life of nature more and more manifest.

Diary, April 22, 1812

The German has the word *"Gestalt"* to designate the complex of being of an actual organism. In using this term he ignores the factor of mobility; he assumes that a composite entity is precisely delimited and fixed.

But when we examine whatever confronts us in the way of *Gestalt*, we find that nothing fixed, static, or precisely delineated occurs and that everything is in a ceaseless state of flux. For this reason our language quite appropriately uses the word *"Bildung"* to designate the product as well as the activity that gives rise to it.

In introducing a study of morphology, therefore, we must not talk of *Gestalt*. Or, granting the use of the word, we must keep in mind the idea, the concept of something that appears fixed in experience only for the moment.

That which is formed is straightway transformed again, and if we would to some degree arrive at a living intuition of Nature, we must on our part remain forever mobile and plastic, according to her own example.

Preface to the first issue of Morphology (1817); 39, 251-2

"Natural system"—a contradiction in terms. Nature has no system. It has—it is—life and consistency expanding from an unknown center to limits that we cannot discern. That makes the study of nature a limitless pursuit, regardless of whether you proceed by analysis of individual features, or whether you plot out the height and breadth of the whole.   *Problems.* [Botany.] (1823); 39, 342

The vintner's occupation . . . Nature, from whatever angle you approach her, has a glorious way of becoming ever truer, ever more manifest, unfolding ever more, ever deeper, although she remains herself, always the same.

To Meyer, Aug. 10, 1828

"Nature does nothing for nothing" is an old Philistine saying. She is eternally alive, prodigal and extravagant in her workings, to keep the infinite ever present, because nothing can endure without change.

To Zelter, Aug. 13, 1831

THE INCOMMENSURABLE

The true, which is identical with the divine, transcends our grasp as such. We perceive it only as reflection, parable, symbol, in specific and related manifestations. We become aware of it as life that defies comprehension, and for all that we cannot renounce the wish to comprehend.

Essay on Meteorology (1825); 40, 55

Man was not born to solve the problems of the universe but rather to try to put his finger on the problem and then to keep within the limits of the comprehensible.

To measure the acts of the universe, our faculties do not suffice; and to attempt to span the universe with reason is an altogether futile endeavor for so limited a scope as ours. Man's reason and the reason of Godhead are two altogether different things.

Eckermann, Oct. 15, 1825. *Biedermann* 2364

I shall tell you something that may serve as a guide in life: There is in nature what is within reach and what is beyond reach. Ponder this well and with respect. A great deal is already gained if we impress this general fact upon our mind, even though it always remains difficult to see where the one ends and the other begins. He who is unaware of the distinction may waste himself in lifelong toil trying to get at the inaccessible without ever getting close to truth. But he who knows it and is wise will stick to what is accessible; and in exploring this region in all directions and confirming his gains he will even push back the confines of the inaccessible. Even so he will have to admit in the end that some things can be mastered only to a certain degree and that nature always retains a problematic aspect too deep for human faculties to fathom. *Eckermann, April 11, 1827. Biedermann 2484*

The phenomena of meteorology are something living that we see at work every day, and they certainly presuppose a synthesis. However, the contributing factors are so manifold that this synthesis is beyond man's grasp and eludes his most painstaking researches and observations. We set our compass toward hypotheses, toward imaginary islands, but the true synthesis will probably remain an undiscovered land.
Eckermann, Feb. 13, 1829. Biedermann 2657

The highest thing man can attain to is to marvel. When the *Urphaenomen* [proto-phenomenon] makes him marvel, let him be content. It cannot afford him an experience beyond this, and to seek something else behind it is futile. Here is the limit. But as a rule men are not satisfied to behold an *Urphaenomen*. They think there must be something beyond. They are like children who, having looked into a mirror, turn it around to see what is on the other side. *Eckermann, Feb. 18, 1829. Biedermann 2661*

[Wilhelm on the observatory.] How can man face the infinite? How, except by taking all his spiritual energies that are drawn in sundry directions, collecting them in his innermost, deepest self, and asking: Can you dare even to think of yourself in the midst of this eternally living order without there asserting itself within you too something that is in ceaseless motion and describes its orbit about a pure center? And even if you were to find it difficult to locate this center within you, you would recognize it by the fact that a kind and soothing effect emanates from it and testifies to its existence.
Wilhelm Meister's Journeyings I, 10 (1829); 19, 137

There are some problems in natural science which cannot properly be discussed without recourse to metaphysics—not in the sense of scholastic verbiage, but as that which was, is, and shall be before, with, and after physics.

Maxims and Reflections 546 (1829)

Man must cling to the belief that the incomprehensible is comprehensible. Else he would give up investigating.

Maxims and Reflections 563 (1829)

It were the height of insight to realize that everything factual as such is, in a sense, theory. The blue of the sky exhibits the basic law of chromatics. There is no sense in looking for something behind phenomena. They *are* theory.

Maxims and Reflections 575 (1829)

"Lo, he goeth by me, and I see him not: he passeth on also, but I perceive him not." [Job ix, 11.]

Goethe's Entry in Eckermann's Album, April 21, 1830.
Biedermann 2817

Although we gladly acknowledge Nature's mysterious *encheiresis,* her faculty of creating and furthering life, and, without being mystics, admit the existence of ultimate limits to our explorations, we are nevertheless convinced that man, if he is serious about it, cannot desist from the attempt to keep encroaching upon the region of the unexplorable. In the end, of course, he has to give up and willingly concede his defeat.

To Wackenroder, Jan. 21, 1832

The highest happiness of man as a thinking being is to have probed what is knowable and quietly to revere what is unknowable.

Maxims and Reflections 1207 (posthumous)

IDEA AND EXPERIENCE

We arrived at Schiller's house. Our unfinished conversation induced me to enter; and there I vividly sketched my theory on the metamorphosis of plants. . . . But when I had finished he shook his head, saying: "That is not an experience; that is an idea."

Annals. Biographical Details. First Acquaintance with Schiller (1794); 30, 391

That the observation of nature leads to thinking; that its abundance makes us resort to a variety of methods in order to manipulate it even to some degree—on this there seems to be general agreement. But only a limited few are equally aware of the fact that the contemplation of nature suggests ideas to which we ascribe the same degree of certainty as to nature itself—a greater degree, in fact; and that we have a right to be guided by these ideas both in our search for data and in our attempts to arrange what we have found.

To Steffens, May 29, 1801

Whereas you strive for the universal, my constitution compels me to seek the specific. My tendency is to incorporate ideas, yours to dematerialize them; and it is just in this operation—from opposite points of approach —that we coincide.　*To von Willemer,* April 24, 1815

Idea and experience will never coincide in the center. Only art and action can effect a synthesis.

To Schopenhauer, Jan. 28, 1816

Everything that takes place is a symbol. In representing itself perfectly it suggests what lies beyond. In this

95

reflection extreme modesty and extreme pretentiousness seem to me combined. *To Schubarth,* April 2, 1818

If we conscientiously persist in our efforts we may finally admit the philosopher to be right who claims that no idea finds its adequate correspondence in experience, but concedes that idea and experience can be analogous, and indeed they must.

The difficulty of bringing idea and experience into relation with one another makes itself very painfully felt in all investigation of nature. The idea is independent of space and time. Research is limited in space and time. Hence in the idea simultaneous and successive features are most intimately linked, whereas these are always separated in experience; and to think of a process of nature as simultaneous and successive at once, in accordance with the idea, makes our heads spin. The understanding is unable to conceive of those sense data as jointly present which experience transmitted to it one at a time. Thus the contradiction between ideation and perception remains forever unresolved.

Doubt and Resignation (1820); 39, 35

But in referring you to the reality immediately at hand —which you might almost deem unworthy of artistic imitation—I would add that the spirit of reality is true ideality. We must not spurn the sensuous-moral life about us, otherwise we ride without ballast.

To Leopoldine Grustner von Grusdorf, March 30, 1827

An *Urphaenomen* [proto-phenomenon] is not to be regarded as a basic theorem leading to a variety of consequences, but rather as a basic manifestation enveloping the specifications of form for the beholder. Contemplation, knowledge, divination, faith—all these feelers with which man reaches out into the universe must set to work jointly if we are to fulfill our important but difficult task.

To von Buttel, May 3, 1827

GENIUS

I believe that all that genius does as genius happens unconsciously. A man of genius can also act reasonably, deliberately, from conviction, but he does so on the side as it were. No work of genius can be improved or freed of its faults by reflection and its immediate consequences. Action and reflection can serve, however, gradually to refine genius to such a degree that it ends by producing faultless works. The more highly the age itself is endowed with genius, the more does the individual benefit.

To Schiller, April 3-4, 1801

For what is genius but that productive energy which finds expression in deeds that can bear the scrutiny of God and Nature and which for that reason have an inner consistency and a lasting effect? All of Mozart's works have this quality. They are possessed of procreative energy that transmits itself from generation to generation and is not likely to be exhausted or consumed for a long time to come. The same holds true for other great composers and artists. . . . Lessing deprecated the high label of genius for his own person, but his enduring effects bear testimony to the contrary. There are literary names of note, on the other hand, that passed for great men of genius while they lived but whose effect was limited to their own lifetime. These proved to be less than they and others thought. For, as I have said, there is no genius without a continuing productive energy, and it makes no difference, furthermore, what activity, art, or calling the individual of genius may pursue. An individual may manifest genius in science, like Oken or Humboldt, or in war and civil administration like Frederick, Peter the Great, and Napoleon, or he may write a song like Béranger—it is all the same provided the thought, the intuition, the deed have vitality that endures.

Eckermann, March 11, 1828. Biedermann 2578

[On Mozart] But where should the deity find room to work miracles, unless the occasional appearance of extraordinary individuals pass for such—individuals we gaze at in astonishment without comprehending whence they come? *Eckermann, Feb. 14, 1831. Biedermann 2915*

THE DAEMONIC

You will find that a man's career frequently takes a turn in middle life. Whereas everything favored him in his youth and one success followed another, now of a sudden everything changes, and he is beset by one accident and misfortune after another.

Let me tell you my idea about this: The individual has to be ruined again. Every extraordinary person has a certain mission which he is called upon to fulfill. After he has accomplished it he is no longer needed on earth in this form, and Providence makes use of him for something else. But inasmuch as everything here on earth is effected by the operation of natural forces, the daemons engage in efforts to trip him up until they have him down. That was the way with Napoleon. Mozart at the age of thirty-six. Raphael. Byron. All of them had completely fulfilled their missions, and it was time, I daresay, that they departed, so that in this long-range project of a world something might be left for other people to do.

Eckermann, March 11, 1828. Biedermann 2578

But let me tell you, the world is not meant to arrive at its goal as quickly as we think and wish. The retarding daemons are ever-present, putting up interference and opposition everywhere, so that there is progress by and large, to be sure, but of a very slow sort.

Eckermann, Oct. 10, 1828. *Biedermann* 2635

The higher a man's status, Goethe said, the more he is under the sway of daemons, and he must always be on his guard lest he be diverted from the main course he has set himself.

Thus there was something peculiarly daemonic about my coming to visit Schiller. We might have been thrown together earlier or later. But the fact that it happened just during that epoch when my Italian journey had been achieved and Schiller was beginning to tire of philosophical speculation, was significant and led to the greatest results for us both.

Eckermann, March 24, 1829. *Biedermann* 2671

When you are old, Goethe said, your way of thinking about the things of the world is different from what it was when you were young. Thus I cannot brush aside the notion that the daemons, in order to mock and tease mankind, have a way at times of putting on display individuals so alluring that everyone emulates them and so great that everyone else falls short of the mark. Thus they set up Raphael, who was equally perfect in conception and execution. One or the other master has subsequently approached him but none is his equal. Thus they set up Mozart as something out of reach in the sphere of music. And thus, in poetry, Shakespeare. I know what you can object with regard to him, but I am speaking only of his endowment, the great gift he was born with. And in a similar way there is Napoleon without a match.

Eckermann, Dec. 6, 1829. *Biedermann* 2747

The daemonic, Goethe said, is that which defies analysis by the understanding and by reason. I am not endowed with it, but I am subject to its influence.

Napoleon, I said, seems to have had this daemonic quality. He did so, said Goethe, in the highest degree, so that scarcely anyone else can be compared to him. Also the late Grand Duke [Carl August] had a daemonic endowment. He was restless and full of boundless energy, so that his own territory was too small for him and even the greatest would have left him dissatisfied. Such daemonic beings the Greeks numbered among the half-gods.

Do not events also show a daemonic aspect? I asked. Decidedly, said Goethe; those in particular that the understanding and reason cannot analyze. And it manifests itself in the greatest variety of ways in all nature, in the invisible as well as the visible realm. Some creatures are daemonic throughout; in others the daemonic is partially effective.

Does not Mephistopheles, too, have daemonic traits, I asked. No, said Goethe. Mephistopheles is far too negative a being, whereas the daemonic asserts itself through positive energy. Among artists, Goethe continued, musicians are pre-eminently disposed to it, painters less so. Paganini shows it to a high degree, which accounts for the spell of his performance.

Eckermann, March 2, 1831. *Biedermann* 2927

In poetry there is something decidedly daemonic—especially in unconscious poetry, which fails to satisfy the intelligence and for that reason transcends everything conceptual in its appeal.

It is the same with music, in the highest degree. Its loftiness is beyond the grasp of the understanding. It casts an all-powerful spell that defies rational analysis.

That is why religion cannot do without music. It is one of the prime means for evoking a miraculous response.

Similarly the daemonic essence likes to take possession of outstanding individuals, especially those in high places like Frederick and Peter the Great. The late Grand Duke [Carl August] was possessed of it to a degree that made him irresistible. . . . If he had only had it in him to take hold of my ideas in the higher realm of the spirit. For when the daemonic spirit passed out of him and only his human self remained, he did not know what to do with himself and was in a wretched state.

Eckermann, March 8, 1831. *Biedermann* 2931

He [adolescent Goethe] fancied that in nature, animate and inanimate as well, he could perceive something manifesting itself only in contradictions and incapable for that reason of being reduced to a concept, much less to a word. It was not divine, for it seemed devoid of reason; not human, for it lacked intelligence; not diabolic, for it was benevolent; not angelic, for it often manifested malicious pleasure. It was like chance in being inconsistent. It resembled Providence, in suggesting a pattern. Everything that finds us blocked seemed penetrable to it. It seemed to manipulate the necessary elements of our life in arbitrary fashion. It controlled time and expanded space. It seemed to take pleasure only in the impossible and spurn the possible with disdain. This essence, that seemed to move in the midst of all others, uniting and separating them, I termed daemonic after the example of the ancients and those who had perceived something similar. . . .

Although this daemonic essence can manifest itself in everything corporeal and incorporeal—it exhibits itself in animals in the most remarkable ways—nevertheless it is pre-eminently in the human sphere that it shows its exceedingly strange workings. It is a power either opposed to the moral order of the universe or at least at cross-purposes with it, so that the one may be regarded as the warp and the other as the woof of the tissue.

The phenomena produced in this way go by innumerable names. All philosophies and religions have attempted to solve this puzzle in poetry and prose and have finally tried to dismiss the matter. We shall not chide them for continuing their efforts along these lines.

But the most fearsome and uncanny manifestation of this daemonic essence is seen when it dominates an individual. During my lifetime I have had occasion to observe this, sometimes near at hand, sometimes at a distance. These are not necessarily individuals of outstanding intelligence and talents, and they are rarely distinguished by a genuinely kindly disposition. But an enormous energy radiates from them, and they exercise an incredible power over all creatures, even including the elements. And who can say how far such an effect will extend? All moral forces acting in unison are of no avail against them. It is in vain that the more enlightened part of mankind tries to brand them as deceived or as deceivers: the masses are attracted by them. Rarely or never more than one such individual exists at a time, and such a one can be conquered only by the universe itself to which it has thrown down the gage. Such observations may have given rise to that strange but momentous saying: *Nemo contra deum nisi deus ipse.*

The Autobiography IV, 20 (posthumous); 25, 124-6

IMAGINATION

The artist is like Sunday's child: only he sees spirits. But after he has told of their appearing to him everybody sees them.   *Böttiger,* Dec. 28-29, 1797. *Biedermann* 535

The imagination lurks as the most powerful foe. It has an irresistible affinity for the absurd. Even cultured individuals are subject to this impulse to a high degree. It is hostile to all civilized life and it confronts our decorous society with a reversion to the innate rudeness of the savage and his love of grimaces. Annals (1805); 30, 188

[Kant's philosophy.] An observation that struck me in reading it through deserves mention. Paragraph three [of the *Critique of Pure Reason*] seems to harbor a major deficiency which makes itself felt in the whole development of that philosophy. Here the major faculties of the mind are listed as sensation, understanding, and reason. But the imagination is overlooked, causing an irreparable gap. Imagination is the fourth major faculty of our mental constitution. It supplements sensation in the form of memory. It submits a pattern of the world to the understanding, in the form of experience. It creates or finds sensuous shapes corresponding to the ideas of reason. Thus it gives life to the totality of the self, which would otherwise stagnate.

Whereas imagination performs such services for its sister faculties, it is only through these dear kinfolk that imagination in turn is introduced to the realms of reality and truth. Sensation presents to it shapes of clean and definite contour; the understanding regulates its productive energy; and reason provides it with complete assurance that it is not playing with dream phantoms but is founded on ideas.

To repeat and amplify: What we ordinarily call the understanding is based on sensation. The pure understanding, however, is self-contained, subject to its own laws. Reason soars above the understanding but without severing the connection with it. Imagination hovers above sensation and is attracted by it. But as soon as imagination spies reason above, it attaches itself firmly to this highest guide. And thus we see the sphere of our modes completely rounded but infinite nevertheless, because one faculty always has need of the others and they all supplement each other mutually.

To the Hereditary Grand Duchess Maria Paulowna,
Jan. 3, 1817

The worst of it is that thinking doesn't help thought. You must have the right start by nature for bright ideas to spring forth like free children of God, as it were, hailing us with the cry: "Here we are."

Eckermann, Feb. 24, 1824. *Biedermann 2228*

THE AGING PROCESS

I remember how Lavater reproached me: "You too act as though we were expecting to live to be three hundred." And yet, in matters of science particularly, there is nothing else we can do. *To S. Boisserée,* June 18, 1819

Everything moves so slowly, as though one planned to live to an age of three hundred years. But one gets to be that old and older, if one but attends to one's daily tasks honestly. *To von Esenbeck,* June 23, 1820

To live long is to survive much—loved, hated, and indifferent people, kingdoms, capitals, even forests and trees that we sowed and planted in youth. We survive ourselves, and we are indeed grateful if even a few gifts of body and mind are still ours. We submit to all transitoriness with a good grace. Provided our thought remains fixed at every moment upon what is eternal, the passage of time does not make us suffer.

To Graefin Auguste Luise Bernstorff, née Stolberg, April
17, 1823

The advantage of old age, despite many lacks, is being able to pass in review a whole century and dwell upon it almost as though it were personally present.

Biographical Monuments by Varnhagen von Ense
(Review; 1824) 37, 279

To mellow in one's judgments, all that is needed is to get older. I see no fault being committed that I too did not commit in my time.

Maxims and Reflections 240 (1824)

You are often cautioned against scattering your energies and having too many irons in the fire; especially the older you get the more you should guard against being involved in new pursuits. That is all very well, dishing out such advice to oneself and to others. The fact is that growing older is tantamount to taking on a new pursuit. All relationships undergo a change in the process, and it becomes a question of either ceasing to act altogether or of adopting the new role willingly and consciously.

Maxims and Reflections 259 (1825)

The man grown old has forfeited one of the major rights of man: he is no longer judged by his own peers.

Maxims and Reflections 371 (1826)

Every entelechy has a share in eternity, and the few years during which it is joined to the earthly body do not age it. If the entelechy is of inferior quality, it will have little power to assert itself during its period of bodily obscuration; the body will dominate, and when it ages the entelechy will not be able to halt or mitigate this decline. But if the entelechy happens to be powerful, as is the case in all men of genius, it will not only permeate the organization of the body with an invigorating and ennobling quality of life, but, by virtue of its spiritual

105

dominance, it will also be tending to assert its prerogative of eternal youth. This accounts for the fact that pre-eminently gifted men experience fresh epochs of special productivity even in old age. They seem to be subject, from time to time, to a burst of rejuvenation, to what I should call a recurrence of puberty.

Eckermann, March 11, 1828. *Biedermann 2578*

In going over the letters I wrote in that period, I see clearly how every age is marked by certain advantages and disadvantages that distinguish it from others. Thus in my fortieth year I had as clear a view of some things as now; in some respects I was even ahead. Nevertheless, now in my eightieth year I possess advantages which I should not be willing to exchange for those.

Eckermann, April 12, 1829. *Biedermann 2680*

Perhaps I may whisper it in your ear: I am experiencing the happiness of having ideas unfold in my old age, which to develop and bring to realization might well be worth living life over again.   *To Zelter*, April 29, 1830

Whereas man undergoes a change in the various stages of his life, he does not thereby improve, and in certain matters his judgment may be as good in his twentieth year as in his sixtieth. The world bears a different aspect, of course, when seen from the plain, as compared to the view afforded from the peaks of the foothills, or from the glaciers of the highest ranges. But that is all, and one cannot say that one view is truer than the others. When a writer leaves behind him monuments that date from various stages of his life, their value is to be judged by the following criteria: Do they exhibit an innate focus and a generous disposition, making for a steady eye and untainted feeling at every stage; and did he express what he thought sincerely and truthfully without hidden motives? If that was the case and what he wrote was right at the time, then it will continue to be right, regardless of the author's subsequent development.

Eckermann, Feb. 17, 1831. Biedermann 3123

To every age there corresponds a particular philosophy. The child appears as a realist, for he finds himself as convinced of the existence of apples and pears as of his own. The youth, beset by inner passions, is compelled to take note of himself and feel his way forward; he is transformed into an idealist. Mature man, on the other hand, has every reason to become a skeptic. He does well to doubt whether the means he has chosen will lead to realization of his objective. Before acting and in acting let him be on the alert to keep his understanding flexible, in order to spare himself regrets over false moves. Old age, however, will always show a predilection for mysticism. It observes that ever so many things seem dependent upon chance. Unreasonable plans succeed, reasonable plans fail, fortune and misfortune strike an unexpected balance. Thus it is, thus it was; and advanced old age finds solace in him who was, is, and ever shall be.

Maxims and Reflections 806 (posthumous)

When one grows older one must consciously arrest one's advance at a certain level.

Maxims and Reflections 987 (posthumous)

It does not behoove the man of years to follow the fashion either in his way of thinking or in his way of dressing. *Maxims and Reflections* 988 (posthumous)

A burned child shuns the fire. An old man who has often been singed is afraid to go and warm himself.

Maxims and Reflections 931 (posthumous)

To become aware betimes in youth of the advantages of age; to preserve in age the advantages of youth—both are but gifts of fortune.

Maxims and Reflections 992 (posthumous)

YOUTH

The attachments of men reach out toward what is alive. Youth models itself on youth.

Riemer. Sept. 13, 1810. *Biedermann* 1335

In my best years friends who had reason to know me would repeatedly tell me that the quality of my living was better than that of my spoken word, that my spoken word was better than my writing, and that my writing was better than what appeared in print.

Autobiographical Notes (After 1810); W. A. *Werke*, 36, 232

The most foolish of all errors is for young people to believe that they lose their originality by accepting the truths which have already been accepted by their predecessors.

Maxims and Reflections 254 (1824)

Everyone believes in his youth that the world began to exist only with his own coming, and that in reality everything exists on his account.

Eckermann, Dec. 6, 1829. *Biedermann* 2747

And to add another reflection, I may properly confess that the first experience of the blossoming forth of the world of sense in my life seemed to put me in touch with genuine, original nature, whereas everything that presented itself to the senses at a later date had something of the air of a copy about it that, while approaching the original, nevertheless lacked the freshness of its spirit and meaning.

Wilhelm Meister's Journeyings II, 11 (1829); 20, 37

The illusory expectations of adolescence suggest trees that bear double flowers, the kind that scarcely ever bear fruit.

Sorel, Aug. 21, 1830. *Biedermann* 2849

That is the way of youth and life generally, that we usually come to understand the strategy only after the campaign is over.

The Autobiography IV, 20 (posthumous); 25, 133

If youth is a fault, it is one that we get over soon enough.

Maxims and Reflections 991 (posthumous)

The immoderate expectations of the adolescent are not to be dismissed as illusions. But just as he then found the divination of things in his heart, so now he must seek the fulfillment in his heart, not on the outside.

Maxims and Reflections 993 (posthumous)

HAPPINESS

Last night I felt a great urge like Polycrates to throw my ring into the water; for in the quiet of the night I cast up the reckoning of my happiness and found a colossal sum.

To Charlotte von Stein, April 22, 1781

Goethe now thinks of all happiness and well-being in terms of proportion and of unhappiness in terms of disproportion.

Caroline Herder, Aug. 14, 1788. *Biedermann* 289

Man does not begin to be happy until his innermost drive determines its own movement.

Wilhelm Meister's Apprenticeship VIII, 5 (1796); 18, 328

Fortunately man can encompass only a certain degree of calamity. What exceeds this either destroys him or leaves him indifferent.

Elective Affinities II, 4 (1809); 21, 164

They have always praised me as one peculiarly favored by fortune; and I will not complain about the course of my life. Yet at bottom it has been nothing but labor and sorrow, and I can say in truth that in my seventy-five years I have not had four weeks of genuine well-being. It was the eternal wrestling with a stone that had to be pushed uphill over and over again.

Eckermann, Jan. 27, 1824. *Biedermann* 2220

And so I have fought my way through life to this day to find that even the extreme of happiness that would lift man above himself is blended with plenty of elements that admonish and compel me from hour to hour to keep hold of myself.

To Rauch, Oct. 21, 1827

A reasonable man needs only to practice moderation in order to experience happiness.

Wilhelm Meister's Journeyings II, 4 (1829); 19, 231

Nemo ante obitum beatus [No one is to be called happy before his end] is a saying that figures in history but turns out to be meaningless. A closer approach to the fact would be: Expect tribulations to the very end.

To Zelter, Nov. 21, 1830

NATURE

Nature with her boundless productivity fills all spaces. Take just our earth, for example: All that we call evil or unhappy is accounted for by the fact that she simply has not room enough to accommodate everything that springs into being, let alone give it enduring existence.

Maxims and Reflections 1251 (posthumous)

Science and Philosophy

THEORY

As for me, I shall owe you the greatest debt of gratitude if through you I succeed in making my peace with philosophers, whom I have never been able to do without and never been able to see eye to eye with.

To Fichte, June 24, 1794

No hypothesis can lay claim to any value unless it assembles many phenomena under one concept.

To Sömmering, Aug. 17, 1795

You can easily surmise what my attitude toward philosophy is. When it specializes in separating, I do not get along with it; and it has harmed me at times, I daresay, by interfering with the natural course of my development. But when it is bent on uniting, or, I should rather say, when it intensifies our original feeling that we are one with nature; when it secures this feeling and transforms it into a deep, steady intuition of the divine life in its ceaseless ebb and flow, even if such is not for us mortals to lead—then I welcome philosophy, and you can gauge my interest in your work accordingly.

To F. Jacobi, Nov. 23, 1801

As for that great philosophical movement begun by Kant, no scholar has ignored it or resisted it or neglected it without detriment to his work, unless it be those genuine students of classical antiquity who seem to be pre-eminently favored above other men by the nature of their subject.

Winckelmann. Philosophy (1805); 34, 37-8

Each item of knowledge involves a second, a third step,

and so on ad infinitum. If we pursue the life of the tree in its roots, or in its branches and twigs, one thing always follows from another. And the more vitally any concern of knowledge takes hold of us, the more we find ourselves driven to pursue it in its ramifications, both up and down.

Annals (1807); 30, 225-6

There would be much less disputing about objects of knowledge, their derivation and explanation, I am convinced, if everyone knew himself above all, and knew what party he instinctively belongs to and what point of view is most congenial to his make-up. We would then utter the maxims that govern us without hedging, and in accordance with them we would quietly communicate our experiences and judgments without getting involved in disputes. For the final upshot of all argument is that two irreconcilably opposed ways of thinking get to be expressed in full clearness, each party maintaining his own stand all the more doggedly and severely.

To von Leonhard, Oct. 12, 1807

It is an odd demand indeed, that is sometimes made, and not lived up to even by those who make it: They want you to report what you experience without any suggestion of a theoretical slant. It is to be left to the reader, the pupil, to work out a pattern according to his pleasure; for merely to look at a thing does not result in benefit. The activity of looking passes over into contemplation; contemplation leads to reflection; reflection brings forth a network of relationships. Thus one can say that every time we attentively open our eyes upon the world we get engaged in theorizing. But to theorize consciously, on the basis of self-knowledge, with freedom, and, I would even venture to say, with irony—what adroitness is needed if the resulting abstraction, which

116

we are afraid of, is to be innocuous, and the yield in cognition, which we hope for, is to become truly alive and useful!   *On Theory of Color.* Preface (1810); 40, 63

Every good book, especially those of the ancients, can be understood and enjoyed only by him who has something of his own to contribute. He who knows something finds infinitely more in them than he who comes merely to learn.

> *On Theory of Color.* Historical Part. Second Division.
> Theory and Use of Color among the Ancients (1810);
> 40, 139

The conflict within the individual between immediate experience and tradition is the real stuff of the history of science. For that which is done by and in the mass takes on real meaning only in the hands of the signally qualified individual who must collect, sift, edit, and unite all these sundry matters, and perhaps it is of no account whether his contemporaries support or oppose these his efforts. What can supporting them mean other than adding to the mass of material and popularizing it? That is useful, to be sure, but does not advance the main undertaking. . . .

Content without method leads to extravagance; method without content to empty sophistry; substance without form to ponderous learning; form without substance to hollow conceit.

> *On Theory of Color.* Historical Part. Third Division.
> Lacuna (1810); 40, 151

We might venture the statement that the history of science is science itself. We cannot really know what we possess until we have learned to know what others have possessed before us.

> *On Theory of Color.* Preface (1810); 40, 66

117

In the sciences everything depends on what one calls an *aperçu*—the discovery of something that is at the bottom of phenomena. Such a discovery is infinitely fruitful.

> *On Theory of Color.* Historical Part. Fifth Division.
> Galileo Galilei (1810); 40, 204

[Goethe reporting on the viewpoint he held in adolescence:] Over against their views I maintained that a special philosophy was not necessary, philosophy being completely embodied in religion and poetry. . . . Since poetry presupposes a certain belief in the impossible, and since religion is based on a similar belief in what passes the understanding, the philosophers seemed to me in an awkward situation in their attempts to prove and explain both within their sphere. A glance at the history of philosophy sufficed to demonstrate that each philosopher went in search of a different basis, and that the skeptic knocked the bottom out of all attempts to explain. . . .

In the oldest men and schools the feature that appealed to me most was that poetry, religion, and philosophy coincided in one undifferentiated whole.

> *The Autobiography* II, 6 (1812); 23, 7-8

The new chemistry. It strikes me as very remarkable that science, which in its origins was enveloped in mystery, must once more, in its infinite development, turn into a mystery.

> *To Seebeck*, April 29, 1812

As in all earthly things, so it is in science: The night is mightier than the day. Think of all the clouds and vapor, all the fog and haze. Even the serenest sky is inevitably dimmed by atmosphere and climatic qualifications. How they reduce the share of light that the sun would uniformly send down to us!

This fact prompted me, both in my *Theory of Color*

and in my utterances on matters of poetry, science, and art generally, to cultivate clearness rather than obscurity and to give preponderance to reason above divination, hoping in the presentation of what is without to give honor in the stillness of the heart to what is within.

To Windischmann, Dec. 28, 1812

I do not like to dispute in scientific matters. To be able to agree is what gives me pleasure.

To von Leonhard, Feb. 8, 1814

We are originals only because we know nothing.
On the Metamorphosis of Plants.
The Fate of My Manuscript (1817); 39, 328

There is in the sciences an eternal circulation. . . . And because our human ways of thinking also form a closed circle, any change of method involves the turning over of the coin, as it were. The atomistic approach will always alternate with the dynamic—not outright, but *a potiori*, for neither can replace the other completely. And this qualification applies to individuals too; for the most out-and-out dynamist will catch himself in atomistic formulations, and similarly no atomist can exclude dynamic conceptions altogether.

My Relation to Science, Especially Geology (1820); 40, 41

If level-headed, thoughtful men disparage science in their old age, it is because they expected too much of it and of themselves. *Maxims and Reflections* 154 (1821)

Even in the sciences, mere knowing is of no avail. It is always a matter of doing.
Maxims and Reflections 415 (1822)

Science helps us above all in facilitating that faculty of

marveling to which we are destined. Its other function is to provide life in its ceaseless evolution with new techniques for warding off what is harmful and promoting what is useful. *Maxims and Reflections* 417 (1822)

Theories are as a rule impulsive reactions of an over-hasty understanding which would like to have done with phenomena and therefore substitute images, concepts, or often even just words, in their place. One has an inkling, sometimes even a clear realization, of the fact that a theory is only a dodge. But are not passion and partisanship always on the lookout for dodges? And rightly so, since they are so much in need of them.

Maxims and Reflections 428 (1823)

Man was not born to solve the problems of the universe, but rather to seek to lay bare the heart of the problem and then confine himself within the limits of what is amenable to understanding.

Eckermann, Oct. 15, 1825. *Biedermann* 2364

At all times, it has been only individuals who have furthered science, not the age. It was the age that executed Socrates by poison, the age that burned Huss at the stake. Ages have always remained alike.

Maxims and Reflections 313 (1826)

With the sciences I fared like a person who, rising early, awaits first the dawn, then, impatiently, the sun, and is dazzled nevertheless when it appears.

Maxims and Reflections 372 (1826)

The greatest art, both in teaching and in life itself, consists in transforming the problem into a postulate.

To Zelter, Aug. 9, 1828

There is a subtle kind of empiricism that identifies itself intimately with the object and thereby evolves into what is truly theory. But this heightening of the mental faculties presupposes a high degree of intellectual development. . . .

Knowing is possible only when one knows little. As one comes to experience more, one gets gradually assailed by doubts. . . .

No phenomenon can be explained, taken merely by itself. Only many, surveyed in their connection, and methodically arranged, finally yield something that can pass for theory.

To Zelter, Oct. 5, 1828

But on close view this remains definitely true: What I know in truth, I really know only within myself. The moment I present it, I am straightway confronted with conditions, qualifications, and contradictions.

To Zelter, Oct. 30, 1828

Everything clever has already been thought. The point is to try to think it over again.

Maxims and Reflections 441 (1829)

General concepts and great conceit are always poised to make a terrible mess of things.

Maxims and Reflections 471 (1829)

Theory as such is of no use except in so far as it makes us believe in the coherence of phenomena.

Maxims and Reflections 529 (1829)

It is always better to stick to straightforward utterance in one's way of thinking, without being very much concerned about proving one's point. For all proofs that we offer are at bottom only variations of our opinions, and the contrary-minded listen neither to the one nor to the other.

Maxims and Reflections 550 (1829)

What is of prime importance is a man's general sentiments. If they are integrated, ideas will emerge. And the
quality of the sentiments will govern that of the ideas.

Maxims and Reflections 794 (1829)

An age that specializes exclusively in analysis and is,
as it were, afraid of synthesis is not on the right path. For
only both of them together, like breathing in and out,
make up the life of science.

Analysis and Synthesis (1829); 39, 56

The second religion, founded upon reverence for that
which is like us, we call the philosophical. For the philosopher, putting himself in the middle, must draw everything higher down to himself and raise everything lower
to his own level, and only in this mediating function does
he deserve to be called a sage. In so far as his insight
embraces his relation to his own likes—hence to all of
humanity, and his relation to the sum total of his earthly
environment in both its necessary and its fortuitous aspects—he alone dwells in the truth in the cosmic sense
of the term.

Wilhelm Meister's Journeyings II, 1 (1829); 19, 182

Heated argument is to be avoided. But to set opposing
points of view into plastic relief is our obligation.

Diary, Jan. 3, 1832

I was again curiously struck by the fact that practical
men of ability are not impeded in their progress by theoretical errors. . . . This teaches us to be humanely tolerant
of opinions, to make men's actions our sole concern, and
in the case of worthy men of good will to exercise a calm
forbearance with regard to what pertains merely to the
sphere of verbal utterance.

Diary, Jan. 7, 1832

Thinking is more interesting than knowing, but not more so than beholding.

Maxims and Reflections 1150 (posthumous)

All hypotheses get in the way of the *anatheorismos*— the urge to look again, to contemplate the objects, the phenomena in question, from all angles.

Maxims and Reflections 1221 (posthumous)

Hypotheses are scaffoldings that one erects in advance of the building and that one takes down when the building is finished. The worker cannot do without them. But he must be careful not to mistake the scaffolding for the building.

Maxims and Reflections 1222 (posthumous)

SUBJECT · OBJECT

In one word, our senses themselves do the real experimenting with phenomena, testing them and proving their validity, in so far as phenomena are what they are only for the respective sense in question. Man himself is the greatest, most universal physical apparatus.

Riemer, June 28, 1809. *Biedermann* 1189

The eye owes its existence to the light. From indifferent auxiliary animal organs the light generates an organ that shall be like unto itself; and thus by light the eye evolves for the light, in order that the inner light may meet the outer.

This recalls to mind the old Ionian school and its constantly repeated highly significant tenet: Things are known only by their own likes; also the words of an old mystic that we might paraphrase as follows: If the eye were not of the sun's essence, how could it ever perceive the sun? If the divine spark were not native to us, how could it move us to rapture?

On Theory of Color. Didactic Part. Sketch of a Theory
of Color (1810); 40, 70-1

In all that lives and shall live, the subject must predominate. It must be more potent than the object. It must overcome the object, as the flame consumes the wick.

Riemer, 1803-14. *Biedermann* 1603

Goethe was so thorough a realist, it did not make sense to him that objects as such exist only in so far as they are conceived by the subject. The idea! he once said to me, fixing me with his Jove's eyes, light exists only in so far as I see it? You would not exist, if the light did not see you!

Schopenhauer 1813-14. *Biedermann* 1571

Being yourself inclined to construe the world out of the subject, you will not repudiate the reflection that the subject, in its phenomenal aspect, is always but an individual and requires a certain blending of truth with error to maintain its peculiar existence. Nothing differentiates men more than the varying proportions in which these two ingredients are blended.

To Schopenhauer, Nov. 16, 1815

Had I not harbored the world within me by anticipation, I would have remained blind with seeing eyes, and all research and experience would have been a lifeless and futile effort. The light exists and colors surround us. However, if our own eye did not harbor light and colors within it, we would not perceive their like outside us either. *Eckermann,* Feb. 26, 1824. *Biedermann* 2230

You see, said Goethe, there is nothing without that were not at the same time within us; and as the external world has its colors, so the eye has them also.

Eckermann, Feb. 1, 1827. *Biedermann* 2473

To critical and idealistic philosophy I owe an enormous benefit: it has focused my attention upon myself. But it never comes to grips with the object. In this respect we enjoy no advantage over the point of view of common sense: we have to concede the object as given, in order to derive the enjoyment of life from our immutable relation to it.
To Schultz, Sept. 18, 1831

This is what they all come to who exclusively harp on experience. They do not stop to consider that experience is only one half of experience.
Maxims and Reflections 1072 (posthumous)

TRUTH

I fancy that I dwell in the truth too, but in the truth of the five senses.
To Lavater, Oct. 28, 1779

[With reference to Lavater.] Truth always strikes one as something brand new; and when one happens on a man so wholly truthful, one feels as though one were just landing in the world for the first time.
To Charlotte von Stein, Nov. 30, 1779

Nothing is great but the true, and the smallest aspect of the true is great.
To Charlotte von Stein, June 8, 1787

When I quoted the saying of the ancients that the right way is one and of wrong ways there are many, Goethe remarked: The particular is the lie, the universal the truth.
Riemer, 1803-14. *Biedermann* 1604

Just as the water which has been displaced by the ship straightway forms a wake behind it, similarly error, thrust aside for the moment by superior minds in their striving for elbow room, is quick to close up behind them, as is but natural.

The Autobiography III, 15 (1814); 24, 255

There is wisdom only in truth.

Maxims and Reflections 78 (1821)

Truth is like a torch, but of gigantic proportions. It is all we can do to grope our way with dazzled eyes, in fear even of getting scorched.

Maxims and Reflections 236 (1824)

Error finds ceaseless repetition in deed, for which reason one must never tire of repeating the truth in words.

Maxims and Reflections 292 (1826)

Error is to truth as sleep is to waking. As though refreshed, one returns from erring to the path of truth.

Maxims and Reflections 331 (1826)

The first and last thing demanded of genius is love of truth.

Maxims and Reflections 382 (1827)

A most reliable criterion for distinguishing what is true from what is specious: The true is always fruitful and favors him who possesses and cultivates it, whereas the merely specious lies dead and fruitless—like a necrosis, in which the dying tissue prevents the living from accomplishing the healing process.

Philosophy of Nature (1827); 38, 118

The chief thing is to have a soul that loves the truth and harbors it where it finds it. And another thing: The truth requires constant repetition, because error is being preached about us all the time, and not only by isolated individuals but by the masses. In newspapers and encyclopedias, in schools and universities, everywhere error rides high and basks in the consciousness of having the majority on its side.

Eckermann, Dec. 16, 1828. Biedermann 2642

Indeed, as long as it lasts, illusion carries an invincible conviction, and it is only manly, doughty spirits who are uplifted and strengthened by recognition of an error.

Wilhelm Meister's Journeyings II, 5 (1829); 19, 253

It is not always necessary that the truth should find tangible embodiment. Enough, if it hovers as a spiritual essence and induces harmony by its vibration, like a bell-tone of solemn serenity.

Maxims and Reflections 466 (1829)

He who contents himself with pure experience and acts accordingly has a sufficient portion of the truth. The child in its process of maturing is wise in this sense.

Maxims and Reflections 528 (1829)

They say that given two diametrically opposed opinions, the truth lies midway between them. Not at all! It is the problem that lies between them, that which defies intuition: life eternally active conceived as at rest.

Maxims and Reflections 616 (1829)

For truth is simple and without fuss, whereas error affords opportunity for dissipating time and energy.

To Zelter, Jan. 2, 1829.

[Goethe's autobiography] I called it *Dichtung und Wahrheit* because its higher aims lift it out of the region of common reality. . . . A fact of our life has validity not by its being true, but rather by its being significant.

Eckermann, March 30, 1831. Biedermann 2948

In tearing down a position, all false arguments carry weight; not so in building up. Only the truth is constructive.
                    Maxims and Reflections 895 (posthumous)

It requires a much higher organ to seize upon truth than it does to defend error.
                    Maxims and Reflections 1220 (posthumous)

ANTINOMIES

[Seyton:] Our disposition seems to consist of two sides that cannot exist without one another. Light and darkness, good and evil, height and depth, nobility and vulgarity—these and many other pairs of opposites blended in variable proportions seem to be the ingredients of human nature; and when the artist has painted an angel white, light, and beautiful, how can I blame him for conceiving the idea of painting a devil black, sullen, and ugly?   *The Good Women* (1801); 16, 309

Close observers of nature, however diverse their points of view, will agree that everything of a phenomenal nature must suggest either an original duality capable of being merged in unity, or an original unity capable of becoming a duality. Separating what is united and uniting what is separate is the life of nature. This is the eternal systole and diastole, the eternal *synkrisis* and *diakrisis,* the breathing in and out of the world in which we move and have our being.
                    On Theory of Color. Didactic Part (1810); 40, 83

Kant's *Critique of Pure Reason* had long made its appearance, but it lay completely outside the range of my interests. It was frequently discussed in my presence, however, and by being moderately alert I soon observed that it centered on a renewal of the old problem, how much the self and how much the outside world contributes to our mental existence. As for me, I had never separated the two factors, and when I philosophized about things in my own way I did so with unconscious naïveté and I fancied that my opinions were immediate sense data. But as soon as this dispute arose, I instinctively inclined to that side which assigns the more honorable part to man, and I fully agreed with all those friends who claimed with Kant that even though all our cognition begins with experience, it does not on that account all derive from experience. Cognitive acts *a priori* appealed to me too; likewise the synthetic judgments *a priori*. Had I not been alternately making use all my life, as poet and observer, of both methods, the synthetic and the analytic? And was I not used to regarding the systole and diastole of the human mind as a continuous pulsation, analogous to breathing, and never as a succession of separate states?

Effect of Recent Philosophy (1820); 39, 29-30

In Kant's scientific writings I had grasped the idea that attraction and repulsion are essential constituents of matter and that neither can be divorced from the other in the concept of matter. This led me to the recognition of polarity as a basic feature of all creation, a principle permeating and animating the infinite range of phenomena.

Campaign in France. Pempelfort, Nov. 1792 (1822);
28, 155

I think of the earth with its atmosphere after the analogy of a great living being that is engaged in a perpetual process of breathing in and out. When it takes in breath, the earth draws its vapory envelope down closer to its surface, causing it to condense into clouds and rain. This state I refer to as the affirmation of water. If it were to continue beyond reasonable limits it would drown the earth. This, however, the earth avoids by letting out its breath, thereby causing the vapors to rise and become diffused through the whole expanse of the higher atmosphere. There they are attenuated to such a degree as not only to give free passage to the sun's radiance, but also to render the eternal opacity of infinite space as a clear blue. For this condition of the atmosphere I use the term negation of water.

Eckermann, April 11, 1827. *Biedermann* 2484

What makes that essay fall short of fulfillment is its ignoring of the two great drives of all nature: the concept of polarity and that of *Steigerung*, the former belonging to matter in its material aspect while the latter pertains to matter in its spiritual aspect. The former reveals itself in ceaseless attraction and repulsion, the latter in a perpetual surge upward. But inasmuch as matter can never exist as an active principle divorced from spirit and vice versa, so matter has the faculty of dynamically rising to higher levels and the spirit, conversely, asserts matter's prerogative of attraction and repulsion on its part. . . .

Elucidation of the Aphoristic Essay on Nature (1828); 39, 349-50

Thinking and doing, doing and thinking—that is the sum of all wisdom, recognized and practiced from of old, yet not understood by everyone. Like breathing in and out, both should occupy life in a ceaseless alternating flux; like question and answer, neither should occur without the support of the other. The genius of the human understanding whispers this maxim into the ears of every newborn babe. He who abides by it, checking thinking against doing, doing against thinking, cannot go astray, or if he should, he will soon find himself back on the right path.

Wilhelm Meister's Journeyings II, 9 (1829); 20, 25

As regards the somewhat paradoxical title *Wahrheit und Dichtung* for the intimate account of my life, I chose it because the public always questions the veracity of such autobiographical attempts to a certain degree. To take the edge off this attitude, I rose to the challenge and acknowledged an element of fiction, rather needlessly; for I had been most conscientious in my attempt to set forth and express the basic truth regarding my life, as I saw it. But to do this from the vantage point of later years recourse must be had to memory—to the imagination, that is to say, and thus, in a sense, the poetic faculty is called into play. From this it follows that the account will emphasize the results and the reconstruction of the past rather than the events as they occurred in all their detail. Even the most matter-of-fact chronicle cannot help being tinged in some degree by the spirit of the times in which it was written . . .

All that aspect of my account which concerns the narrator and the medium of narration I tried to suggest by the term *Dichtung*, making it serve as the vehicle for the truth that I had in mind.   *To Zelter*, Feb. 15, 1830

This instance should bring home to each of us the fact that separating and co-ordinating are two inseparable acts of life. Perhaps it is better to say that whether we wish it or not, it is unavoidable for us to proceed from the whole to the parts and from the parts to the whole. And the more vitally these two functions of the mind are conjoined, like breathing in and out, the better it will be for science and its friends.

Principes de Philosophie Zoologique. Part Two. (1832); 39, 233

RELATIVISM

Even a truth picked up in reading must subsequently be reinvented by us. The brain cavities are full of seeds that require the soil and the potshard of feeling to germinate.

> Jean Paul [Friedrich Richter], 1798. *Biedermann* 550

I do not pretend to piety; I am pious when the occasion is fitting. It costs me no effort to observe all conditions with a clear innocent eye and then to depict them with the same purity. But all manner of caricaturing distortion with which conceited people violate the integrity of the object has always been distasteful to me. When I encounter something that goes against my grain, I avert my eye. But there is much that, without exactly approving, I like to discern in its specific character. And in most cases, as a result of this, I am led to see that the others have just as valid a claim to their mode of existing as I have for my own.

> *Campaign in France.* Münster, Nov. 1792 (1822);
> 28, 191

In keeping with his dislike for all mechanically transmitted learning, Goethe maintained that philosophy, too, could be meaningful only if loved and lived. But do we of this age still know what it is to live? he would add. The Stoic, the Platonist, the Epicurean, each has to come to terms with the world in his own way. That is the task of life from which there is no dispensation, regardless of the school one adheres to. The philosophers on their part have only patterns of life to offer us. How these fit our individuality, whether by virtue of our nature and endowment we can supply the content that conforms to a particular pattern, that is our affair. We must test ourselves, and, as with the food we eat, we must scrutinize most carefully everything that we take into ourselves from without; otherwise we and philosophy work our mutual destruction.

The strict sobriety of Kant, for instance, requires a philosophy that conformed to his innate inclinations. . . . Every individual has a claim to principles that do not negate him as an individual. Here, I daresay, we have the origin of all philosophizing. . . . We must first be in harmony with ourselves before we are able in some manner to cope with the disharmonies pressing in upon us from without. I claim that there is even such a thing as an innate disposition toward eclecticism in philosophy; and where eclecticism derives from a man's inner disposition, I shall never find it a cause for reproach.

Falk (undated; died 1826). *Biedermann* 3095

True conviction springs from the heart. As the real seat of conscience, it is a far more reliable judge than the understanding of what is permissible and what is not. The latter, for all its subtlety and discernment, is likely to miss the central point. *To Thomas Carlyle,* March 14, 1828

When one is at harmony with oneself one is so also with one's fellows. I have often observed that I regard that idea as true that is fruitful for me, that fits in with the rest of my way of thinking and at the same time advances me. Now it is not only possible but natural that the particular idea may not fit in with the cast of mind of another person. It may even block his progress instead of advancing it; hence he will regard the idea as false. Once one has come to a thorough realization of this, one will never try to make converts. *To Zelter,* Dec. 31, 1829

Every man must think in his own fashion; for on his way he always finds a truth or an aspect of truth that helps him to live his life. Only he must not allow himself to drift; he must exercise control. To rely on mere instinct is not in keeping with the status of man.

Maxims and Reflections 460 (1829)

LIFE

Across from the door one saw on a rich sarcophagus the solemn marble image of a man reclining on a pillow. He held a scroll in his hand, his eye fixed upon it in calm contemplation. The position of the scroll was such that one could read the words inscribed on it without difficulty. They read: Remember how to live.

> *Wilhelm Meister's Apprenticeship* VIII, 5 (1796);
> 18, 312

The purpose of life is life itself.

> *To Meyer*, Feb. 8, 1796

All that is alive tends toward color, individuality, specification, effectiveness, and opacity to an infinite degree. All that is done with life inclines to knowledge, abstraction, generality, transfiguration, and transparency.

> *On Theory of Color*. Didactic Part. (1810)
> W. A. Werke, Zweite Abteilung, 1, 234

Man cannot dwell for long in a conscious state, or in consciousness. He must again take refuge in the unconscious, for that is where his life is rooted.

> *Riemer*, Aug. 5, 1810. *Biedermann* 1317

All satisfaction in life is grounded in a regular recurrence of the things about us. The rhythm of day and night, of the seasons; that of the blossoms and fruits; all things the enjoyment of which is contingent on periodicity—these are the basic stimuli of earthly life. The more receptive we are to these enjoyments, the happier we feel. If, however, these phenomena rotate about us without our participating; if we are unreceptive to such lovely offerings, then we fall a prey to the greatest evil, the gravest malady; then life comes to be felt as a loathsome burden.

The Autobiography III, 13 (1814); 24, 158

When they asked Plato how he had lived in this world he answered: I entered with pain. I never ceased to marvel. I depart with reluctance. And I have learned nothing except that I know nothing.

Divan. Notes. Recent and Contemporary Figures (1819); 5, 198

We experience beauty when we behold that which is alive in conformity with natural law in its acme of vitality and perfection; and this in turn raises our own vitality and activity to the highest pitch and incites us to recreation.

Campaign in France. Münster. Nov., 1792 (1822); 28, 185

The life of man, faithfully recorded, never presents itself as a rounded whole. . . . Even less does a human life deserve to be disparaged; for what counts in life is living as such and not any result that may be scored up. We should rather look upon the lowliest individual with respect, if in the unfolding of his simple fate we observe the invisible touch of a higher power that has deigned to take the morose, depressed, and momentarily helpless individual by the hand and guide his faltering step over a rough passage.

Introduction to The German Gil Blas (1822); 37, 202-3

The highest gift we have received from God and nature is life, the rotating movement of the monad about itself, knowing neither pause nor rest. The impulse to nurture this life is ineradicably implanted in each individual, although its specific nature remains a mystery to ourselves and to others.

Maxims and Reflections 391 (1822)

Everything living forms an atmosphere about itself.
Maxims and Reflections 435 (1823)

The maxim that only he who is alive is in the right befits a mind like Schiller's. For indeed, he who would effectively influence life must not dwell upon the past with an excess of love. *To Süvern, June 21, 1825*

Years and decades take their course. And of all our striving, enterprise, and venturing, of all our accelerating and retarding drives only that leaves a valid trace which in its basic manifestations nurtured and transmitted a truly living existence. The only influence in the true sense of the word is that of procreation, birth, growth, and un-trammeled development.
Errors and Truths, by Wilhelm Schulz (Review; 1827) 38, 89

Where object and subject touch, there is life.
Parthey, Aug. 28, 1827. Biedermann 2526

What is genuinely alive keeps growing by regenera-tion, just as the vicious proliferation of the Hydra's heads is not to be stamped out either. *To Zelter, Aug. 26, 1828*

This house can be said to have shaped its occupants. For when the inanimate is alive, it can also bring forth life. *Wilhelm Meister's Journeyings* II, 2 (1829); 19, 13

Life belongs to the living, and he who lives must be prepared for change.
Wilhelm Meister's Journeyings I, 2 (1829); 19, 27

Our life at long last resembles the Sibylline books. The less there is left of it, the more precious it becomes.
To Schultz, June 29, 1829

Life makes its abode in the tiniest mouse as it does in

the colossus of the elephant, and it is always the same. Similarly in the smallest moss as in the largest palm.

von Müller, July 2, 1830. *Biedermann* 2845

Let us remain in league with advancing life and test ourselves when opportunity offers. Then the passing moment provides a criterion whether we are alive, and subsequent scrutiny, whether we were alive.

Well-Meant Reply. Another Word for Young Poets (1832); 38, 326

Goethe was steeped in the conception that nothing in nature is lifeless. Even in this piece of sugar there is life, he once told me. *Eckermann* (undated). *Biedermann* 3132

SPIRIT

To us who have not inherited political power and are not disposed to acquire riches, nothing is more welcome than what extends and confirms the rule of the spirit.

To Charlotte von Stein, June 17, 1784

The words are good, but they are not the best. The best does not become plain through words. The spirit in which we act is the highest.

Wilhelm Meister's Apprenticeship VII, 9 (Journeyman's Graduation Letter) (1796); 18, 259-60

How few of us feel inspired by that which presents itself only to the spirit. The senses, the emotions, the heart exert a much greater sway over us, and rightly so; for our concern is life, not contemplation.

Preface to the First Issue of Morphology Apology for the Undertaking (1807); 39, 249-50

They say of the human heart that it is a stubborn and faint-hearted thing. Something similar may well be said of the human spirit. It is impatient and pretentious and at the same time unsure of itself and timid. It strives for experience as the means to a wider range of more integrated activity, and then again it shrinks away from it, not without reason. In advancing, man feels more and more, being conditioned as he is, that he must lose in the process of gaining; for both the true and the false are bound up with necessary conditions of existence.

On Theory of Color. Historical Part. Fourth Division.
Transitional Reflection (1810); 40, 184

So much has already been said about Shakespeare that it might seem there were nothing more to be said; and yet this is the quality of spirit, that it eternally stimulates the spirit. *Shakespeare and No End* (1813); 37, 37

The highest characteristic of oriental poetry is what we Germans call *Geist,* the predomination of the supreme principle. Here all other qualities are gathered together without any one of them claiming undue prominence. *Geist* is pre-eminently a matter of old age or of an aging epoch. These poets easily relate the remotest matters with one another, thereby approaching that which we call wit. Yet wit does not stand on so high a plane, being self-seeking, a stricture that does not apply to the spirit. . . .

Divan. Notes. Extreme Generalizations (1819); 5, 195-6

All that we term invention, discovery in a higher sense, is the significant activation of an innate sense of truth which, having germinated within us undetected, bursts forth in a trice into a fruitful act of cognition. It is a revelation from within, outwardly manifest, and allows man to sense his participation in the divine essence. It is a synthesis of world and spirit, vouchsafing the happiest confirmation of the eternal harmony of existence.

Maxims and Reflections 562 (1829)

138

Jacobi was thinking of spirit, I of nature. We were divided by what should have united us. . . . Strange that persons who developed their power of thinking in such manner were incapable each of making the other see his point of view, letting themselves be thwarted and confused by a misunderstanding, a terminological idiosyncrasy, that should have been easy to clear up. Why did they not say betimes: He who wills the highest must will the whole; he who treats of the spirit must presuppose and include nature, and vice versa? Thought cannot be separated from the object, the will from what is moved!

Annals. Biographical Details. Jacobi. 30, 403

IMMORTALITY - ENTELECHY

To me this seems the noblest of our sentiments—the hope to persist, even after fate has seemed to reduce us again to the general state of nonexistence. This life is much too short for the soul. Evidence of this, that every man, the lowliest and the highest, the most ineffective and the most deserving alike, sooner tires of everything else than of living. Further evidence, that no one reaches the goal that he so anxiously strove to attain. . . .

Shakespeare Anniversary Speech (1771); 36, 3

Everything perfect of its kind must rise above its kind; it must become something different and incomparable. In some of its notes the nightingale is still a bird; but then it rises above its class and seems to wish to suggest to every winged creature: This is song.

Elective Affinities II, 9 (Ottilie's Diary) (1809); 21, 225

[The day of Wieland's funeral.] Do not interrupt me if I am to develop my ideas fully and calmly. That Nature should allow such high spiritual energies to perish is wholly out of the question; she never squanders her capital in such fashion. Wieland's soul is by its nature a treasure, a veritable gem. And his long life has not diminished but rather augmented these fine spiritual talents. Once again, give careful thought to this aspect: Raphael was hardly in his thirties, Kepler only in his early forties when they suddenly put an end to their lives, whereas Wieland—"What!" I broke in on Goethe with some astonishment, "are you not speaking of dying as if it were an act independently willed?" I allow myself to do that on occasion, he replied, and if it pleases you I should like to tell you my ideas on this subject in full because this moment affords me license to do so. . . .

You have long known that ideas which lack a firm foundation in sense experience do not carry conviction with me, regardless of what value they may have, because over against nature I want knowledge, not mere speculation or belief. As for personal survival after death, this is what I arrive at by my approach: The idea is not contradicted by the observations I have been making for many years concerning our own constitution and that of all other creatures; on the contrary, it is reinforced by them. But how much or how little of this personality merits surviving is another question, and this is something that we must leave to God. For the time being I will say this: I assume that there are gradations of class and rank differentiating the ultimate constituents of all beings, the starting points, as it were, of all phenomena in nature. Let us call them souls, or even better monads—let us keep this Leibnizian term by all means; a better could scarcely be found to express the simplicity of the simplest essences. Now, as experience shows, some of these monads or starting points are very tiny and insignificant, while others are strong and powerful. These latter have a way of drawing everything that approaches them into their orbit, assimilating it and transforming it into a body whether it be a plant, an animal, or, still higher, a star. They continue this activity until the world, be it large or small, that is spiritually prefigured in them, becomes visible in outward embodiment. Only the latter I would call souls in the narrower sense of the term. It follows from this that there are world-monads, world-souls, just as there are ant-monads, ant-souls, and that both are sprung from the same source, or at least from a related one. Every sun, every planet is charged with a higher intention, a higher mission, by means of which its development must take place with the same regularity and according to the same laws as govern that of a rose, with its leaves, stem, and flower head. Whether you prefer to call this an idea or a monad is all the same to me; the main thing is that this intention invisibly anticipates its visible development in nature. The larvae or intermediate states which characterize the idea in its transitions must not confuse us. It is always the same power of metamorphosis which turns the leaf into a flower, or a rose, the egg into a caterpillar, and the caterpillar into a butterfly. . . . But all monads are by nature so indestructible that even in the moment of dissolution their activity does not come to rest but is rather continued straightway. Thus they simply disengage themselves from their old relationships to enter into new ones. In the accomplishment of this change everything hinges upon the degree of energy contained in this or that monad. The monad of a cultivated human soul and that of a beaver, a bird, or a fish—there is an enormous difference. And this brings us back to the gradation of souls according to rank, an idea which we have to postulate if we would account for the phenomena of nature in any way. . . .

The inferior assortment, he continued after a pause and more calmly, demands an insufferable degree of elbow room. It is a regular monad rabble which we have been jumbled up with in this planetary nook; and if they were to hear of this on other planets we should derive little honor from this company. . . .

If we are to indulge in surmises for a moment, Goethe continued, I really do not see what should hinder the monad to which we owe the phenomenon Wieland on our planet, from entering into the highest combinations of this universe in its new phase. . . . I would be little surprised, I would find it quite in keeping with my views, in fact, if I were someday, after millennia, to meet this same Wieland as a world-monad again, as a star of the first magnitude, and become witness to its quickening and cheering effect upon everything in the range of its mellow light. Indeed, to irradiate the nebulous nature of some comet or other with light and clarity—this might be an appropriate task for the monad of our Wieland. Generally speaking, as soon as we think of the universe as eternal, we cannot imagine any ultimate destiny for the monads except to share in the joys of the gods as participants in the creative power. The emergence of creation is entrusted to them. Summoned or not, they throng hither on all the ways, from all the mountains, from all the stars. Who can check their course? As you see me here, I have surely existed a thousand times before and expect to return a thousand times more. . . . In one of our earlier conversations I referred to man as the first dialogue of Nature with God. I do not doubt that this dialogue can be accomplished on other planets in a much loftier, deeper, and more intelligent way.

Falk, Jan. 25, 1813. *Biedermann* 1490

And then let us not trouble ourselves about the future. In our father's realm there are many provinces; and since he prepared so delightful a dwelling place for us here, we shall surely be taken care of in the beyond too. Perhaps we shall then succeed in what we have been unable to do here, in getting to know each other face to face and loving each other all the more. . . . May we all be reunited in the arms of the all-loving father.

To Graefin Auguste Luise Bernstorff, née Stolberg,
April 17, 1823

Goethe maintained very decidedly that for a thinking being it is quite impossible to conceive of itself as ceasing to exist and think and live. This is in a way a proof of immortality that everyone automatically carries within himself. But as soon as one tries to enter the field of objective argument and attempts to prove and understand dogmatically one's own personal survival, as soon as one dresses up that inner perception with Philistine trimmings one gets lost in contradictions. In spite of this, however, a man is always impelled to postulate the impossible. Almost all laws are syntheses of the impossible —for instance, the institution of marriage. And it is good that it is so, for only by postulating the impossible is the utmost possible achieved.

von Müller, Oct. 19, 1823. *Biedermann* 2172

At the sight of the setting sun, as we drove back to Weimar, Goethe lapsed for a while into reverie, then quoted to me from one of the ancients: "Setting even, it is ever the self-same sun." When one is seventy-five years old, he then continued with great serenity, one cannot but think at times of death. As for me, this thought leaves me perfectly calm, for I have the firm conviction that our mind is a wholly indestructible essence, active through all eternity. It resembles the sun which seems only to our mortal eyes to set, whereas it really never sets but ceaselessly shines. *Eckermann,* May 2, 1824. *Biedermann* 2254

Let us continue to be active until, summoned in our turn by the world-spirit, we return into the ether. Let us hope that the eternally living spirit may then not refuse to assign to us new activities analogous to those in which we have already proved our competence. If he then chooses in his fatherly way to endow us with recollection of the right and good things that we have willed and accomplished here on earth, we shall then adjust ourselves to the cosmic mesh-work all the more zestfully.

The monad or entelechy must only make it its business to continue ceaselessly active. If this becomes second nature to it there can be no want of a sphere of activity throughout eternity. Forgive these abstruse terms. But one has always got tangled up in such regions; one has always resorted to such ways of speaking where reason no longer avails and man is nevertheless reluctant to concede the field to unreason. *To Zelter*, March 19, 1827

I must admit, I would not know what to do with heavenly bliss if it did not offer new tasks and new difficulties to be overcome. But they are surely provided for. We need only look at the planets and the sun. There will be nuts enough to crack there.
von Müller, Sept. 23, 1827. *Biedermann* 2551

The philosopher does not need the authority of religion in order to prove certain doctrines as, for example, that of eternal survival. Man is meant to believe in immortality; he has a right to do so; it is in accordance with his nature; and he is warranted in trusting to the assurances of religion. But if the philosopher resorts to a legend for proof of the immortality of our souls, that is very weak and means little. The conviction that we are destined to endure is rooted only in the concept of activity; for if I continue ceaselessly active to the end of my days, Nature is under obligation to assign to me another form

144

of existence, when the present one is no longer able to
contain my spirit.

Eckermann, Feb. 4, 1829. Biedermann 2652

Of all the philosophizing about immortality! And what
tangible yield has it given us? I do not doubt that we are
destined to endure, for Nature cannot do without the entelechy; but we are not all immortal in the same way, and
in order to manifest oneself in the beyond as a great entelechy, one first has to be one.

Eckermann, Sept. 1, 1829. Biedermann 2731

MAN AND HISTORY

When you look at such a way of existing that is two
thousand years old and older and has undergone so many
changes of a fundamental sort and is still the same soil,
the same mountain, often even the same wall and column,
and traces of ancient character are still discernible in the
people—then you feel as though you were sitting in on
the great deliberations of Fate.

To J. G. and Caroline Herder, Rome, Nov. 10, 1786

I would try my hand at historical subjects too, if history were not the most thankless and most dangerous of
subjects.

To F. Jacobi, July 7, 1793

What does an outline sketch of a human life amount
to? As compared to the homely detail of a significant
life, all generalizing biography must crawl into a hole.

To Meyer, Feb. 8, 1796

Former ages thought in terms of images of the imagination, whereas we moderns have concepts. Formerly the
guiding ideas of life presented themselves in concrete

visual form as divinities, whereas today they are concep-
tualized. The ancients excelled in creation; our own
strength lies rather in destruction, in analysis.

Riemer, May 10, 1806. *Biedermann* 865

On closer consideration I find I am more sympathetic-
ally inclined to the so-called Dark Ages than you. There
are many apartments in my father's house, and the dark
cellar below is as much a part of the palace as the roof
garden. My present task of arranging and editing my materials on the history of the theory of color necessitates
my entering into the history of art, of science, and of the
world in general. And I just cannot help feeling that even
in those ages that appear dark and mute to us a loud
paean of humanity rose up to the gods that they might
well have taken pleasure in inclining their ear to. And to
me it is always a thrilling sight to behold this dark and
deep teeming of energies. What a touching thing to see
the individual nations and races preserve and pass on the
sacred flicker of consciousness; what a grand thing to
dwell on those select individuals in whom it rises once
more to a steady flame. *To F. Jacobi*, March 7, 1808

What gives a man lasting significance is not the accu-
mulation he leaves behind, but rather the activity and
zest that permeates his life and passes itself on to others.
The Autobiography II, 7 (1812); 23, 75

The historian is on the lookout for results and we do
not blame him; but this involves the sacrificing of the individual act as well as of the individual human being. . . .
History, even the best of its kind, always suggests the
corpse and the scent of the tomb. In fact, as time wears
on, history makes more and more disagreeable reading;
for every historian is under pressure to outdo his predecessors in achieving an ever more concentrated and subtle

distillate of world events, with the final upshot that what does not fall by the wayside as *caput mortuum* goes up in smoke.

If there shall and must be history, however, the biographer can render it a great service by preserving and transmitting that which, being alive, escapes the scrutiny of history.

Draft of Preface to *The Autobiography* III, 1814;
W. A. Werke, 28, 358

There can and will be new inventions, but there can be no inventing of anything new as regards the moral nature of man. Everything has already been thought and said; the most we can do is to give it new forms and new phrasing.   *Grüner*, Aug. 24, 1823. *Biedermann* 2130

We all know that to cut a figure in the world requires two things: an outstanding intelligence, and a great inheritance.   *Eckermann*, May 2, 1824. *Biedermann* 2254

The cutting of the Isthmus of Panama; the linking of the Danube with the Rhine; the English in possession of a canal at Suez. These three great things I should love to live to see, and for their sake I would consider putting up with another fifty years of this existence.

Eckermann, Feb. 21, 1827. *Biedermann* 2476

The world of reason is to be regarded as a great immortal individual that irresistibly keeps performing what is necessary and thereby even obtains mastery over what is subject to chance.   *Maxims and Reflections* 444 (1829)

We call a feeling for human values historical, when it is cultivated in such fashion that in its appraisal of contemporary merits the achievements of the past are felt as participating in the scale of values.

Maxims and Reflections 494 (1829)

The best thing that history yields us is the enthusiasm that it generates.   *Maxims and Reflections* 495 (1829)

To be a judge of history, you must have experienced history in your own life. This holds good for entire nations. The Germans have learned to pass judgment on literature only since they have come to have a literature of their own.   *Maxims and Reflections* 517 (1829)

Galileo died in the same year as that in which Newton was born. This is the Christmas festival of the modern age.   *Diary*, June 24, 1831

The day as such is too slight a substance. Unless you grasp a whole armful of years, you will never get a sheaf.
Maxims and Reflections 910 (posthumous)

The day is committed to error and floundering; success and achievement are matters of long range.
Maxims and Reflections 911 (posthumous)

Men should be regarded as organs of their age that for the most part move unconsciously.
Maxims and Reflections 957 (posthumous)

The Social Sphere

BILDUNG

If you have a vivid awareness of what infinite operations on the part of Nature and Art are required to produce a *gebildet* [formed and modeled] human being; if you yourself contribute to the extent of your capacities to further the *Bildung* of your fellow-men—then you are tempted to despair when you see how often it happens that a man deliberately ruins his endowment, or comes to have it ruined through his own fault or through inadvertence. When I consider this, life itself seems to me so fortuitous a gift that I feel like commending anyone who does not value it more highly than it deserves.

Wilhelm Meister's Apprenticeship VII, 2 (1796); 18, 176

With what interest Wilhelm now looked at the tree nurseries and the buildings. . . . He no longer eyed the world like a bird of passage. . . . All the improvements he planned to make were to punctuate the stages of his child's growth; all that he planned to build would be intended for a succession of generations. In this sense his apprenticeship was ended, and simultaneously with the feeling of fatherhood he had come into possession of all the virtues of a citizen. He felt this, and his joy knew no bounds. "How unnecessary the stern discipline of morality," he exclaimed, "when Nature in her gracious way sees to shaping us in the direction of what is right! How misguided the strange demands of society that begins by confusing and misleading us in order to present demands later that exceed those of Nature!

Woe to every kind of *Bildung* that destroys the most effective means of true *Bildung* and has only the ultimate

end in view instead of awarding gratification in the process!"
Wilhelm Meister's Apprenticeship VIII, 1 (1796);
18, 266-7

Not all people are genuinely concerned about their *Bildung*. Many desire only a sort of nostrum that will put them at their ease—recipes for acquiring wealth and every kind of happiness.
Wilhelm Meister's Apprenticeship VIII, 5 (1796);
18, 323-4

It is incredible how much a person of *Bildung* can do for himself and others, when, without ambition to rule, he leads them to do at the right time what conforms to their own promptings, and helps them to the realization of ends which for the most part they clearly envisage while they flounder in their choice of the means.
Wilhelm Meister's Apprenticeship VIII, 10 (1796);
18, 393

Moral education is closely related to aesthetic education. They form one body, as it were, and neither one can be thought of as attaining perfection without a corresponding development on the part of the other.
Annals, (1803); 30, 121

Bildung begins along one specific line, to be sure, but it cannot end there. One-sided *Bildung* is no *Bildung*. There must be a specific point of departure, but the movement must also pursue a variety of directions. It does not matter whether one's *Bildung* takes its starting-point from mathematics, from philology, or from art, provided one has it. But *Bildung* cannot consist in the mastery of these sciences as such. The individual sciences are only the sense organs, as it were, which we train upon objects; philosophy, or the science of sciences, is the *sensus communis*. However, just as it would be ridiculous to compensate and supplant sight by hearing, hearing by sight, to try to see tones instead of to hear them, so it is ridiculous to substitute the formulas of mathematics for the other forms of cognition and vice versa. The upshot of this can only be fantastic speculation. Nowadays there are plenty of men of this type who, lacking an adequate knowledge of the specific sciences, nevertheless contrive by fantastic combination of facts popularly known to give the impression of deep insight into the nature of all the sciences. *Riemer, July 24, 1807. Biedermann 1020*

But who is so *gebildet* [cultured] as to refrain from cruelly stressing, at times, the qualities in which he excels! *Elective Affinities* I, 2 (1809); 21, 15

To communicate one's personality is an impulse of nature. To accept what is communicated in the spirit in which it is offered is *Bildung*.
Maxims and Reflections 5 (1809)

It is a matter of indifference in what circle we begin our work of self-cultivation, it is all the same from which point we orient the progress of our *Bildung*, provided there is a circle and there is a point of departure. To acquire a productive *Bildung* that proceeds from a nucleus should be a young man's concern; and even in advancing years, when our development broadens out along historical lines, we must compress the diffusion of our interests and recapture the sense of unity.
To Schubarth, July 8, 1818

Bildung is a prison. Passers-by can take offense at its iron gratings or run danger of colliding with its walls. The man confined within, undergoing the treatment, is subject to hard knocks too, but the result is the gaining of true freedom. *Laube, 1818-21. Biedermann 1963*

[When someone proposed a toast to Remembrance.]
I do not subscribe to remembrance in your sense of the
word. That is an inept way of putting things. Whatever
great, beautiful, or significant experiences have come our
way must not be recalled again from without and recap-
tured, as it were; they must rather become part of the tissue of our inner life from the outset, creating a new and
better self within us, continuing forever as active agents
of our *Bildung*. I do not admit of anything past that we
would be warranted in longing to recall; I admit only the
existence of what is eternally new as it shapes itself out
of the expanded elements of the past. True longing must
always be productive and create something that is both
new and better.

von Müller, Nov. 4, 1823 *Biedermann* 2185

But what would all *Bildung* amount to if it did not involve the effort to counteract our natural impulses! To expect of people that they should harmonize with our individuality is great folly. I have never done this. I have always regarded a man as a self-contained individual whom
it was up to me to explore and come to know in his peculiarity, without demanding any sympathetic response
on his part. By this means I have learned how to handle
all sorts of men; and it is only in this way that one comes
to know the varieties of human character and learns how
to get on in life. For it is precisely in our contacts with individualities that do not appeal to us that we are put on
our mettle. The need of somehow getting along with
them stimulates a variety of facets in us and develops
them, and in that way one soon comes to feel equal to
any confrontation of personalities.

Eckermann, May 2, 1824. *Biedermann* 2254

Byron's boldness, his temerity, his lofty sweep—does
not all this mold our contours? We must guard against

confining the idea of *Bildung* to what is strictly pure and moral. Everything great molds us from the moment we become aware of it.

Eckermann, Dec. 16, 1828. *Biedermann* 2642

All living, all doing, all artistic creation presupposes craftsmanship, which can be acquired only by self-limitation. To know and to practice one thing right bestows a higher *Bildung* than is achieved by dabbling in a hundred spheres of interest.

Wilhelm Meister's Journeyings I, 12 (1829); 19, 171

Piety is not an end in itself—only a means of attaining to the highest *Kultur* through the purest tranquillity of the spirit. *Maxims and Reflections* 519 (1829)

Everyone who knows how to assimilate, of that which surrounds him and transpires about him, that which conforms to his nature, is an eclectic. And this covers all that we call *Bildung* and progression, in its theoretical and its practical aspects. *Maxims and Reflections* 649 (1829)

May the study of Greek and Roman literature forever remain the basis of higher *Bildung*.

Maxims and Reflections 762 (1829)

To further his own moral *Bildung* [education] is the simplest and most feasible thing that a man can undertake. The impulse to do so is innate. Through intelligence and love he is led, even impelled, in this direction in his association with his fellow-men.

The Autobiography IV, 16 (posthumous); 25, 19

The highest point of *Kultur* that man can rise to is the conviction that he does not figure in the concerns of others. *Maxims and Reflections* 928 (posthumous)

HUMANITY

I look forward with great pleasure to the third part of Herder's work. . . . No doubt he has admirably developed that lovely wish-dream of mankind that someday things will be better. And I must admit I, too, believe that *Humanität* will eventually triumph; only I fear that at the same time the world will become a vast hospital where each will play the role of warder to the other patients.

To Charlotte von Stein, Rome, June 8, 1787

Only all men taken together make up mankind, only all forces in their co-öperation the world. . . . Every aptitude is important and needs to be developed. If one person promotes only what is beautiful, another only what is useful, only the two of them jointly constitute a human being. The field of what is useful needs no special furtherance, for it is the concern of many minds and none of us can do without it; beauty on the other hand requires patronage, for, though it is the need of many, there are few who produce it.

Wilhelm Meister's Apprenticeship VIII, 5 (1796);
18, 326-7

The reason why Nature is unfathomable is that no single individual can fathom her, although mankind as a whole need not necessarily fail in the attempt. But because the human race is never alerted as a whole, she has an easy time playing her game of hide-and-seek with us.

To Schiller, Feb. 21, 1798

All the ancients clung to what was immediate, true, and real; even their poetic imagery has bone and marrow. Man and everything pertaining to man stood highest in

their scale of values; and the same lofty sweep character-
izes their treatment of all man's inner and outer relations
cal lines, we must compress the diffusion of our interests
with the world, both in the contemplation of reality and
in its artistic projection. As yet feeling and contemplation were no piecemeal matters; as yet that cleavage—
probably beyond healing—had not begun to sap the
wholeness of man's vitality.

Winckelmann. The Way of Life of the Ancients (1805);
34, 13

Mankind? That is an abstraction. It has always been
only individuals who exist, and it will never be otherwise.
Luden, Aug. 19, 1806. *Biedermann* 874

For nearly a century now the humanities have ceased
to permeate the people engaged in these studies as a living force. We have reason to feel happy over the fact
that Nature has intervened and become the focus of interest, opening a new approach to *Humanität* for us from
her angle. *To von Knebel,* Nov. 25, 1808

Let the individual continue to feel free to concern himself with what attracts him spontaneously and gives him
pleasure. But the proper study of mankind is man.
Elective Affinities II, 7 (Ottilie's Diary) (1809); 21, 213

As we survey the varied development of individual
epochs, regions, and localities in detail, we see emerging
from all angles of the obscure past fine and outstanding
individuals, brave, good, handsome, and of commanding
stature. Mankind's paean of praise, so pleasing to the ear
of the Deity, has never been silenced; and we too feel a
divine happiness as we listen to the harmonious outpour-
ings distributed through all times and all localities, now
as solo voices, now as individual choruses, now in the

form of fugues, and now in a glorious total symphony.
On Theory of Color. Historical Part. Third Division
(1810); 40, 148

It is a lovely thing to realize that only men taken together constitute man in the true sense of the word, and
that the individual can be cheerful and happy only when
he has the courage to feel himself as part of the whole.
The Autobiography II, 9 (1812); 23, 208

To be gentle requires no effort on my part, as any hard-
ness and sternness are only put on in self-defense.
To von Reinhard, Nov. 14, 1812

Among the gains I derived from my last journey I
would give top listing to an increased sense of tolerance
with regard to the individual human being. When one has
come to observe several hundred people at close range
and thousands rather more remotely, one must admit that
in the end each of us is kept quite busy finding a niche
for himself and maintaining it; one should never try to
lord it over others and force one's advice on them; for in
the end it remains for the individual himself to make his
adjustment in fortune and misfortune.
To von Knebel, Nov. 9, 1814

As far as I am concerned, the contemplation of classical
antiquity—in any of its fragmentary remains—puts me
into a state that makes me feel: I am a human being.
To Zelter, Nov. 6, 1827

The development of mankind, I said, would seem to
be a plan requiring thousands of years.

Who knows, Goethe replied, millions perhaps. But
however long the time span you care to give it, mankind
will never be lacking in obstacles to buck up against;
there will always be crises to develop its energies. Intel-

ligence and insight will increase, but mankind will never become better, happier, and more energetic, or at best only periodically. I see the time coming when God will no longer look with pleasure upon his creation; he will have to smash it to bits to rejuvenate it. I am sure this is all according to plan, and in the distant future the time and the hour have already been fixed for this epoch of rejuvenation. But that prospect would seem to be rather far in the offing, and we can continue for thousands and thousands of years to amuse ourselves on this dear old earth of ours as it is constituted.

Eckermann, Oct. 23, 1828. *Biedermann* 2635

MAN AMONG MEN

One does not get to know that one exists until one rediscovers oneself in others.

To Auguste Stolberg, Feb. 13, 1775

The way I feel about it, the company of children makes me happy and young.

To Krafft, July 13, 1779

Since I am now as pure and quiet as the air, I find the breath of good and quiet people very welcome.

To Charlotte von Stein, Sept. 28, 1779

The most interesting object to man is man; perhaps he should be the exclusive object of his interest. Everything else that makes up our environment is either only the element in which we live or a tool that we make use of. If we make these latter things our concern and allow ourselves to be preoccupied by them, our sense of our own value and our social sense will suffer and diminish in proportion.

Wilhelm Meister's Apprenticeship II, 4 (1795); 17, 113

It is never too early for us to learn that we are anything but indispensable to the world. What important persons we fancy ourselves to be! We think it is only ourselves that give life to the circle in which we are active; once we are gone, we fancy life, sustenance, and breath must come to a standstill—and the gap we leave is all but unnoticed, it closes up so quickly, and its place is occupied, often enough, by something better or, at least, something more agreeable.

Wilhelm Meister's Apprenticeship VII, 8 (1796); 18, 233

If we take people only as they are, we make them worse; if we treat them as though they were what they ought to be, we steer them in the right direction.

Wilhelm Meister's Apprenticeship VIII, 4 (1796); 18, 302

It is after all our own individuality that always hinders us from becoming aware of the individualities of others in their full extent. *To von Knebel,* Jan. 3, 1807

There is in man among other things an impulse to serve. This accounts for the chivalry of the French.

Riemer, Jan. 8, 1808. *Biedermann* 1062

Do not let trifles nettle you or make you suspicious, and learn betimes to practice the art of compromise in the world wherever possible. There are plenty of relations where it is ruled out.

To August von Goethe, Dec. 5, 1808

Do not ever neglect to include in your endeavors the co-öperation of like-minded friends. Conversely I advise you, also on the strength of my own example, never to waste an hour with people into whose ways you do not fit, and vice versa. Such contacts advance you little but may lead to all kinds of embarrassment ending in a sense of frustration.   *Falk,* Feb. 28, 1809. *Biedermann* 1153

To subordinate oneself is easy; but to do so on a descending scale, to recognize as above us something on a lower level, is difficult.

We like to yield place to antiquity, but not to posterity. Only a father does not begrudge a son his gifts.
                    Riemer, June 9, 1809. *Biedermann* 1183

The sum total of man's endeavors is directed upon man as their object through the medium of personality; youth impinges most strongly upon youth, and here we have the purest transmission of human energies. It is this activity of youth which animates the world and preserves it from extinction both morally and physically.
            The Autobiography II, 10 (1812); 23, 279-80

To live with someone, and to live in someone—those are fundamentally different things. There are people in whom we can live, without living with them, and vice versa. To combine both requires the purest love and friendship. Apply this reflection to Herder.
        A Note for The Autobiography, Book 10 (1813); 23, 327

Trying to please everybody Goethe always referred to as the most ridiculous of pretensions.
                    Riemer, 1806-14. *Biedermann* 1608

To be loved for what one is, is the greatest exception. The great majority love in another only what they lend him, their own selves, their version of him.
                    Riemer, 1806-14. *Biedermann* 1630

Continue, with unruffled disposition, to watch out for two things: what people are aiming at, and how they mask themselves to this end. Be careful to display only a moderate sense of ease lest people begrudge you your good fortune.   *To August von Goethe,* Jan. 14, 1814

We attain to certainty concerning our own basic organization only by recognizing the organization of other individuals as on a par with our own, as equally determined by natural law.

> *Meteors of the Literary Heaven.* Priority (1820); 39, 38

He who is and remains honest with himself possesses the most beautiful quality of high endowment.

> *Maxims and Reflections* 383 (1827)

[Montan:] My idea was to withdraw from men. You cannot help them, and they get in the way of our helping ourselves. If they are happy, you should not interfere with their follies; if they are unhappy, you should rescue them without touching these follies. And as for yourself, no one ever asks whether you are happy or not.

> *Wilhelm Meister's Journeyings* I, 3 (1829); 19, 34

One is truly alive only when one enjoys the good will of others.   *Maxims and Reflections* 518 (1829)

For each individual the world as given—the finished product with all its rules and regulations—is no more than an element from which he endeavors to create a particular world shaped to his own needs. Men of capacity seize upon it without hesitation and come to grips with it as best they can; others approach it in a half-hearted manner; some even doubt its existence.

If this basic truth were to become second nature to us we should never engage in dispute with anyone. Any individual's particular view of things, along with our own, would range itself, instead, among phenomena to be noted.   *Maxims and Reflections* 594 (1829)

When all is said and done, one knows what one knows only for oneself. If I speak to another of that which I think I know, he straightway thinks he knows better, and I am again driven to retreat into myself with my knowledge.

Maxims and Reflections 595 (1829)

The question to ask is not whether we are perfectly agreed, but whether we are proceeding from a common basis of sentiment.

Maxims and Reflections 893 (posthumous)

Man can live only with his own equals, and not even with these; for in the long run he cannot endure anyone's being his equal.

Maxims and Reflections 1405 (posthumous)

MAN AND THE WORLD

The tissue of this world is woven of necessity and chance. Man's reason takes up its position between them and knows how to control them, treating necessity as the basis of its existence, contriving to steer and direct chance to its own ends. Only in so far as reason stands firm and unshakable does man deserve to be called a god of the earth. Alas for the wretch who accustoms himself from youth to think of necessity in terms of chance, and to attribute to chance a sort of reason and even dress it up with religious sentiment. What is this but the renunciation of one's reason and the free indulgence of one's inclination! As if there were something pious in drifting without forethought, in yielding to the determination of pleasant chance, and in invoking the name of divine guidance for the result of such haphazard living! . . .

I can take pleasure only in a man who knows what is good for himself and others and who works to limit his arbitrary caprice. Everyone's hands are at work molding his own fortune, like the plastic artist shaping his raw material. But it is with this art as with all others: The capacity is innate, but only learning and solicitous effort bring it to fruition.

Wilhelm Meister's Apprenticeship I, 17 (1795); 17, 78-9

Probably the greatest thing that can be said to a man's credit is that he succeeds in determining circumstances to the greatest extent possible and to the least extent is subject to their determination. The whole world lies before us like a great quarry before the architect. But only he deserves this name who succeeds in using these natural blocks to give substance to an archetypal intuition with the greatest economy, purposiveness, and solidity. Everything outside us is only material (and I would include even the outer layer of the self in this term); but deep down in the core there is this creative power, the capacity to create what is to be, and the urge to tolerate no letdown until we have given it shape in one way or another, either outside ourselves or in our own person.

Wilhelm Meister's Apprenticeship VI (1795); 18, 150

When man's healthy natural faculties co-öperate as a totality; when man feels the world about him as a great, beautiful, dignified, and spacious whole; when this sense of ease and harmony culminates in a state of pure, free delight—then the universe, if it were endowed with feeling, would exult in a sense of final achievement and admire the crowning glory of its own evolving essence. For all this lavish display of suns, planets, and moons, of stars and galaxies, of comets and nebulae, of worlds formed and in process of forming—what does it all avail in the last resort unless there be harmonious man unconsciously rejoicing in his existence! ·

Winckelmann. The Values of Classical Antiquity
(1805); 34, 12

So divinely is the world organized that everyone in his place, in his time, balances everything else.

Riemer, July 3, 1810. *Biedermann* 1305

All men of good endowment come to realize as their *Bildung* progresses that they have a double role to play in the world—a real role and an ideal one—and this feeling is the basis of everything noble. The real role assigned to us becomes sufficiently evident; as concerns the second, we rarely arrive at a clear realization of it. Regardless of whether he seeks his higher destiny on earth or in heaven, in the present or in the future, man always remains subject to a sense of fluctuation from within and disturbing interferences from without until he makes up his mind once and for all that the right thing for him is that which conforms to his nature.

The Autobiography III, 11 (1814); 24, 19-20

There is nothing insignificant in the world. It all depends on the point of view.

Lobe, July, 1820. *Biedermann* 1920

If I know my relation to myself and the world about me, I call it Truth. In this way each individual can have his particular truth, and it is nevertheless the same truth.

Maxims and Reflections 198 (1823)

Modestly enough, I gave the title *Dichtung und Wahrheit* to a work of exacting fidelity, to express the deep conviction that man, in modeling his environing world, gives it the stamp of his personal peculiarities. If this holds true for the active present, how much more does it apply to the recollected past!

Annals, 1811 (1830); 30, 258

MAN AND FATE

Provided he remain true to himself, man finds a helpful maxim for coping with every situation. In my case, as soon as the danger became great, the blindest fatalism came to my aid; and I have noticed that men whose occupation exposes them to extraordinary danger find themselves braced and strengthened by such a faith. The Mohammedan religion affords the best proof of this.

Campaign in France. October 7 and 8, 1792 (1822); 28, 97

Fate, the other smilingly replied, is a distinguished but expensive tutor. I would rather look for support to the rational guidance of a human master. I accord all due reverence to the wisdom of Fate; but Chance, through which it works, would seem an awkward executive agent. For it rarely seems to carry out in pure and exact terms what Fate has decreed.

Wilhelm Meister's Apprenticeship II, 9 (1795); 17, 137

Great necessity elevates man, petty necessity casts him down. *Riemer,* Oct.-Nov., 1803. *Biedermann* 707

. . . Just as in the most momentous crises, when everything is at stake, people continue somehow to live as though it were nothing.

Elective Affinities I, 13 (1809); 21, 110

For Providence has a thousand means to raise the fallen and support the prostrate. Sometimes our fate re-

sembles a fruit tree in winter. Who would think at beholding so sad a sight that these rigid branches, these
jagged twigs, would turn green again in the spring and
blossom and bear fruit? But we hope it, we know it!

Wilhelm Meister's Journeyings I, 12 (1829); 19, 171-2

Remember that with each breath we take, an ethereal
current of Lethe penetrates our whole being, so that we
remember our joys with moderate vividness, our suffer-
ings scarcely at all. This great gift of God I have always
appreciated, made use of, and cultivated.

As for the blows and buffetings on the part of Fate,
lovers, friends, and foes—the good, the resolute man has
long since cast the smart of their memory to the winds.

To Zelter, Feb. 15, 1830

MAN AND SOCIETY

The moment you enter society, you draw the key from
your heart and put it in your pocket. Those who fail to
do so are fools.   *Lavater*, June 26, 1774. *Biedermann* 52

Rosencrantz and Guildenstern . . . There should be at
least a dozen of them, if that were possible; for they are
something only collectively. They are society.

Wilhelm Meister's Apprenticeship V, 5 (1795); 18, 24

A distinguished bearing, being an essentially negative
qualification, is difficult to imitate and requires long application. Any display of dignity is a wrong move, as this
tends to formality and aloofness. The point is to avoid
anything that is undignified and vulgar. One must never
let oneself out of hand, one must always keep watch over
oneself and others, never make a *faux pas*, never do too
much or too little to others; one should never display

emotion, never act impetuously; one should be in control of oneself at every moment and maintain an outward equilibrium regardless of what goes on under the surface. The noble individual can neglect his manners on occasion, the distinguished individual never. The latter is like an impeccably dressed gentleman; he leans against nothing, and everyone takes care not to brush against him; he stands out quite distinct from the rest, and yet he must not stand aloof; for as in every art, so in this, even the most difficult feats must be performed with elegance. Thus the man of distinction, regardless of the difference that marks him off, must always seem to be in contact with others. Never stiff, always flexible, he must always appear in the lead without ever elbowing his way forward.

It is clear, therefore, that to appear distinguished, one has to be distinguished. It is clear why women, on the average, give themselves this appearance more readily than men; why courtiers and military men enjoy a great advantage in this regard over the rest of us.

Wilhelm Meister's Apprenticeship V, 16 (1795); 18, 87-8

Apropos of the present vogue in society, to spy on each other's vanity, Goethe remarked: This is to ruin social intercourse; for now the one group will become purely passive by reasoning: If I am not to display the agreeable quality that I possess I shall act as though I had no qualities whatever. And now these begin to spy on the others, with the result that the worst, the most impudent member of the group takes over control.

Riemer, May 21, 1807. *Biedermann* 994

He who discourses alone at length without flattering his listeners arouses ill will.

Maxims and Reflections 8 (1809)

You can force anything upon society in the way of entertainment except the consistent pursuit of a topic.

Maxims and Reflections 26 (1809)

Everything that we call good society tends to polish off the edges of our individuality more and more, threatening a reduction to absolute zero—unless we cultivate the talent, while indulging our own vanity, of flattering the vanity of others.

Divan. Notes. Book of Ill-Humor (1819); 5, 237

The only reason why everyone attaches such value to the prerogatives of birth is that they are unchallengeable. By way of contrast, everything that we earn and achieve through personal effort remains forever at the mercy of diverse judgments and points of view. To try to reconcile them is impossible and makes matters even worse. The bourgeois population, for instance, is not reconciled to the luxury of a court table by having a few of their number invited occasionally to join in the feast.

von Müller, Feb. 14, 1824. *Biedermann* 2224

Of the best society they used to say: Its conversations are instructive, its pauses *bildend* [cultivating].

Maxims and Reflections 365 (1826)

To live in a closed social circle at home among familiar and intimate people without a change of scene eventually leads to a very curious situation: we get so used to exercising mutual tolerance and forbearance, to sharing in each others' affirmations and renunciations, that a certain temperate climate of resignation results from the mutual canceling out of joy and pain, irritation and well-being, under the force of habit. All feelings tend to be reduced to a neutral mean, and in our striving for accommodation we are rendered incapable at last of responding spontaneously to either pain or pleasure.

Italian Journey. Report, October, 1787 (1829); 27, 149

The significance of the most innocent words and acts grows with the years. Where my contacts are of more than a transitory nature I try to make my associates aware of the differences that exist between frankness, confidence, and indiscretion. Strictly speaking, there is not a difference, but rather an imperceptible gradation from the most innocent to the most offensive attitude, something to be observed or rather sensed.

Maxims and Reflections 482 (1829)

In society all are equal. Equality, not freedom, is the principle of all social life. Equality is what I look for society to offer. Freedom—I mean the moral freedom of being willing to subordinate my individuality—is what I contribute myself.

Maxims and Reflections 951 (posthumous)

THE INDIVIDUAL AND THE PUBLIC

One thing remains certain: This public, so honored and so despised, is almost always wrong in its judgment of particulars, but is guided nearly as often by a sound instinct as regards the whole.

To Charlotte von Stein, Dec. 10, 1781

There is nothing that the *Menschenpack* [human rabble] is so much afraid of as reason. Stupidity is what they should fear if they knew what is fearful. But the former is embarrassing and therefore to be brushed aside; the latter is only disastrous and permits of an attitude of wait and see.

Wilhelm Meister's Apprenticeship VII, 3 (1796); 18, 184

The greatest respect one can show to the public is not to treat it as rabble.

The Weimar Court Theater (1802); 36, 191-2

Men in the mass are never moved to act jointly except through prejudice and when stirred by passion. Thus even the most praiseworthy purposes are always adulterated and sometimes distorted. In spite of this a great deal of good is accomplished, if not at once, yet in the course of time; if not directly, yet indirectly.

To Blumenthal, May 28, 1819

Popular philosophy is not to my taste either. There is an esoteric element in philosophy as well as in religion. That is something the common man can well be spared. Nothing is worse than the forcible injection of such matters into popular discussion. Epicurus says somewhere: This is right because it offends the preconceptions of the common man. *Falk* [undated]. *Biedermann* 3095

A man must cling to every kind of property. He must make himself the center from which the common weal can emanate. He must be an egoist in order not to become egotistical. He must gather in order that he may distribute.

Wilhelm Meister's Journeyings I, 6 (1829); 19, 77

[On Saint-Simonianism:] I do not know why they want to sacrifice the interest of the individual to that of the masses. I maintain that each should remain what he is and work and produce according to his inner conviction. In writing, I never had the interest of the masses in mind; I have tried, rather, to say what is true and to write only what I thought and believed good as such. This has resulted in benefit to my fellow-men without this having been my primary aim. To say that each should sacrifice himself for the good of all, therefore, seems to me a false principle; each should render sacrifice to his own conviction! *Soret,* Oct. 20. 1830. *Biedermann* 2871

KNOWLEDGE OF HUMAN NATURE

We do not learn to know men by their coming to us.
We must go to them to find out what they are like.

Maxims and Reflections 27 (1809)

Fools and wise men are equally harmless. It is only the
half-fools and the half-wise who are really dangerous.

Maxims and Reflections 51 (1809)

[Graphology.] That a man's handwriting bears a relation to his disposition and character, and that at least a
suggestion of his way of existing and acting is to be derived from it is scarcely to be doubted, just as there is no
denying the fact that not only the build and the features,
but also the play of features, the tone of voice, the movements of the body are significant and in keeping with the
individual's whole make-up. But this too is a matter of
feeling rather than of clear perception. One might venture to formulate some detailed observations, but I doubt
whether it will ever be possible to do so in a comprehensive methodical way that carries conviction.

To Preusker, April 3, 1820

SPIRITUAL COMMUNITY - FRIENDSHIP

As you get older and your world keeps shrinking, you
sometimes think with amazement of the times when you
trifled away friendships—insensitive in the reckless folly
of youth to the wounds you inflicted and indifferent to
healing them.

To F. Jacobi, Oct. 2, 1782

Give as much of yourself to the Herders as you can.

172

Strange, that a sort of veil or cloud can persist between
the best and most reasonable people.

To Charlotte von Stein, May 25, 1787

On the point of arriving at the development of his energies, aptitudes, and ideas, a man sometimes gets into a fix
from which a good friend could easily extricate him. He
is like a wayfarer who falls into a current not far from
the inn. If someone were to reach out at once and pull
him ashore he would be none the worse except for the
wetting, instead of having to scramble ashore by his own
efforts on the opposite bank and making his way by a la-
borious circuit to his destination.

Wilhelm Meister's Apprenticeship III, 8 (1795); 17, 207

The surest means of cultivating and preserving a
friendly relation is to communicate to each other what we
are doing. For men are much more apt to agree in what
they do than in what they think.

To S. A. W. Herder, Dec., 1798

We love our friends, we esteem them, we are even
ready to render them a drastic service on occasion at
some sacrifice to ourselves. But as to indulging some
fleeting wish, some momentary fancy, some crotchet of
theirs, we are—shall I say—too indolent, too unimagina-
tive, too rigid and aloof, and we fail to realize that it is
the satisfaction of just these whimsies which affords the
greatest pleasure.

To Marianne von Eybenberg, April 4, 1803

Sentiments are what unites people, opinions what sep-
arates them. Sentiments are a simple bond that gathers
us together; opinions represent the principle of variety
that scatters. The friendships of youth are founded on
the former, the cliques of old age are to be blamed on

the latter. If we could only realize this early and arrive at a liberal view as regards others in cultivating our own attitude of mind, we would be more conciliatory and try to collect by the bond of sentiment what opinion has dispersed.

To F. Jacobi, Jan. 6, 1813

For only sentiments of mutual good will and trust can promote what is most insistently needed and sought after in the City of God and of good morals.

To the Senate of the University of Jena, Nov. 24, 1825

Since it would be futile to battle the broad floodwaters of the day, those of us who are serious in their hearts must lead the quiet, even subdued, existence of a community of spirits, trying withal to keep our footing steadfastly until the rush of the current has abated.

Further Remarks on World Literature (1829); 38, 203

Looking at the present course of the world, we must ever and ever rehearse the conviction that there have been and will be men of quality who deserve a word of encouragement, both spoken and left behind on paper. That is the community of saints to which we adhere.

To Zelter, June 18, 1831

CRITIQUE OF THE TIMES

On this journey I hope to satisfy my heart as regards the fine arts, impress their sacred image firmly on my soul and preserve it for quiet enjoyment. But then I plan to turn my attention to artisans, and after my return study chemistry and mechanics. For the era of beauty is ended; necessity and stern need monopolize our days.

Diary of the Italian Journey. Venice, Oct. 5, 1786

Your own epoch you cannot change. You can, however, oppose its trend and lay the groundwork for auspicious developments. *To Schiller,* July 21, 1798

And supposing they could clarify and study all sources, what would they find? Nothing other than one great truth that has long since been discovered and does not need elaborate confirmation—the truth, that is, that life has been a wretched business at all times and in all lands. People have always worried and toiled; they have pestered and tormented each other; they have made their little span of life miserable for themselves and their fellows, and they have known neither how to respect nor how to enjoy the beauty of the world and the sweetness of existence that this beautiful world offers them. Only few have fared comfortably and pleasurably. Most men, I daresay, after being carried along in the current of life for a time, would have preferred to take their exit rather than begin over again. What little attachment they have or had for life is due to the fear of dying. That is how it is; how it has been; how it will be in all probability. *Luden,* Aug. 19, 1806. *Biedermann* 874

The modern age has a false sense of superiority because of the great mass of data at its disposal. But the valid criterion of distinction is rather the extent to which man knows how to form and master the material at his command. *On Theory of Color.* Historical Part. Third Division. Transition. Lacuna (1810); 40, 150

[After the suicide of Zelter's son.] When you see how people in general and the young generation in particular are not only giving free rein to their desires and passions, but when you see that even their higher and better aspirations are distorted and caricatured by the serious follies of our times, so that everything that should lead to their salvation turns into a factor of damnation, not to mention all the unspeakable outward tribulation involved—then you are no longer surprised to see people vent their destructive rage against themselves and their fellow-men. . . . Most young people of superior endowment make greater demands upon themselves than is reasonable. They are driven to this by the enormous pressure of circumstances. . . . We do not stop to think that reason and the brave exercise of will are given us to ward off not only what is evil but also an excess of what is good.

To Zelter, Dec. 3, 1812

[Referring to the Wars of Liberation.] I am continuing in my fashion. In contrast to the course of the world, I try to preserve, to arrange in order, to establish; and in like manner I am appealing to such friends of the arts and sciences as remain at home to preserve the sacred fire which the next generation will be so badly in need of —even if it were but a spark under the ashes.

To von Knebel, Nov. 24, 1813

Werther created a stir because it appeared, not because of the moment when it appeared. In every age there is so much unexpressed suffering, so much secret dissatisfaction and pessimism, so much maladjustment and so many conflicts between individual temperaments and bourgeois institutions that *Werther* would create a stir even if its appearance had been delayed until this day.

Eckermann, Jan. 2, 1824. *Biedermann* 2213

What the next years will bring, nobody can predict; but I fear we are not soon due for a state of tranquillity. It is not given to the world to practice moderation—neither to the rulers to refrain from the abuse of power, nor to the mass to content itself with a tolerable state in expectation of gradual reforms. If humanity could be made perfect, a perfect state of things would be thinkable too. But as it is there will be eternal fluctuation; one part will suffer while the others enjoy well-being. Egotism and envy will always be at work as evil demons, and the struggle of parties will continue without end.

The only reasonable course is for everyone to practice the calling to which nature and training have designed him, and not to prevent one's fellows from practicing theirs. *Eckermann, Feb. 25, 1824. Biedermann 2229*

The history of our own times moreover is great and significant. The battles of Leipzig and Waterloo stand out so boldly that those of Marathon and others tend to lose their lustre in comparison. Nor do our individual heroes lag behind. The French marshals and Blücher are wholly on a par with those of antiquity.

Eckermann, Nov. 24, 1824. Biedermann 2299

All epochs that are regressive and in process of dissolution are subjective; all progressive epochs, on the other hand, bear an objective stamp. Our whole present age, being subjective, is regressive.

Eckermann, Jan. 29, 1826. Biedermann 2388

There is among men no end of strife, and it always flares up anew because of the currents and crosscurrents of opinion that refuse to be reconciled. Now when it happens that one particular current gains the lead and succeeds in capturing the fancy of the public and triumphing to such a degree that the opposition has to pull in its horns and retreat and go into hiding, then we call this preponderance the *Zeitgeist* and for a while it holds the field unchallenged.

Homer Once More (1827); 38, 77-8

Transposed from the crude setting of the old folk tale

to the higher level of modern culture, Faust's character represents an individual who chafes impatiently at the limits imposed by earthly existence, who regards the highest knowledge and the most coveted possessions as wholly inadequate to satisfy his longing—a spirit who, though he turns in all directions, always turns back in disappointment.

This state of mind is so characteristically modern that a number of reputable writers have felt the urge to wrestle with the solution of this problem.

Helena. Intermezzo to Faust (1827); 38, 112

All of us old Europeans are in a wretched fix, more or less. Our status is much too artificial and complicated; our eating and living habits are divorced from nature, and our social intercourse is without genuine love and good will. Everyone is courteous and polished, but no one has the courage to be warm and genuine, so that an honest man with natural inclinations and sentiments has a hard time of it. One should often wish to have been born a so-called savage on one of the South Sea Islands, in order for once to enjoy human existence as such, pure and unadulterated.

When you let yourself go in moods of depression to dwell on the misery of the times, you feel as though the world were pretty nearly ripe for Judgment Day. And this keeps piling up from generation to generation! Not enough that we suffer for the sins of our fathers: we transmit these inherited ailments, augmented by our own, to posterity.

Eckermann, March 12, 1828. *Biedermann* 2579

The greatest evil of our time, which allows nothing to ripen, I find in the fact that each moment eats up the moment that has gone before, the day is frittered away, and life has become a hand-to-mouth affair with nothing being accumulated. We already have newspapers for every time of day, though somebody's ingenuity will contrive to subdivide it still further! In this way everything that a man does or pursues, everything he intends to do, in fact, is dragged into the public forum. No one is allowed to rejoice or suffer except as a pastime for the public. And this giddiness leaps from house to house, from town to town, from state to state, from continent to continent finally—all in a mad whirl.

Maxims and Reflections 479 (1829)

The Moral Sphere

FREEDOM

Let a man but declare himself free, straightway he will feel himself limited. But let him be bold enough to declare himself limited, and he will experience a sense of freedom.

Maxims and Reflections 44 (1809)

Freedom is a curious thing, and everyone is likely to have enough of it provided he knows how to limit and find himself. And what is the good of a superabundance of freedom that we do not know how to make use of? See this room and this adjoining chamber in which you see my bed through the open door. Neither of them is large. They are restricted, moreover, by all kinds of furnishings, books, manuscripts, art objects; yet they are sufficient for me. I have lived in them all winter long, scarcely setting foot in my front rooms. Now what benefit did I derive from my commodious house and from the freedom of passing from one room into another, since I did not feel the need to use them!

If one has sufficient freedom to live in good health and go about his business one has enough, and that amount is likely to fall to everyone's lot.

Eckermann, Jan. 18, 1827. *Biedermann* 2469

Freedom is nothing but the possibility of doing the rational thing under all circumstances. The absolute stands even above the reasonable. That is why sovereigns often choose to act unreasonably, in order to retain their sense of absolute freedom.

von Müller, June 20, 1827. *Biedermann* 2506

Whatever aspect of our life we may choose to consider, we find ourselves outwardly conditioned from the first breath to the last. Despite this, however, we are in possession of the highest freedom—that of developing our inward selves in such a way as to make our lives harmonize with the moral world order. In this way, whatever obstacles may confront us, we can arrive at peace with ourselves.

To Graf Brühl, Oct. 23, 1828

Whatever liberates our spirit without giving us mastery over ourselves is destructive.

Maxims and Reflections 504 (1829)

CONSCIENCE

The worst ills—natural or civic, physical or economic—that can befall us when we move within the pale of the law are infinitesimal, I venture to say, compared with the miseries that have to be faced if we skirt the edge of the law or actively defy law and custom while yet at the same time we feel the need of remaining in a state of balance as regards ourselves, our fellow-men, and the moral order of the universe.

To Schubarth, Nov. 7, 1821

Whereas all this is calculated to serve public and communally moral functions, the core of religion belongs to the inner life of each individual, for it is concerned only with conscience. Conscience is to be aroused or assuaged. Aroused, when it is dull and languid and inactive; assuaged, when the restlessness of remorse threatens to poison life. For conscience is very closely related to worry, and worry threatens to turn into consuming grief when through our own fault we have brought an affliction upon ourselves or others.

Wilhelm Meister's Journeyings I, 7 (1829); 19, 94

184

LAW AND ORDER

[Goethe, in answer to remonstrances about the risk he had incurred in saving a fugitive—an alleged pillager—from the mob:] I cannot help being made that way. I would rather commit an injustice than countenance disorder.   *Campaign in France.* Siege of Mainz, July 25, 1793
                                                 (1822); 28, 251

All laws are attempts to make the course of life and of the world conform to the designs of the moral order of the universe.   *Maxims and Reflections* 831 (posthumous)

It is better for you to suffer injustice than for the world to be without law. Therefore let everyone submit to the law.   *Maxims and Reflections* 832 (posthumous)

It is better that acts of injustice occur than that they be redressed by unjust means.
                    Maxims and Reflections 833 (posthumous)

AUTHORITY

Speaking of tradition, we are impelled to join its discussion with that of authority; for, on close view every authority is a kind of tradition. We accept the existence, the dignity, the sway of whatever it be, without clearly seeing or understanding its source, its origin, its value. . . . Thus reason and, allied with it, conscience exercise an enormous authority because they are unfathomable; similarly that which we designate by the name of genius. The understanding, on the contrary, commands no authority whatever, just as all education confined to the understanding leads to anarchy.

185

Man's attitude toward authority, as to many other things, is a perpetual seesaw. His sense of inadequacy makes him feel that without support from something outside himself his strength does not suffice. But when a feeling of pride and power begins to exert its sway, he thrusts aside such aid and fancies that he can manage for himself and for others.

The infant, for the most part, accommodates itself patiently to the authority of parents; the boy struggles against it; the youth casts it off; and the man accepts it again, because he has occasion more or less to command it in his own person and because experience has taught him that he can accomplish little without the co-operation of others.

Mankind as a whole exhibits this same seesaw. Now we see friends, disciples, adherents, companions, contemporaries, neighbors, fellows-in-arms throng about a man of distinction. Now again such a society, such a realm breaks up into numerous factions. Now monuments of older ages, documents of earlier continents are invested with divine sanction and accepted literally; everyone yields up his senses and his understanding to their authority; all energies are concentrated on pointing up the value of such remains, on making them known, commenting upon and explaining them, and transmitting them to future generations. And now again an iconoclastic frenzy is turned against these very objects of veneration; there is an urge to obliterate to the very last traces what has been valued so highly. No pronouncement of former times continues to carry any weight; all that passed for wisdom is to be branded as folly, all that was salutary as noxious; and what was long regarded as making for progress suddenly takes on the aspect of an impediment.

The epochs of the natural sciences exhibit such a seesaw in more than one way. . . . The natural sciences have expanded admirably, but not steadily or even gradually. It has been an up-and-down matter, progression and recession, a rectilinear and a spiral pattern. And as a matter of course every epoch fancied itself vastly superior to its predecessors.

On the Theory of Color. Historical Part. Third Division. Authority (1810); 40, 157-8

FAULTS - VIRTUES

Human frailties are regular tapeworms. You succeed now and again in tearing off a stretch, but the head remains embedded. Even so, I am determined to prevail. No one except him who denies himself utterly is worthy to rule and capable of ruling. *Diary,* May 13, 1780

Our love of self exaggerates both our virtues and our faults.

Wilhelm Meister's Apprenticeship IV, 12 (1795); 17, 282

Man's good intentions, resolutions that always succumb to ingrained habit, are like the cleaning, scrubbing, and adorning that we practice on Sundays, holidays, and feast days. We always get dirty again, to be sure, but such a partial cleaning process has the advantage of upholding the principle of cleanliness.

Riemer, Nov., 1806. *Biedermann* 913

It is man's foibles at bottom that make him lovable.

Riemer, May 17, 1807. *Biedermann* 989

If we happen to meet someone who owes us thanks, we think of it straightway. But how often do we meet someone to whom we owe thanks without thinking of it!

Maxims and Reflections 4 (1809)

187

Certain defects are necessary to the constitution of the individual. It would be disagreeable to us if old friends were to divest themselves of certain crotchets.

Maxims and Reflections 18 (1809)

Passions are deficiencies or virtues, only on a higher plane. *Maxims and Reflections* 21 (1809)

Our passions are regular phoenixes. As the old one is consumed, straightway the new rises out of the ashes.

Maxims and Reflections 22 (1809)

Great passions are diseases past hope of cure. Remedies applied only serve to make the danger acute.

Maxims and Reflections 23 (1809)

Patience, hope, faith, love, all these virtues are reason *actu*, in practice, they are practical reason.

Riemer, 1810. *Biedermann* 1364

Entangling relations are always a misfortune. But for him who happens to get involved in such, they are touchstones of character and will power under acute conditions of stress. *Maxims and Reflections* 173 (1823)

Ingratitude is always a kind of weakness. I have never observed men of substantial worth to be ungrateful.

Maxims and Reflections 185 (1823)

What is virtue other than conduct that truly conforms to a given situation?

von Müller, Aug. 23, 1827. *Biedermann* 2520

[Makarie:] As we are constituted by nature, there is not a fault that could not turn into a virtue, and not a virtue that could not turn into a fault.

Wilhelm Meister's Journeyings I, 10 (1829); 19, 146

HUMILITY · REVERENCE · MYSTERY

The greatest men I have known, those who took in heaven and earth with a clear eye, were humble and knew the gradations of esteem.

To Lavater, July 24, 1780

This morning early we had all the murderers, thieves, and fences lined up for questioning . . . an impressive study of mankind and physiognomy that makes you feel like putting your hand over your mouth and rendering glory to God, whose alone is the power and the understanding and so forth, for ever, Amen.

To Charlotte von Stein, Sept. 9, 1780

When self-esteem asserts itself by despising others, even the humblest, the effect is distasteful. A frivolous person can better afford to make fools of others and expose them to humiliation and contempt, because he does not take himself seriously. But whoever has a sense of his own worth would seem to have renounced the right to look down upon others. And are any of us so made that we have much to brag about?

To F. Jacobi, May 5, 1786

All paths open up before me because I walk in humility.

To Herder, Rome, January 13, 1787

If certain manifestations of human nature, regarded from the angle of morals, compel us to ascribe to it a sort of radical evil and original sin, other manifestations demand that we attribute to it likewise an original virtue, an innate goodness and righteousness and especially an inclination to reverence. This disposition, if cultivated in man, rendered active and brought into the open, we call "piety" as the ancients used the term.

A powerful current of this shows in the relations of parents to children, less so of children to parents. Its beneficent effects extend from the nearest of kin to all men united by bonds of blood, tribe, and country. It colors the relation to rulers, benefactors, teachers, patrons, friends, protégés, household servants, animals, to the soil, to country and city. It embraces everything, and, having the world for its domain, it turns its last and best manifestation heavenward. It alone is a counterbalance to egotism. If, through a miracle, it would come to the fore in all men in a moment, it would heal the earth of all its present, possibly incurable ills.

Salvandy's *Don Alonzo, ou l'Espagne* (Review; 1824); 37, 288-9

There are great advantages in mystery. For when you always tell a man straightway what is at issue he fails to be impressed. Certain mysteries, even though they be manifest, must be accorded respect by veiled reference and silence in the interest of modesty and good morals.

Wilhelm Meister's Journeyings II, 1 (1829); 19, 175

CHARACTER · PERSONALITY · INDIVIDUALITY

Among all possessions on earth a heart of one's own is the most priceless, and there are scarcely two among thousands possessed of it.

Review of Wieland's *Thoughts on an Old Inscription* (1772); 36, 76

Goethe aptly remarked that an individual cannot represent a character type in its extreme purity. He would not be able to live. He must have mixed qualities in order to exist. *Caroline Herder*, Oct. 4, 1788. *Biedermann* 298

How shallow, mean, and empty is their judging of another's personality! How they direct their darts at the
outer work of appearance without the faintest inkling of
how inaccessible a fortress the man lives in who takes
himself and things seriously!   *To Schiller,* Dec. 5, 1796

However much one may develop in the direction of
the universal, one always remains an individual. And it is
the nature of individuality to exclude certain qualities
by virtue of possessing others.

                    To W. von Humboldt, July 16, 1798

But every individual may be regarded as a charade of
many syllables of which the individual himself succeeds
in spelling out only a few, while others are apt to decipher
the whole word.   *Winckelmann.* Character (1805); 34, 42

Fate grants us our wishes, but it does so in its own way
in order to be able to give us something more inclusive.
                    Elective Affinities II, 10 (1809); 21, 227

There is more repetition than is commonly realized in
the ordinary pattern of every person's experience, because
it conforms to an innate disposition. Character, individuality, inclination, focus, locale, environment, and habits
form a whole in which each person is suspended as in an
element or an atmosphere and to which it is adjusted.
And thus, despite all the complaints concerning man's
variability, we find people unchanged, to our astonishment, after many years and, despite an infinite host of
outer and inner stimuli, unchangeable.
                    Elective Affinities II, 17 (1809); 21, 287

Our attempts to express the essence of a thing are
really doomed to failure. What we perceive is effects, and
a complete account of these effects would presumably

encompass the essence of that thing. In vain we labor to depict the character of a man; but give us a comprehensive report of his actions, his deeds, and it will fuse into a picture of his character.

On the Theory of Color. Didactic Part. Preface
(1810); 40, 61

Every creature aware of itself as a separate entity wants to maintain its own status without division or alteration. This is an eternal, necessary gift of nature, and in this way one can say: Every individual has character, down to the worm that turns when stepped on. In this sense we may ascribe character to the weakling, even to the coward; for he yields up what is priceless in other men's eyes—honor, glory—but what is not part of his own nature, in order to maintain his personality. Usually, however, the word "character" is used in a higher sense, to signify a personality of outstanding qualities that will not allow itself to be swerved from its own course by any outside force.

We speak of a strong character in the case of one that resolutely faces all outward obstacles and strives to maintain its peculiar existence. We speak of a great character when strength appears combined with great qualities and with capacities of infinite range, leading to the manifestation of quite original and unexpected designs, plans, and deeds.

Although everyone is quick to realize that it is the overweening scope which constitutes greatness in this case, it would be a mistake to think of this in terms of the moral sphere. The main foundation of morality is the good will which by its very nature is focused upon what is right. The main foundation of character on the other hand is resolute willing, without any bearing on right or wrong, on good or evil, on truth or error, and this is what every party values so highly in its adherents. Good will pertains to the realm of freedom; it relates to the inner man and to purpose. Resolute willing pertains to the realm of nature, and it relates to the outer world and to action. And because the exercise of will is always limited in its aim it almost follows that in practice that which is right in a higher sense can be willed never or only by chance. *On the Theory of Color.* Historical Part. Newton's Personality (1810); 40, 263-4

Wherever a man may happen to turn, whatever a man may undertake, he will always end up by returning to that path which nature has marked out for him.
The Autobiography I, 4 (1811); 22, 150

Our desires are anticipations of the faculties that lie in us, precursors of what we shall be able to accomplish.
The Autobiography II, 9 (1812); 23, 207

[With reference to Moses] It is not talents, not an aptitude for this and that, which constitute the man of action. Everything depends on personality. Character is based on personality, not on talents. Talents can be joined to character, but not vice versa; for in character everything can be dispensed with but itself.
Divan. Notes. Israel in the Desert (1819); 5, 266

The element of longing in my make-up that I had perhaps unduly cultivated in my earlier years I strove vigorously to curb as life advanced. It no longer seemed to comport with the status of manhood, and I sought instead complete satisfaction within the limits of the finite.
Campaign in France. 1792 (1822); 28, 148

. . . Peculiarities. There are certain human phenomena that are best designated by this term. Aberrations as to their outward effect, they are integral as regards the inner organization, and psychologically they are highly significant. It is they which constitute the individual. Through them the universal is particularized. And the most extreme individual oddity is not without a trace of sense, reason, and benevolence that attracts and holds us.

Laurence Sterne (1827); 38, 85

The heart is a world of its own and must contrive its own creation and destruction.

To Louise Adele Schopenhauer, Nov. 16, 1827

The botanists distinguish a class of plants that they call *Incompletae.* Similarly there are men who deserve the designation incomplete. They are the ones whose longing and striving is out of proportion to their deeds and achievements.   *Maxims and Reflections* 473 (1829)

The humblest individual can be complete provided he moves within the limits of his talents and accomplishments. But even high deserts are obscured and annulled when this indispensable balance is absent. Cases of such disharmony are bound to multiply in our epoch; for who can do justice to the demands of an age so intense and so rapid in its movement?

Maxims and Reflections 474 (1829)

What is part of you, you cannot get rid of, even if you throw it away.   *Maxims and Reflections* 645 (1829)

Animals are taught by their organs, the ancients said. Men likewise, I add; but they have the advantage of teaching their organs in turn.

Every act, every talent, therefore, presupposes something innate that acts of itself and unconsciously brings the necessary *Anlage* [disposition] into play, so that, although conforming to rule, it can nevertheless run its own course without ultimate aim or purpose.

The sooner a person discovers that there is a craft or an art which can spur his native *Anlagen* to a graduated rise, the better for him. Whatever he may receive from without will not harm his innate individuality. The best endowment of genius is that which knows how to absorb and assimilate everything without in the slightest impairing that fundamental pattern which we call character, accentuating it rather and increasing its vitality.

To W. von Humboldt, March 17, 1832

EDUCATION

Attempts to amend ineradicable defects in men and circumstances are a waste of time and make matters worse. One should rather treat these deficiencies as a basic datum and then try to counterbalance them. The finest way of sensing the ideal would be to sense more and more keenly the reason why we cannot attain it.

Diary, Dec. 14, 1778

A leaf that is destined to grow large is full of grooves and wrinkles at the start. Now if one has no patience and wants it smooth offhand like a willow leaf, there is trouble ahead.

To F. Jacobi, Sept. 9, 1788

[Serlo:] Man is so inclined to busy himself with the most vulgar concerns; the mind and the nerves are so easily dulled to impressions of the beautiful and the perfect that one should try in every way possible to preserve the capacity for their appreciation. For we can never quite come to do without their enjoyment, and it is only because they are unaccustomed to the enjoyment of what is good that many people delight in the silly and trivial, provided it has the attraction of novelty. Every day one

195

should hear at least one little song, read one good poem, see one outstanding picture, and, if it could be contrived, speak a few sensible words.

Wilhelm Meister's Apprenticeship V, 1 (1795); 18, 5

When I strictly scrutinized my own and other men's development in life and art I often found that what can properly be called an aberration turned out to be an indispensable digression for the individual on the way to his goal. Every return from error exerts a mighty formative effect on man, specifically and generally, so that it is easy to understand how the prober of hearts can take greater pleasure in one repentant sinner than in ninety-nine righteous. As a matter of fact we often consciously strive in the direction of an apparently mistaken goal, just as the ferryman heads diagonally against the current when his only concern is to land exactly across from his starting-place.

To Eichstädt, Sept. 15, 1804

Aptitudes are what we count on to start out with. They must be transformed into accomplishments. This is the purpose of all education.

Elective Affinities I, 5 (1809); 21, 46

In any case it would not be a bad thing if the future manual of good manners, after telling how to act in company while eating and drinking, were to contain a rather detailed chapter on how to behave in art collections and museums.

Elective Affinities II, 6 (1809); 21, 195

We submit to having our faults passed in review; we submit to censure; we endure a variety of things on their account with patience. But when it is demanded that we cast them off we react with impatience.

Maxims and Reflections 17 (1809)

There is not a single outward mark of courtesy that does not have a deep moral basis. The right kind of education would be that which transmits both the outward mark and its basis.   *Maxims and Reflections* 38 (1809)

Sketching develops and compels attention, without doubt the highest of all accomplishments and virtues.
von Müller, Nov. 30, 1816. *Biedermann* 1756

We are definitely opposed to the uniform. It conceals the character, and more than any other simulation it hides the individual qualities of the children from the eye of their supervisors.
Wilhelm Meister's Journeyings II, 2 (1829); 19, 194

Man has to run through a variety of stages, and every stage is accompanied by its own peculiar virtues and faults which, for the stage in question, are to be regarded as natural and in a sense right. On the next stage man is no longer the same; of his former virtues and faults not a trace remains, but other positive and negative qualities have taken their place. And thus it continues all the way to the final transformation, the nature of which we do not know in advance.
Eckermann, March 6, 1831. *Biedermann* 2929

The higher maxim of pedagogy: Not to disturb children, nor the un- and half-educated in their reverence for higher things.   *Diary*, April 24, 1831

LOVE

If the author had ever loved he would know that love has nothing to do with any feeling of our own perfection or of pleasure at the appreciation of our worth on the part

197

of others. He would have known that love is an independent emotion that aims at nothing but itself; that the embracing and fusing of kindred souls, the dwelling upon the beloved object, the expansion of one's own existence, the constant outflow and return of the warmest feeling, the natural receiving and bestowing of happiness and a thousand other ecstasies make of love the greatest boon that God could bestow upon man.

History of Selbstgefühl (Review 1772);
W. A. Werke, 38, 371

Love does not dominate, it cultivates. And that is more.
The Fairy-Tale (1795); 16, 300

For such is the nature of love that it thinks it alone is in the right and all other claims melt away in its presence.
Elective Affinities I, 12 (1809); 21, 98

If one love but a single being from the very heart, all the others seem lovable also.
Elective Affinities I, 12 (1809); 21, 101

Hatred is partial, but love is more so.
Elective Affinities I, 13 (1809); 21, 108

There is a courtesy of the heart; it is akin to love. The most unaffected courtesy of outward behavior derives from this source. *Maxims and Reflections* 40 (1809)

Confronted by outstanding merit in another, there is no way of saving one's ego except by love.
Maxims and Reflections 45 (1809)

The only means to gain one's ends with people are force and cunning. Love also, they say; but that is to wait for sunshine, and life needs every moment.
Riemer, April 27, 1810. *Biedermann* 1287

One gets to know nothing except what one loves; and the more deeply and exhaustively this knowledge is to penetrate, the more vigorous, intense, and vital a love—nay, a passion—is called for.

To F. Jacobi, May 10, 1812

I will not deny that I am aware of having exerted a good influence these past few summers at the Rhine and the Main, for I have only been preaching the admonition of St. John: "Children, love one another," and, if that is asking too much, at any rate: Be fair to one another.

To Zelter, Nov. 7, 1816

In all things we learn only from those whom we love.

Eckermann, May 12, 1825. *Biedermann* 2331

Every thoughtful person who looks at his calendar or his watch will remember to whom he owes these benefits. But if we respectfully yield time and space to the mathematicians as their domain they will come to see on their part that we perceive something common to all that transcends these matters and that conditions their special activity—the Idea and Love.

Maxims and Reflections 711 (1829)

Now the conversation turned to "Greek love." Goethe developed the view that this aberration has its root in the fact that according to purely aesthetic standards man·is far more beautiful and perfect than woman. Where this feeling exists it is easy for it to stray into the domain of animal nature. Homosexuality is as old as mankind, and in a sense it is natural even though contrary to nature.

von Müller, April 7, 1830. *Biedermann* 2815

MARRIAGE

Among all festivals the wedding feast is the least appropriate. No other festival is so much in need of being celebrated in seclusion, in humility and hope.

Wilhelm Meister's Apprenticeship V, 13 (1795); 18, 59

Whoever attacks matrimony, Mittler cried, whoever undermines this basis of all moral society by words or by deeds, will have to settle with me. Or if I cannot cope with him I'll have nothing to do with him. Marriage is the beginning and the peak of all cultivation. It makes the boor gentle, and the most cultivated man has no better opportunity to show his gentleness. It must be indissoluble; for it makes for so much happiness that all individual unhappiness weighs as nothing in the balance. And what do they prate of unhappiness? It is a fit of impatience that seizes a man from time to time, and then it is his sovereign pleasure to find himself unhappy. Let such a moment pass, and he will congratulate himself on the continuance of a relation of such long standing. For separating there are absolutely no sufficient grounds. This human state has so wide a range of sorrows and joys that there is simply no computing what a pair of married folks come to owe to each other. It is an infinite debt that only eternity can square. It may be uncomfortable at times, that I will believe, and that is as it should be. And are we not married to conscience also, and would we not often like to be rid of it, because it is more uncomfortable than a husband or wife ever could be?

Elective Affinities I, 9 (1809); 21, 80

Thou shalt not commit adultery, Mittler continued, how coarse, how indecent! How much better it would

sound to say: Thou shalt have reverence for the marriage
bond. Where you see married people who love one another you shall rejoice in this and take part in it as in the
joy of a smiling day. If anything tend to trouble their relations you should endeavor to straighten it out. You
should endeavor to mollify and pacify them, to make
them see their mutual advantages. Practicing a fine un-
selfishness, you should make them realize how every duty
is a source of happiness, and this duty in particular which
ties husband and wife by an indissoluble bond.

Elective Affinities II, 18 (1809); 21, 292

Both sexes display a characteristic cruelty toward each
other. Every individual probably has these impulses at
times even if they do not get a chance to come into the
open. In men it is the brute violence of voluptuousness.
In women cruelty takes the form of ingratitude, indifference, nagging, etc.

Riemer, July 7, 1811. *Biedermann* 1420

Elective Affinities. The very simple text of this ramified
little book is the words of Christ: Whosoever looketh on
a woman to lust after her, etc. I do not know whether
anyone has recognized them in this paraphrase.

To Zauper, Sept. 7, 1821

You know how I hate all happy-go-lucky ways. Above
all, an engagement or a marriage on the spur of the moment I have always regarded as a regular abomination.
Love can be kindled in a moment, and every genuine inclination must at some time have flamed up like a flash of
lightning. But why marry the moment one is in love?
Love is an ideal thing, marriage a real thing; and a confusing of the real with the ideal never goes unpunished.
Such an important turning-point of life wants to be considered from all angles and over a considerable time to

see whether the lives of the two individuals harmonize in all respects or, at least, in most.

von Müller, Sept. 14, 1823. *Biedermann* 2144

Almost all laws are syntheses of the impossible, Goethe said; for example, the institution of marriage. And yet it is good that this is so; for by postulating the impossible a maximum of the possible is achieved.

von Müller, Oct. 19, 1823. *Biedermann* 2172

In my *Elective Affinities* I endeavored to make the inner true catharsis as pure and perfect as possible. But I do not delude myself for all that with thinking that any handsome young man who reads the book can thereby be purged of the desire to lust after the wife of another. The sixth commandment, which seemed necessary enough to Jehovah-Elohim in the desert for him to carve it with his own hand in tablets of granite, will always have to keep its place in our pulp catechisms.

To Zelter, Jan. 29, 1830

KNOW THYSELF

[In search of his true vocation.] Thoughts on the instinctive aptitude for any concern. Every work that a man engages in has its own smell, so to say. Just as, literally speaking, the rider smells of horses, the bookshop has a slightly musty odor, and there is the smell of dogs about the huntsman. This holds true in more subtle ways. The material a person shapes, the tools he uses, the muscles he exerts in the act—all this together makes for a certain domestic setting, a marriage between the artist and his instrument. This intimacy with all the strings of the harp, this assurance of his touch, is a mark of the master in every domain. He goes straight for what can be observed, he does not fall to dreaming about plastic art as the like of us used to do. When at work, his hand reaches directly for what is needed at the moment. Tilling the fields is glorious, because everything responds so precisely when I go about it rightly or stupidly, and well-being or congestion results for the organs of elimination. But I sense in advance that I was not cut out for this either. I must not stray from the way marked out for me. It so happens that my existence is not simple. I only wish that gradually everything pretentious in me would dry up but without diminution of that glorious strength for pumping the liquid through the right pipes ranged side by side and filling them to the same level.* You envy any man whose eye you see fixed on his potter's wheel, when there issues forth from under his hands now a jug, now a bowl, according to his will. Finding the point of focus for the diversity [of creative impulses] always remains a secret, because one must settle that with one's own individuality and listen to no advice.   *Diary*, July 14, 1779

O thou sweet Poetry I sometimes exclaim and praise the good fortune of Marcus Aurelius (who himself gives praise to the gods on this account) that kept him from getting involved with poetry and eloquence. I divert the waters from these fountains and cascades to the best of my ability to sluice them into millraces and ditches, but before I know it an evil genie has thrown the switch and everything shoots sky-high. And when I think I am sitting on my nag and jogging along in the line of duty, before I know it the mare under me is sublimely transformed and grows wings and is seized with an irrepressible urge, and off we go.

                    To Charlotte von Stein, Sept. 14, 1780

[* An allusion to Lessing's *Hamburgische Dramaturgie*, Issues 101-104, April 19, 1768.]

It is good for a man, when he makes his debut in the world, to regard himself highly, to aim at perfecting himself in a great number of ways, to take the broadest view of his possibilities. But after he has arrived at a certain degree of self-perfection it is of advantage for him to learn to lose himself in a crowd, to live for the sake of others, and to forget himself in activity prescribed by duty. Only then does he begin to know himself; for it is in what we do that we truly measure ourselves against others.

Wilhelm Meister's Apprenticeship VII, 9 (1796); 18, 255

To be sure, it is a tedious and at times melancholy business, this overconcentration on ourselves and what harms and helps us. But considering the ominous idiosyncrasy of human nature on the one hand and the infinite diversity of modes of life and enjoyments on the other, it is a sheer miracle that the human race has not long since wrought its own destruction. It must be that human nature is endowed with a peculiar tenacity and versatility enabling it to overcome everything that it contacts or takes into itself, or, if the thing defies assimilation, at least to render it innocuous.

The Autobiography II, 8 (1812); 23, 161

We act well, strictly speaking, only in so far as we are acquainted with ourselves. If we are in the dark concerning ourselves we are not likely to succeed in doing what is good in the right way, which amounts to the good not being done at all. But as for conceit, it certainly leads us to evil; present in any degree, in fact, it leads to bad conduct even though I would not necessarily go so far as to say that the man who acts badly is bad.

To von Knebel, April 8, 1812

The highest stage man can reach is to be conscious of

his own thoughts and sentiments, to know himself. This affords him the cue for arriving at intricate knowledge even of personalities constituted differently from his own.

Shakespeare and No End (1813); 37, 37

But what troubles the sensitive youth most is the inescapable recurrence of his faults. For how late do we learn to realize that in developing our virtues we at the same time cultivate our faults. This is the most difficult aspect of knowledge of one's self, making it well-nigh impossible.

The Autobiography III, 13 (1814); 24, 159

"It takes the endowment of a robust constitution to practice introspection without morbidity." To look into oneself soundly without undermining oneself; to venture into the unexplored deep not with illusion and make-believe, but with a pure gaze, is a rare gift. But then, too, the results of such exploration for the world and for science constitute a rare good fortune.

Seeing, in Its Subjective Aspect, by Purkinje (Notes; 1820) W. A. Werke, Zweite Abteilung, 11, 269f.

[Magnetism, mesmerism.] Only under the guidance of your trusted hand did I venture a few steps in the direction of the occult. But with the best will in the world I had to turn back very soon, for this simply happens to lie outside my province. I look to be deeply refreshed by natural slumber. When I consider the fact that Gassner and Mesmer produced a great stir in my most impressionable years and that I was a friend of Lavater, who attached religious value to this marvelous phenomenon, I sometimes find it strange that I did not respond to the attraction—like a man walking beside a river without feeling any urge to go in bathing. My nature must somehow be responsible for this attitude; how else would you account for its having persisted into old age?

To von Esenbeck, July 23, 1820

Often in life, when we have been pursuing our course with the greatest assurance, we realize with a start that we have been caught up in error. We had drifted into intimacy with persons and things on fictitious premises under a sort of day-dream spell, and the moment we open our eyes the whole fabric of illusion has dissolved into thin air. Yet we are unable to disengage ourselves; a power that seems beyond comprehension holds us fast. Sometimes, however, it happens that we become fully alerted and then we realize that illusion has been just as efficacious a spur to activity as a genuine interest. Inasmuch as initiative is the decisive factor in all concerns of life, an active illusion can result in positive gains, because every act is infinite in its effects. Positive productivity is always to be preferred, to be sure, but even a destructive act can thus involve fortunate consequences.

Among all the illusions that give us pause there is none so intriguing as that which involves the limits of our own faculties. We devote ourselves to a worthy undertaking that exceeds our capacities; we strive for a goal that is beyond our reach. The torments that we suffer in consequence are excruciating in proportion to the sincerity of the efforts we expended on the quest. Even so, when that to which we aspired has faded quite out of reach, we are more likely than not to have already happened upon some other desirable interest that is in keeping with our capacities and conforms to the sphere of our native endowment. *Maxims and Reflections.* To be pondered. 67-8 (1820)

For a man to measure up to all that is demanded of him he must overestimate his possibilities.
Maxims and Reflections 69 (1821)

I confess that the great and high-sounding task, Know Thyself, always seemed suspect to me as a device of

priests secretly leagued to confuse man by impossible demands and to divert him from activity in the world about
him to a false introspection. Man knows himself only in
so far as he knows the world, becoming aware of it only
in himself, and of himself only in it. Every new object,
attentively looked at, brings a new inner faculty into
play.　　*A Single Suggestive Term Opens New Vistas* (1823);
39, 49

I claim that man can never learn to know himself; he
can never learn to regard himself purely as object.
Others know me much better than I do myself. It is only
my relations to the world about me that I can learn to
know and appraise correctly. We should confine ourselves
to this. With all our striving for self-knowledge, as
preached by priests and moralists, we get no further in
life; we arrive neither at any definite conclusions nor at
genuine inner improvement.

von Müller, March 8, 1824. *Biedermann* 2235

Man should learn—this is the view of our group—to
think of himself without lasting outward ties. He should
look for consistency not in circumstances but in himself.
There he will find it and nurture it lovingly. He will develop and accommodate himself with a view to being at
home everywhere. Those who devote themselves to matters of urgent necessity will always have the least difficulty in advancing to their goal. Those, on the other
hand, whose concern is with higher and more delicate
matters, will have to exercise caution even in deciding
what path to pursue.

Wilhelm Meister's Journeyings III, 9 (1829); 20, 144-5

All ages have said and repeated that one should strive
to know oneself. This is a strange demand which no one
up to now has measured up to and, strictly considered, no

one should. With all his study and effort, man is directed to what is outside, to the world about him, and he is kept busy coming to know this and to master it to the extent that his purposes require. Of himself he has knowledge only when he enjoys or suffers, and thus it is only through pain and pleasure that he finds out what he has to seek and what to avoid. But in general man has to grope his way. He knows not whence he comes nor whither he goes; he knows little of the world and himself least of all.   *Eckermann,* April 10, 1829. *Biedermann* 2678

False tendencies are unproductive, or at most, that which is produced is of no value. To become aware of this in others is not particularly difficult; but to do so in oneself is another story and requires a great degree of spiritual freedom. And even diagnosis does not always help. One doubts and hesitates and cannot make up one's mind. It is as difficult as trying to disengage oneself from a girl one loves despite repeated proofs of her infidelity.
                Eckermann, April 12, 1829. *Biedermann* 2680

Act with Circumspection is the practical side of Know Thyself. Neither of these maxims must be regarded as a law or a rigid command. They are set up like the bull's-eye of the target on which the sights must always be trained, even if we do not always hit it. Men would be more sensible and happy if they knew how to sense the difference between the infinite goal and the limited aim, and if they could gradually master the trick of realizing the extent of their means.   *To Rochlitz,* Nov. 23, 1829

How can one learn to know oneself? Introspection is a hopeless method, whereas action may lead to success. Try to do your duty, and you know your mettle straight-way.   *Maxims and Reflections* 442 (1829)

But what is your duty? The summons of the day.
Maxims and Reflections 443 (1829)

If then we examine the significant adage, Know Thyself, we must not put an ascetic interpretation upon it. It does not point to the self-probing of our modern hypochondriacs, humorists, and self-tormentors. It means very simply: Keep a moderate watch upon yourself in order that you may become aware of your relations as regards your fellow-men and the world. For this no psychological self-tormenting is needed. Every worth-while individual knows and experiences what it means. It is a good piece of advice, of the greatest practical benefit to everyone. *Maxims and Reflections* 657 (1829)

POSITIVE VALUES

We human beings so often complain that of good days there are so few and of evil days so many, and, as I think, without warrant for the most part. If we always had an open heart to enjoy the good things that God prepares for us every day, we would then have strength enough too to bear affliction when it comes. . . .

With ill humor it is just as with indolence, for it is a kind of indolence. Our nature leans very much that way, and yet, once we muster the strength to shake it off, work goes smoothly and we find a real delight in activity.
The Sorrows of Werther I, July 1 (1774); 16, 34-5

May God grant further aid and light to keep us from standing in our own way. May he allow us to do our proper task from morning to evening and give us clear conceptions of the consequences of things. Not to be like people who complain all day about headaches and use headache remedies and then in the evening drink too much wine. May the idea of purity, extending even to the bite I put in my mouth, become ever brighter within me.

Diary, Aug. 7, 1779

He who is morally active does not exert himself in vain, for much more of the seed falls on fertile ground than the Gospel all too modestly estimates in the parable of the sower. *The Autobiography* III, 14 (1814); 24, 199

In one's inward self one must not deviate from the highest maxims of life and of art by even a hair. But in practice, in the current of daily life, I would rather be overgenerous and let something of middling quality pass than fail to recognize something really good or depreciate it by fault-finding. *To Zelter,* Nov. 11, 1816

[Speaking of Byron:] All fault-finding attacks on the social order have a negative bias, and the negative is nothing. If I call bad what is bad, what is the great gain? But if I call bad what is good, great harm is done. He who would work effectively must never scold. He must simply ignore what is wrong and just go on doing what is good. For what is needed is not tearing down but building up something in which mankind can take pure satisfaction. *Eckermann,* Feb. 24, 1825. *Biedermann* 2310

We should put into words only such higher maxims as the world can profit from. Others we should keep locked in our bosom, but they will irradiate what we do, like the light of a sun obscured by haze.

Eckermann, Oct. 15, 1825. *Biedermann* 2364

In general, I must keep myself very much under control these days and avoid getting involved in polemics more than ever. One really has plenty to do carrying one's own positive contribution to the end. Fortunately, the conviction remains as a last resort that many things can and must exist alongside one another that would like to crowd each other out. The world-spirit is more tolerant than one thinks.   *To von Reinhard,* May 12, 1826

I would rather hang myself than be forever saying no, be forever in the camp of the opposition, forever with my finger on the trigger to snipe at the faults and imperfections of my contemporaries and neighbors. You are still awfully young and reckless if you can approve of such an attitude. That is an old leaven that has infected the character and dates from the Revolution.
                    von Müller, June 18, 1826. *Biedermann* 2423

There are simultaneously so many fine and substantial things in the world, but they are not in touch with each other.   *Maxims and Reflections* 352 (1826)

If only men after finding what is right did not distort and obscure it again, I would be content. For mankind would seem to be in need of something positive to be transmitted from generation to generation; and it would be well if the positive were at the same time the right and the true.   *Eckermann,* Feb. 1, 1827. *Biedermann* 2473

It faut croire à la simplicité! One must believe in simplicity, in primal creative forces at work, if one would find the right way. But it is not given to everyone to do this. We are born into an artificial environment, and it is decidedly easier to intensify this artificiality than to return to simplicity.   *To Zelter,* March 29, 1827

Everything noble has a quiet way about it and seems to sleep, until by its opposite it is awakened and challenged.   *Eckermann,* April 1, 1827. *Biedermann* 2483

[Dissection an inferior method of studying the human organization] Building up teaches more than tearing down, joining together more than separating, reviving the dead more than keeping on killing what is dead.

Wilhelm Meister's Journeyings III, 3 (1829); 20, 68

The rational world is to be regarded as one great immortal individual that unswervingly pursues its necessary course and thereby masters even what is subject to chance.

Maxims and Reflections 444 (1829)

Love of truth asserts itself in the ability to find and appreciate what is good wherever it be.

Maxims and Reflections 493 (1829)

If I am to listen to the opinion of another person it must be couched in positive terms. I have enough problematic stuff in myself.

Maxims and Reflections 499 (1829)

I love and honor what is positive and lean on it for support, in so far as its vitality dates from time immemorial and may serve us as a true foundation for our life and activity.

To Schultz, Jan. 10, 1829

ACTIVITY

With my own unsettled disposition, I derive unspeakable benefit from associating with these people, every one of whom has a definite, simple, steady, and important task to perform. It is like a cold bath after voluptuous relaxation. Every nerve becomes taut and tingles with new life.

To Charlotte von Stein, Dec. 9, 1777

The pressure of business is very good for the soul. After

it has discharged its task the soul moves with greater ease and enjoys life. There is nothing more wretched than well-being without work. This is enough to make the finest of nature's gifts turn sour. *Diary*, Jan. 13, 1779

Solitude is a fine thing when one is at peace with oneself and has something definite to do.
To Charlotte von Stein, March 4, 1779

The needs of my nature compel me to engage in a diversity of activities. In the lowliest village or on a desert island I should have to try my hand at all sorts of things just to keep alive. Even though it turns out that for some among these I have no aptitude, I come to take this with good grace because it is an article of faith with me that through steadfastness and fidelity in our present sphere we become worthy and capable of entering the higher stage of one to follow, whether it be in this life or in that beyond. *To von Knebel*, Dec. 3, 1781

I have come to know happy individuals, by the way, who are happy only because they are whole. Even the lowliest, provided he is whole, can be happy and in his own way perfect. *To Charlotte von Stein*, June 9, 1787

The physician showed me how these sentiments, cultivated as such without being anchored to any object outside us, have a great tendency to hollow us out, so to say, and undermine the basis of our existence. Man was designed, he said, first and foremost to be active, and all those times in between, when he is compelled to rest, should be employed in acquiring a clear understanding of outward things, to be turned to advantage in subsequent activity.

Wilhelm Meister's Apprenticeship VI. *Confessions of a Beautiful Soul* (1795); 18, 162-3

Anything that merely adds to my information without augmenting my activity or communicating an immediate vital impulse I find odious.   *To Schiller*, Dec. 19, 1798

I see more and more that everyone should pursue his own business seriously and take all the rest lightly. A few verses that I have to put into shape interest me more than far more important things over which I have no control, and if everyone does the same domestic and state affairs will be in good shape.

Riemer, Oct.-Nov., 1803. *Biedermann* 711

The safest thing is for us to try to transform everything in and about us into action. Then let the others talk and argue about it as they please.   *To Zelter*, Oct. 30, 1828

Versatility really does nothing but prepare the field in which the specialist can now exert his energies with sufficient elbow room. This is indeed an age of specialization. Good speed to him who grasps this truth and labors accordingly for himself and others. In some things this is a matter of course: Train yourself to be a first-class violinist and be assured that the concertmaster will assign you your place in the orchestra. Make a function of yourself and be prepared to have mankind accord you a proper sphere of activity in the general economy. . . . I insist, it is necessary in all things to begin serving from the bottom up. To concentrate on a craft is the best procedure. For the person of inferior gifts it will always remain a craft. The more gifted person will raise it to an art. And as for the man of highest endowment, in doing one thing he does all things; or, to put it less paradoxically, in the one thing that he does properly, he sees a symbol of all things that are done right.

Wilhelm Meister's Journeyings I, 4 (1829); 19, 39

To heal psychic ailments that we have contracted through misfortune or faults of our own, the understanding avails nothing, reason little, time much, but resolute activity everything.

Wilhelm Meister's Journeyings II, 11 (1829); 20, 46

To become expert in some field, to acquire mastery in some specific activity to a degree not easily shared by anyone else near by—that is what counts.

Wilhelm Meister's Journeyings II, 11 (1829); 20, 47

[After the death of Goethe's son] Here it is only the great concept of duty that can bear us up. My only concern is physically to keep myself in balance; everything else follows automatically. The spirit is willing; the body has to follow suit. And he who sees the most necessary course charted out for his will need not waste time making up his mind.

To Zelter, Nov. 21, 1830

There is no situation that could not acquire dignity by performance or patient endurance.

Maxims and Reflections 856 (posthumous)

The spirit, alive and gifted, focusing with practical intent on the most immediate concerns, is the finest thing on earth.

Maxims and Reflections 1205 (posthumous)

TIME

I confess that my old adage takes on more and more importance: *Tempus divitiae meae, tempus ager meus.*

To Fritz von Stein, April 26, 1797

They always say, the span of life is short. However, one can accomplish much if one knows how to use time wisely. I have not smoked tobacco, I have not played chess, in short, I have indulged in nothing that could squander time. I have always felt sorry for people who do not know how to spend or use their time.

Grüner, Aug. 21, 1822. *Biedermann* 2038

We instill the highest respect in all our pupils for Time as the greatest gift of God and Nature and the most attentive companion of our life. . . . Our moral teaching, which has a wholly practical focus, tries above all to inculcate thoughtfulness, and this is stimulated in the extreme by the time schedule and attention to each hour. Something is assigned to be done for every moment, and how could it be accomplished without regard for the task as well as the hour?

Wilhelm Meister's Journeyings III, 11 (1829); 20, 161

It is better to do the most trifling thing in the world than to regard half an hour as a trifle.

Maxims and Reflections 752 (1829)

The day is of infinite length for him who knows how to appreciate and use it.

von Müller [undated]. *Biedermann* 3108

FOLLOW-THROUGH

Follow-through! The only attitude by which everything is accomplished, and without which nothing can be accomplished—why is it so rarely sustained? Why is it so difficult to create in ourselves and those we try to influence?

Riemer, Aug. 18, 1809. *Biedermann* 1209

There are only two ways, I often heard Goethe maintain, to achieve great and significant ends—tyrannical power and single-mindedness. Tyrannical power is apt to be resented and to provoke opposition; it is the prerogative, moreover, of few favored individuals. Single-mindedness, however, an unflinching, systematic attitude of follow-through, is in the power of even the most modest individual to employ, and it will rarely fail of its aim since its quiet momentum irresistibly mounts with the passing of time. Where I cannot apply myself with this attitude of follow-through, where I cannot exert my influence without interruption, I find it more advisable to withdraw altogether. Fitful, capricious action, besides affording no guarantee of progress in the right direction, has a way, moreover, of interfering with the natural course of things and disturbing those healing agencies that would automatically come into play.

von Müller, 1832. *Biedermann* 3101

Character—in things great and small—is indicated when a man pursues with sustained follow-through what he feels himself capable of doing.

Maxims and Reflections 839 (posthumous)

NEGATIVISM

Most people, because they are themselves formless, because they are unable to give form to themselves and their nature, endeavor to strip objects of their form, so as to leave nothing but loose and disjointed matter such as they themselves represent. They reduce everything in the end to the so-called effect. To them everything is relative; and so everything becomes relative except nonsense and trite commonplaces, which then hold absolute sway.

Wilhelm Meister's Apprenticeship VIII, 7 (1796); 18, 352

... at a season which is to me the most insufferable
time of the year, making it perfectly plausible to me how
Henry III had the Duke of Guise shot simply because the
weather was nasty, and making me envy Herder when I
hear he is being buried.

To Charlotte von Schiller, Dec. 20, 1803

That chance aspect of the real which at the moment
fails to suggest either a law of nature or one of freedom,
we term the vulgar.   *Maxims and Reflections* 103 (1821)

There is in us an organ of malevolence and discontent,
just as there is one of contradiction and skepticism. The
more we foster it and give it play, the more powerful it
becomes until it develops from an organ into a festering
cancer that keeps on expanding, consuming, and infect-
ing all healthy tissues. Then it gets incrusted with remorse, self-reproach, and other absurdities. We become
unjust toward others and toward ourselves. We lose
pleasure in the success and achievements of ourselves and
of others. In despair we finally look for the root of all evil
outside ourselves instead of finding it in our own con-
trariness. If we could only take each individual and each
event for what it is worth and emerge from the confines
of the self to return to it with a new sense of expansion.

von Müller, Feb. 2, 1823. *Biedermann* 2061

The empirical moral world consists for the most part
only of malevolence and envy.

Maxims and Reflections 170 (1823)

[Goethe commenting on his refusal to see his daughter-
in-law while her face was disfigured by a fall from her
horse:] I never can rid myself of such disagreeable impressions again; they leave a permanent scar on my
memory. My faculty of sensuous perception is so strange-

ly constituted that all contours and forms get fixed in my memory in the sharpest focus, and any deformations and flaws affect me very vividly. The finest, costliest etching, once it has got a spot or a tear, is ruined for my appreciation. *von Müller*, May 17, 1826. *Biedermann* 2403

There are moments so cruel that they would make us regard the brevity of life as the greatest boon, to keep intolerable torment from being interminable.

To Rauch, Oct. 21, 1827

Art

FUNDAMENTALS: BEAUTY - STYLE

In art it's not thinking that turns the trick, but making.
Italian Journey. Rome, July 5, 1787. 27, 72

Art exists in order to be seen, not to be discussed, except—at most—in the presence of the object.
Italian Journey. July 29, 1787. 27, 79

There is much more in art that is positive—I mean what can be transmitted by teaching—than people realize, and there are many mechanical devices by which highly subtle effects can be achieved, granted that it takes brains. When one knows these little tricks, many things that pass for very profound are reduced to mere play. There isn't a place in the world, I believe, where one can learn more, in high matters and low, than in Rome. *Italian Journey*. Rome, Dec. 8, 1787. 27, 167

The highest aim of art, in my opinion, is to depict human forms as sensuously significant and beautiful as possible. Among moral themes art must restrict itself to those that are intimately conjoined with sensuous nature and lend themselves to representation through figures and gestures. *To Meyer*, April 27, 1789

Whereas *simple imitation* flourishes under tranquil and satisfying conditions of existence, and whereas *mannerism* calls for a light touch and a fresh individuality, that which I call *style* rests on the deepest foundations of cognition, on the inner essence of things, in so far as this is given us to comprehend in visible and tangible forms.
Simple Imitation of Nature, Mannerism, Style (1789); 33, 56-7

ART

For our understanding a genuine work of art, like a work of nature, always remains incommensurable. We contemplate it; we feel it; it is effective; but it eludes exact cognition, and its essence, its quality, cannot be expressed in words. *On Laocoön* (1798); 33, 124

Art is constitutive—the artist determines beauty. He does not take it over. *Notes for publications on art* (1798) W. A. Werke, 47, 292

All the arts, owing their development to the interaction of hand and brain, practice and theory, remind me of cities that are built on foundations the record of which is lost. *To Zelter,* June 22, 1808

It is hard to get it through people's heads that the highest, indeed the only, function of both nature and art is the creation of form, and within the realm of forms the aim is specification, in order that each product may become, be, and remain both specific and significant. It is altogether too easy to employ talent for the convenient indulging of one's humors. Something is always bound to result, like the serpent-boy monster that owed its existence to the spilled semen of Vulcan. *To Zelter,* Oct. 30, 1808

It is the highest task of every art to employ appearance to create the illusion of a higher reality. But it is a false endeavor to carry the realization of appearance to such a point as to leave nothing in the end but ordinary reality. *The Autobiography* III, 11 (1814); 24, 49-50

To begin with, plastic art is a servant of architecture. A frieze on a Doric temple demands figures that conform to the proportion of its over-all profile. This consideration tended to give preference to what is compact and bold.

But to grant this relation, why should we meet with disproportion over and above this? How is this to be excused? It is not to be excused; rather to be praised; for when the artist deliberately departs from the norm he stands higher than we, and we must revere him instead of reproving.

. . . The master touch is revealed in the very fact that he deliberately commits a breach to a higher end. Verisimilitude is the condition of art, but within the sphere of verisimilitude the highest manifestations must be demanded. The merely correct is not worth sixpence if it has nothing further to offer.

Relief of Phigalia (1818); 35, 160-1

According to Hemsterhuis we experience beauty and the pleasure of beauty when we can easily span a very great number of perceptions at one moment. I had to maintain, on the contrary, that we find ourselves in the presence of beauty when we behold that which is alive in conformity with natural law in its acme of vitality and perfection; and this in turn raises our own vitality and activity to the highest pitch and incites us to re-creation. Upon close view, both of us will be found to have been saying the same thing, and I refrain from further comment. For the beautiful contains more of promise than of fulfillment, whereas the ugly, arising from an inhibition, inhibits in turn and stimulates neither hope, desire, nor expectation.

Campaign in France. Münster, Nov., 1792 (1822);
28, 185

Art bridges the realm of what lies beyond words to utter. That is why it seems folly to try to bridge our direct reception of art by words. Even so the mind derives profit from such attempts and this in turn redounds to the benefit of the creative faculty.

Maxims and Reflections 384 (1827)

I have to laugh at the aestheticians who agonize over trying to formulate in a few abstract words that indefinable thing we call beauty. Beauty is an *Urphaenomen* [archetypal phenomenon]. While it never materializes as such, it sheds its glow over a thousand different manifestations of the creative spirit and is as multiform as nature itself.

Eckermann, April 15, 1827. *Biedermann* 2485

No art can do without sensuous appeal, and the full flavor of this is present in subjects like those of Ostade's paintings. But where the artist tries to move in a higher region and approach the sphere of the ideal, it is difficult to provide sufficient sensuous content, and the treatment is apt to be dry and chilling. Youth and age enter in as favorable and unfavorable factors, and the artist must choose his themes to comport with his years. My *Iphigenie* and my *Tasso* turned out successful because I was young enough to transfuse the ideality of the subject matter with my sensuous vitality. Now that I am old such ideal subjects would not be suitable for me, and I do well to choose themes that have a natural affinity to the world of sense.

Eckermann, Feb. 4, 1829. *Biedermann* 2652

There are quite a few instances of isolated beauty in the world, but it is the task of the spirit to discover relations and thereby produce works of art. The charm of the flower is enhanced by the insect that clings to its calyx, by the dewdrop that moistens it, by the vessel perchance from which it draws its last nourishment. Not a shrub, not a tree but can be set into relief by a neighboring rock or a spring or made more appealing by being placed at a moderate distance. The same is the case with human figures and with animals of every type.

Maxims and Reflections 452 (1829)

ART AND NATURE: THE SUBJECT

It is not the subjects as such that count for the artist. It is a matter rather of his finding the subjects whose inner life responds to his own disposition and of his being able to project them again with all the workings of their life. If his eye penetrates through the outer shell into their innermost being; if they move his soul to inspiration so as to make him see their forms transfigured; if he has the mastery of stroke and color so as to objectify his inner vision, then he is a great artist. Let the subject be ever so humble, it will enchant us.   *To Müller,* June 21, 1781

The study and appreciation of nature comes easier than that of art. The lowliest product of nature embodies the sphere of its perfection within itself, and to discover these relationships all I need is eyes to see. I am certain that within a small sphere a wholly true existence is confined. In a work of art, on the other hand, the principle of its perfection lies outside itself. There is—most important of all—the artist's idea, rarely if ever matched by his execution. There are furthermore certain implicit laws which, though stemming from the nature of the craft, are not so easy to understand and decipher as the laws of living nature. In works of art there is always a large traditional factor, whereas the works of nature are like a word of God spoken this instant.

To the Duchess Luise, Rome, Dec. 23, 1786

When the artist selects a subject from nature, the subject no longer is under nature's jurisdiction. One can say, in fact, that the artist creates the subject at that moment when its significant, characteristic, interesting features dawn upon him—at the moment, I should rather say, when he endows the subject with higher value.

Introduction to the Propyläen (1798); 33, 112

When Nature begins to reveal her manifest mystery to a man, he feels an irresistible longing for her worthiest interpreter—art. *Maxims and Reflections* 201 (1823)

But now, in commending to you that reality which is most closely at hand—subjects that might seem almost unworthy of imitation on your part—I would add that the spirit of the real is in reality the truly ideal. We must not disdain what is immediately visible and sensuous, otherwise we shall be sailing without ballast.

To Leopoldine Grustner von Grusdorf, March 30, 1827

I am well aware that Nature often enchants us in a way that art cannot match, but I do not by any means believe that she is beautiful in all that she displays. Her intentions are always good, but not so the conditions necessary to make these manifest. The oak, for instance, is a tree that can be very beautiful. But what a favorable juncture of circumstances is required before Nature succeeds for once in producing a truly beautiful specimen!

Eckermann, April 18, 1827. *Biedermann* 2485

ART, RELIGION, AND MORALS

Throughout the whole [Volume 8 of Herder's *Letters on Humanität*] he keeps harping on the old Philistine half-truth that the arts must recognize the moral law and subordinate themselves to it. The former they have always done and always must do, because their laws derive

from reason no less than the moral law. If they were to
do the latter, however, they would be lost, and it would
be better to fasten a millstone around their necks and
drown them rather than make them suffer gradual atrophy
in catering to utilitarian interests.

To Meyer, June 20, 1796

The most wretched painting can appeal to sentiment
and imagination by activating them and setting them free
and leaving them to their own devices. The best work of
art also appeals to sentiment, but it speaks a higher language, one that needs to be understood. It ties down the
feelings and the imagination; it restricts our license. That
which is perfect is not subject to our whims; we are compelled to surrender to it in order to find ourselves restored
finer and better than we were.

Introduction to the Propyläen (1798); 33, 115

Conflict of good and evil cannot be aesthetically rendered, for something has to be added to evil and sub-
tracted from good to put them into a state of balance.—
Milton's *Paradise Lost*, where the interest is really on the
side of the devils.

Outlines and Jottings for *The Autobiography*
W. A. Werke, 27, 389

A good work of art can and will have moral effects, but
to demand moral aims of the artist is to ruin his craft.

The Autobiography III, 12 (1814); 24, 111-2

,Religion bears the same relation to art as do all the
other higher interests of life. For art it is nothing but matter that enjoys equal rights with all other matters of life.
Belief and disbelief, moreover, are by no means the
organs with which a work of art is to be assimilated;
here a wholly different set of human powers and apti-

tudes comes into play. It is only proper that art should exercise its function for the specific organs with which we assimilate it. If it fails to do this it misses its aim and the characteristic effect of art is lost. There is no reason why a religious subject should not lend itself well to artistic treatment, provided it makes a universally human appeal. Thus a virgin with the child is an excellent theme. Although it has been treated hundreds of times, we never tire of it.   *Eckermann,* May 2, 1824. *Biedermann* 2254

Music, no more than any other art, can affect morals directly, and it is always wrong to make such demands on the arts. Only philosophy and religion can do this. Our sense of reverence and of duty has to be stimulated, and it is only by accident that the arts accomplish this. They do have a civilizing effect upon rude manners, but this quickly leads to the degeneration of manly virtue.
              Gleanings apropos of Aristotle's Poetics (1827); 38, 84

The world—and I may include myself—is infinitely indebted to our old Kant for the energetic way in which he ranges art and nature alongside one another in his *Critique of Judgment* and accords to both the right to act from great principles, without purpose. Even earlier, Spinoza had confirmed me in my violent repudiation of those absurd final causes. Nature and art are too great to envisage purposes. They can well do without, for interrelations are found everywhere, and interrelations make up life.   *To Zelter,* Jan. 29, 1830

STUDY OF THE ANCIENTS

The wind that blows from the graves of the ancients wafts a fragrance as from a mound of roses.
              Italian Journey. Verona, Sept. 16, 1786. 26, 43

You have forced me to glimpse a region which I am
ordinarily at pains to avoid. We poets of this latter age
must revere the legacy of our ancestors, Homer, Hesiod,
and others, as arch-canonical writings. We do obeisance
to them as inspired by the Holy Ghost, and we do not
presume to ask whence and whither. We are quite willing
to assume that they had an old folk-religion to lean on,
but to us the pure characteristic personification without
hidden meaning and allegory is worth everything. We
must pay no regard to later attempts on the part of poets
and philosophers to unravel these mysteries. That is our
confession of faith.

But when the passion for delving into these mysteries
goes so far as to link the Hellenic sphere of god and man
with the remotest regions of the earth; when we are asked
to see analogies in words and images between the Greek
gods and the frost-giants, on the one hand, and the fire-
Brahmas on the other, then our suffering becomes acute
and we hasten to take refuge again in Ionia, where loving
divinities of the flowing spring mate and give birth to
Homer.   *To Creuzer*, Oct. 1, 1817

When we redistill diffuse antiquity we get a potion
that straightway refreshes the heart; and when we revive
obsolete turns of speech through our own vivid experience we feel like that dried fish which, immersed by
pranksters in the fountain of youth, began to swell up,
move about, and dart away, rejoicing in the fact that it
had found the true water.

To S. Boisserée, July 16, 1818

Clearness of focus, serenity of perception, ease of communication—this is what delights us. And when we now
claim that all this is what we find in those genuinely
Greek works, rendered in the noblest medium, with the
most exalted content, with deft and exact execution, then

it is no mystery why they are forever the beginning and
end of our painting. Let each of us be a Greek after his
own manner, but let him be one!

Ancient and Modern (1818); 35, 129

We always advocate study of the ancients. But what
does this mean other than: Concentrate upon the real
world and seek to express it? For that is what the ancients
did in their day.

Eckermann, Jan. 29, 1826. *Biedermann* 2388

What grandeur there is in the ancients, particularly
the Socratic school, in its training of the focus of vision
upon the source and guiding principle of all life and conduct, not as encouragement to empty speculation but as
a summons to living and doing!

Maxims and Reflections 658 (1829)

Caught up in the limitless maze, the fragmentation and
complication of modern natural science, and yearning for
the recapture of simplicity, we must forever ask ourselves: Supposing he had known nature in its present state
of complexity, a basic unity withal, how would Plato have
coped with it? *Maxims and Reflections* 664 (1829)

THE GREEKS: POETRY AND LITERATURE

Man can accomplish not a little by advantageous em-
ployment of individual powers. Extraordinary things
may result from the combined application of several
faculties. But the unique performance surpassing all expectation is achieved only by the totality of his powers
in harmonious union. This last was the happy lot of the
ancients, especially the Greeks in their prime. We moderns are restricted by fate to the two earlier alternatives.

Winckelmann. The Way of Life of the Ancients (1805);
34, 11-2

In Homer the world of human affairs is reflected in Olympus, and this duplicate hovers like a mirage above the earthly sphere. Such a mirroring enhances the value of any poetic work. It achieves a totality as it were and really answers a human need. . . . Over the *Nibelungs* there is a brazen sky, no trace of gods or of fate. Only man, left to his own resources and his passions.

Riemer, 1807. *Biedermann* 942

A prime factor in the much-vaunted good fortune of the Greeks was the fact that they were not deflected from their course by any outside influence. In modern times few individuals are so favored by fate, and among nations there is not a single instance. For even perfect models have a disturbing effect in that they lead us to skip necessary stages in our *Bildung*, with the result, for the most part, that we are carried wide of the mark into limitless error.

On Theory of Color. Historical Part. The Romans (1810)
W. A. Werke, Zweite Abteilung, 3, 120-1

Plato's relation to the world is that of a beautiful spirit who chooses to make his abode here for some little time. He is less concerned—by virtue of his foreknowledge—with getting to know it than with graciously imparting what he has to offer and it is in such need of. He penetrates to its depths, not so much to explore them as to fill them with his own essence. He soars to its heights, full of longing to return to his source. His every utterance is imbued with an awareness of what is eternally whole, good, true, and beautiful. What he assimilates in the way of specific earthly knowledge melts—evaporates, one might say—in his method, in his discourse.

Aristotle, on the other hand, faces the world as a man, as an architect. He has been assigned to this sphere, and he has a task to perform. He explores the soil but no deeper than necessary to lay a secure foundation. What extends beyond this to the center of the earth does not concern him. He marks out a vast circle for his edifice, he assembles materials from all quarters, he orders them, one on top of the other, and thus he rears his structure in the form of a regular pyramid, whereas Plato, like an obelisk or even a pointed flame, aspires heavenward.

On Theory of Color. Historical Part. Third Division.
Interim (1810); 40, 154-5

The Greek language is much more simple and direct, much more suited to the rendering of felicitous aspects of nature in a natural, serene, spirited, aesthetic manner. Its predilection for verbs, especially infinitives and participles, gives a noncommittal flavor to every expression. Nothing is determined, staked down, and fixed by words. Their function is merely suggestive, calling up the object to the inner eye.

The Latin language, on the other hand, by its use of substantives, acquires a decisive and commanding flavor. The concept is completely presented in the word, rigidified in the term, and it is treated accordingly as a real entity.

On Theory of Color. Historical Part. Fourth Division.
Scaliger (1810); 40, 177

Among all nationalities it was the Greeks who dreamed the dream of life most beautifully.

Maxims and Reflections 298 (1826)

With the Greeks, everything is of one piece, in the same grand style—the same marble, the same bronze, that makes possible a Zeus or a faun, and always the same spirit that confers upon everything its appropriate dignity.

On the Cyclops of Euripides (1826)
W. A. Werke, 42 (II), 463

Despite our appreciation of foreign literatures, we must take care not to confuse their specific flavor with absolute standards. In the last resort, it is not the Chinese manner that counts, nor the Serbian, nor Calderón, nor the *Nibelungs*. In our need of a norm we must forever return to the ancient Greeks, whose works are unfailing exponents of human beauty. With regard to everything else a merely historic approach is in order, an attitude of picking and choosing such elements of lasting value as we can find.   *Eckermann*, Jan. 31, 1827. *Biedermann* 2472

When a modern individual like Schlegel has fault to find with so great an ancient figure [Euripides], he should in fairness do so on bended knee.
Eckermann, March 28, 1827. *Biedermann* 2483

Describing or narrating, the Greeks did not discourse on cause and effect. They simply let the phenomena speak for themselves.
Maxims and Reflections 1366 (posthumous)

CLASSICAL ART

For my delectation yesterday I placed in the hall a cast of the colossal Head of Juno, the original of which is in the Villa Ludovisi. This was my first love in Rome, and now I own it. No words can give an intimation of its quality. It is like a canto of Homer.
Italian Journey. Rome, Jan. 6, 1787. 26, 179

Surrounded by classical statues, you feel caught up in the movement of animate nature. You become aware of the multiplicity of human forms. You are reintroduced to man in his purest state. And the beholder too finds himself more alive and more purely human.
Italian Journey. Report, April, 1788 (1829); 27, 267

ART

To arrive at true understanding, fragments suffice.
To Meyer, Sept. 15, 1809

These statues that date from the best period of antiquity are most appropriately designed for chiaroscuro effects. The parts that are exposed to the light are treated simply; those that lie in shadow are broken up to a high degree to make them catch a variety of reflections, after the manner of the polyhedron.
On Theory of Color. Didactic Part. (1810); 40, 106

The high points in my experience of classical art are a few bas-reliefs from the cella of the Parthenon, the Pallas of Velletri, the infinitely beautiful torso of a Venus, and the head of a Venetian horse.
To von Knebel, Weimar, Nov. 9, 1814

[Facsimile of the Frieze of Phigalia] It is an abyss of wisdom and power. You straightway become younger and better by two thousand years.
To August and Ottilie von Goethe, Feb. 10, 1818

Once when we were planning to stage the apparition of the Earth Spirit in *Faust* here, it was my idea likewise to project simply a colossal illuminated head and bust. I had in mind the well-known bust of Jupiter, inasmuch as the words "terrible apparition" can be construed to render the feeling of the beholder (who might indeed be terrified by such an apparition) and need not refer to the features of the figure as such. In no case, of course, would I have tolerated anything distorted and repulsive.
To Graf Brühl, June 2, 1819

On the Elgin horse's head, one of the noblest remains of the highest period of art, the eyes are found to protrude and to be shifted toward the ear, causing the senses of sight and of hearing to appear in immediate co-öperation and enabling the sublime creature by a slight movement both to hear and to see what is behind it. It looks overpowering and spectral, as though it had been modeled in defiance of nature; but in truth the artist has only fashioned an archetypal horse, seen by him—who knows —with the eyes of the body or those of the spirit. To us, at any rate, it seems to conform both to poetry and to reality in the highest degree.

Postscript to D'Alton's Essay: On Artistic Representation of Biological Forms with Special Reference to Osteology (1823) W. A. Werke, Zweite Abteilung, 12, 147

[On Ternite's line reproductions of Pompeian paintings:] Here the most wonderful feature of antiquity for those who have eyes to see: I mean the validity of the passing moment and its value. For these paintings, buried by the most horrible catastrophe, are just as fresh, intact, and full-bodied after nearly two thousand years as they were at that fortunate moment which preceded this awful entombment.

If you were asked what they represent, you might be at a loss what to answer. For the time being I would say: These figures make us feel that the passing moment must be weighty and sufficient unto itself to qualify as a worthy intersection of time with eternity.

To Zelter, Oct. 19, 1829

[On receipt of a line drawing of the Pompeian floor mosaic of the Battle of Alexander:] Now my wish has been fulfilled, and there can be no question, I daresay, but that the mosaic represents Alexander as the victor and Darius as personally caught up in flight at the moment when he has sustained his most grievous loss. The conception of the subject is brilliant: the king shocked out of countenance, less by a sense of his personal danger than by the death of his most faithful follower under his very eyes; his charioteer, gesturing with his whip-handle to the faithful Persians pressing from the rear and flushed with anticipation of victory, to make way for the fleeing royal chariot; the forest of Persian spears poised at the Greeks, paralyzed, as it were, by this gesture. Commentators will exhaust themselves in the effort to render adequate tribute to such a miracle of art; and analysis will always have to make way again for pure admiration.

To Zahn, March 10, 1832

ROME

Here one is subjected to a great schooling. One single day has so much to say, and yet one ventures to say nothing that concerns the day. . . .

He who looks about him seriously here and has eyes to see must become stable. The idea of stability must become more vivid to him than ever before.

To Charlotte von Stein, Rome, Nov. 7, 1786

It is not only the artistic sense but also the moral sense which is experiencing a great renewal.

To Charlotte von Stein, Rome, Dec. 20, 1786

The rebirth that is transforming me from within is proceeding without letup.

Italian Journey. Rome, Dec. 20, 1786

But it is only an illusion if we wish ourselves dwellers in ancient Athens and Rome. Only from a distance, only divorced from all vulgar concerns, only as something that has passed away must antiquity appear to us. We feel the same way as we do about the ruins. My friend and I are always annoyed when some half-buried remains are excavated. At best, archaeology is the gainer at the expense of the imagination. *Winckelmann*. Rome, 1805

COMPOSITION

The highest ambition of the pictorial arts can take two forms. It is either a case of decorating a given space or of designing a space to fit a given decoration. Everything that we call artistic composition derives from this demand. The Greeks excelled in it, and after them the Romans.

Whatever is to appeal to us as decorative must therefore be articulated in a higher sense; it must consist of parts that suggest a mutual interplay. This requires that it have a center, an above and a below, a left and a right. These elements of symmetry represent the lower order of decoration as long as they are on the purely rational level. But as the complexity of the interrelated parts advances, by intertwining, concealment, the alternation of opposites, taking on more and more the aspect of a manifest mystery, the pleasure in the decorative design is proportionately enhanced, and it reaches its highest pitch when the whole no longer calls to mind those primary foundations but strikes us rather as free and spontaneous.

Art and Antiquity on the Rhine and the Main. Heidelberg (1815); 29, 306-7

The prime requisite of great composition was already recognized by the ancients: the grouping of many significant characters around a center that commands their joint interest while stimulating each to give expression to his individuality.

The Paintings of Philostratos (1818); 35, 79-80

A fully satisfying composition, in the plastic and the pictorial arts and in architecture alike, requires that the center of the field be unimpressive or empty. The eye must be led to occupy itself with the periphery without

239

referring the effectiveness of its offerings to a common point of origin.   *Relief of Phigalia* (1818); 35, 163

THE HUMAN FIGURE

Now at last the alpha and omega of all things known to us, the human figure, has taken hold of me and I of it, and I say: Lord, I will not let thee go except thou bless me, even if I get lamed in the struggle.

Italian Journey. August 23, 1787. 27, 96

The possibilities of the human figure have been so thoroughly canvassed by the ancients that we shall scarcely succeed in inventing any wholly new posture without exceeding the bounds of good taste. It is only a question of making it express what we had in mind, and of our being able to reproduce it in conformity with various intentions.   *To Meyer,* April 27, 1789

Only for a very limited space of time does the human body deserve to be called beautiful. . . . For both sexes the moment of puberty is the moment in which the human figure is capable of the highest beauty, and it is indeed for a moment. Mating and propagation involve for the butterfly the sacrifice of life, for man the sacrifice of beauty.

Diderot's Essay on Painting. Translated and Annotated (1798); 33, 221

The ultimate product of Nature in her ceaseless striving to surpass herself is the beautiful human being. It is true that she rarely achieves this, because too many conditions are at odds with her ideas, and even her almighty power cannot dwell for long in a state of perfection and endow beauty with permanence. In the strict sense of the

240

word "beautiful" man is beautiful for but a moment.

This is where art takes over; placed on the pinnacle of nature as he is, man beholds himself as another natural reservoir which in turn strives to achieve a second culmination. He works up to this by impregnating himself with all perfections and virtues, by mastering selection, order, harmony, and significance, and by rising finally to the creation of the work of art that commands a proud place among his other deeds and achievements. Once it is achieved and presented to the world in its ideal actuality, it produces a lasting effect—the highest, in fact. Being the product of the totality of his spiritual powers, it gathers into itself everything that is noble and worthy of reverence and love; and in endowing the human form with soul it raises man above himself; it rounds out the sphere of his life and activity and deifies him for that present moment which includes the past and the future. Such were the feelings of those who gazed upon the Zeus of Olympia, as we can gather from the descriptions and reports of the ancients. The god had become man in order to elevate man to the position of a god. The highest dignity presented itself to view and kindled enthusiasm for the highest beauty. In this sense one can probably agree with those ancient writers who claimed in the fullness of their conviction that it was a misfortune to die without having beheld this work.

Winckelmann. Beauty (1805); 34, 17-8

If the emerald solaces the eye by its glorious color and is even credited with a degree of curative virtue with regard to this noble organ, a vastly more powerful effect emanates from human beauty to influence both the outward eye and the mind's eye. He who beholds it cannot be touched by any ill wind. He feels in harmony with himself and the world.

Elective Affinities I, 6 (1809); 21, 52

The topmost aim of all plastic art is to render the dignity of man within the compass of the human form. To this aim every non-human element, in so far as it lends itself to treatment in this medium, must subordinate itself. Such elements must first be assimilated to the dignity of man in order that they may set it off, instead of calling attention to themselves or even detracting from it. Draperies and all kinds of garments and attributes come under this head, also animals; and to these latter only sculpture knows how to impart that dignity which is theirs by virtue of the fact that they are in a measure akin to that embodiment of the divine which we meet in the human figure.

Society of German Sculptors (1817); 35, 65

Only man unclothed is truly man. The sculptor stands shoulder to shoulder with the *Elohim* transforming the gross and formless clay into the noblest image. Such divine thoughts must be his to harbor. To the pure all things are pure—why not the direct intention of God in nature? But you cannot expect this of our age. It cannot do without fig leaves and pelts, and even they do not satisfy it.

Wilhelm Meister's Journeyings III, 3 (1829); 20, 71

ARCHITECTURE

As regards architectural beauty, Goethe assumes that it is only an idea, and that every specific work of architecture is more or less in conflict with it. If the architect's sole concern is beauty, he must be producing his work, the same as the poet, for an ideal man who is not confined to a specific state and has no practical needs. From this we gather that all works of architecture only approximate such an aim, and in reality this aim can at most find a sort of fulfillment in the case of public buildings, because they do not suffer from any limiting determination and the particular practical needs of any individuals are not a factor governing their design.

Goethe demands of a beautiful building that it should not merely make its appeal to the eye. He claims that even a man led through it blindfold should still be able to sense its spatial arrangement and find it pleasing.

Schiller to W. von Humboldt, Nov. 5-9, 1795.
Biedermann 470

Of Vitruvius I can say and have always said that repeated attempts on my part to use him as an avenue of approach to the older architecture have failed. I never managed to work my way into the book and derive benefit from it; and I blamed myself for this. And coming to look at it, my destined way really led me past Roman architecture to that of the Greeks. Here was something of course that I felt myself drawn to in quite another sense, and I have come to gaze on it more and more as on a strange, sublime fairy world.

To Schultz, Jan. 10, 1829

Temples of the ancients house the God in man; the churches of the Middle Ages strive after the God on high.

Maxims and Reflections 1134 (posthumous)

ART CRITICISM

If I were to set down a general confession of faith regarding ancient and modern art, I would say: While one cannot feel enough reverence for what has been preserved from ancient and modern times, it requires a whole lifetime to condition this reverence properly, to discern the value of each individual work in its way and neither to expect too much of it—a work of man, after all—nor to be too easily satisfied. *To Heyne*, Weimar, July 24, 1788

I as a poet have a totally different interest from that of the critic. My business is to co-ordinate, to unite, to make a whole of differentiated parts; it is the critic's business to resolve, to analyze, to separate the most homogeneous whole into parts. As poet I have therefore raised an insurmountable barrier between myself and the mischievous activity of the critic; but now it turns out that there are a hundred instances when I cannot do without the critic. I read my Homer with admiration, but I suddenly come upon scenes and individual passages that disturb the general impression and leave me completely nonplused. Here I am infinitely grateful to the critic when he tells me: This very passage is spurious.

Böttiger, spring, 1795. *Biedermann* 454

Few Germans, and perhaps few moderns generally, have a feeling for an aesthetic whole. All their praise and blame and their raptures are of a piecemeal character. What great good luck derives from this for our actors, inasmuch as theater productions are always an uneven patchwork.

Wilhelm Meister's Apprenticeship V, 4 (1795); 18, 18-19

The youth, attracted by nature and art, believes that his impulsiveness will soon carry him into the inner sanctum. The man, having walked about for a long time, discovers that he is still in the outer courts. . . .

A discussion of works of art that is genuinely profitable for both parties should really be carried on only in the presence of these works. It is all a matter of seeing what is there, and it is of the utmost importance to use the most specific language possible for purposes of elucidation, otherwise the result is nil.

Introduction to the Propyläen (1798); 33, 102, 119

ART

Genuine works of art carry their own aesthetic theory implicit within them and suggest the standards according to which they are to be judged.

To Cotta, Nov. 14, 1808

Technical facility in alliance with triteness is the worst enemy of art. *Maxims and Reflections* 1129 (posthumous)

HISTORY OF ART

That is the way our time reels it all off: the whim of the artist serves the crotchets of the rich; the author of travel books stands and gapes; and our polished wits—philosophers, we call them—continue to this day to contrive principles and histories of the arts from protoplastic fables—whereas men of true worth are overwhelmed and slain by genius in the outer court of the mysteries.

On German Architecture (1772); 33, 5

One does not get to understand works of nature and works of art when they are complete. One must try to see how they came into being, in order to comprehend them in a measure. *To Zelter*, Aug. 4, 1803

The study of art, like that of the ancient writers, gives us a certain support, a sense of inner satisfaction. By filling our minds with great themes and sentiments it gathers into its focus all those wishes and desires that tended outward but now are harbored in the stillness of the heart. The need for communication becomes less and less; the connoisseur finds himself living like the painter, the sculptor, the architect: he works in solitude to experience pleasures which he can share with others only on the rarest of occasions.

Campaign in France. Transition. 1792 (1822); 28, 149

ART

The plastic arts, generally speaking, have a way of transporting us directly into the conditions, sentiments, feelings, capacities, and accomplishments of the age in which the particular work originated. Sublimity and bathos, broad-mindedness and narrowness, nobility and pettiness, reverence and brashness are instantly communicated loudly and plainly; and irresistibly make us part of the contemporary scene.

To Kronprinz Friedrich Wilhelm von Preussen,
Aug. 14, 1827

POETRY AND THE POET

Let the poet confine his use of individual models to what is necessary to make his subject alive and convincing. As for all the rest, let him rely on the living world as mirrored in his bosom.

Caroline Herder, Feb. 9, 1789. *Biedermann* 334

Untrammeled nature, irresistible inclination, surging passion—supreme requirements of genuine poetry, whether the subject be great or humble, the treatment simple or in the grand manner.

To von Rumohr, Sept. 28, 1807

The touchstone of genuine poetry is that it has the ability, as a secular gospel, to liberate us from the weight of our earthly burden by an inner serenity and an outward sense of well-being.

The Autobiography III, 13 (1814); 24, 161

More than ever the web of this primeval tapestry [the *Orestes* of Aeschylus] makes me marvel. Past, present, and future are so felicitously interwoven that in beholding it you become a seer yourself—that is to say, one akin to God. And that, when all is said and done, is the ultimate triumph of poetry, covering its whole range.

To Wilhelm von Humboldt, Sept. 1, 1816

Deliberation enters into the creative powers of poetry only as regards the factor of form—the subject matter is lavishly supplied by the world; the significance with which it comes to be endowed is a matter of spontaneous expression of values inherent in the poet's personality. Subject matter and values fuse unconsciously into an inescapable whole. Form, however, although pre-eminently an attribute of genius, requires thought and deliberation, in order to achieve a whole in which form, subject matter, and values conform to one another and interpenetrate each other.

Divan. Notes. Interpolation (1819); 5, 212

A genuine poet always feels a call to fill himself with the glory of the world. For that reason he will always be more inclined to praise than to censure.

Divan. Notes. Dschelâleddîn Rumi (1819); 5, 184

In his [Alessandro Manzoni's] defense we venture the seemingly paradoxical statement that all poetry deals in anachronisms. Whatever period of the past we endeavor to evoke for a contemporary audience, we cannot help endowing it with a higher culture than it really possessed. The poet has to square this with his conscience as best he may; as for the reader, we expect him to oblige by not too critical an attitude. The *Iliad* and the *Odyssey*, all the tragedians, and whatever fragments of genuine poetry have been preserved—they all live and breathe in an atmosphere of anachronism. All conditions are presented with modern touches, so as to make them vivid and even tolerable.

Recently we have been doing the same with the Middle Ages, with the consequence that its stylized mask has been taken far too much at its face value in the way we have allowed it to influence our art and our very lives.

Manzoni's Adelchi (Review; 1827). 38, 64

Every poem is in a sense a kiss bestowed upon the world, but mere kisses do not produce children.

Ortlepp, fall, 1825. *Biedermann* 2374

No subject suggested by the real world defies poetic treatment, provided the poet knows how to make proper use of it.

Eckermann, July 5, 1827. *Biedermann* 2507

The poets all write as though they were sick and the whole world a hospital. They all speak of the suffering and the misery of the earth and of the joys of the beyond; and, not enough that they are all discontented to begin with, each fans the discontent of the others. This is really an abuse of poetry, which has been given to man to gloss over the petty dissonances of life and make him contented with the world and his own condition. But the present generation is afraid of everything that has genuine strength, and it feels at ease and poetically touched only by exhibitions of weakness.

I have found a good term to annoy these gentlemen. I shall call their poetry hospital poetry. By contrast I invoke the name of Tyrtaios [the Spartan poet] not only for the poetry of battle but for all poetry that gives man courage to face the battles of life.

Eckermann, Sept. 24, 1827. *Biedermann* 2552

We are going to derive as little profit from the gloomy age of German antiquity as we have done from the Serbian songs and related barbaric folk-poetry. You read it and interest yourself in it for a while, to dismiss it eventually and pass on. Quite enough of a pall is cast over our lives through our own passions and adversities without our having to borrow from the darkness of a former barbaric age. We are in need of clearness and serenity, and we should turn to those epochs of literature and art in which men of quality attained to fully rounded *Bildung* and lived serene lives and in turn radiated the harmony of their culture to distant epochs.

Eckermann, Oct. 3, 1828. *Biedermann* 2622

One might use the term "science" to designate knowledge of the universal—abstract knowledge. In that case art would be science practically applied. Science would be equivalent to reason and art to technique. Thus science and art would stand in the relation of theorem and problem.

Perhaps it might be objected: Poetry is numbered among the arts, yet it has no technique.

. . . But I deny that poetry is an art; neither is it a science. Arts and sciences can be mastered by thinking; not so poetry. Poetry is inspiration. It was conceived in the soul, when it first stirred. One should call it neither art nor science, but genius.

Maxims and Reflections 759 (1829)

[Anticipation] They say of the poet that he has all the elements of the visible world deep in his make-up and simply waiting to develop and emerge, so that he comes to behold nothing in the world at large of which he had not previously experienced prior intimation.

Wilhelm Meister's Journeyings I, 10 (1829); 19, 145

Poetry has something definitely daemonic about it, especially unconscious poetry, where the understanding does not get its due—which is why its effect surpasses all understanding.

Eckermann, March 8, 1831. *Biedermann* 2931

LANGUAGE: THE WORD

"Good night" we northerners can say at any hour of parting in the dark. The Italian says *Felicissima notte* only once, at the parting of day and night, when the lamp is brought into the room, and here the phrase has a very different meaning. So untranslatable are the idioms of every language. From the highest to the lowest word everything has reference to national peculiarities, whether it be character, sentiments, or modes and customs.

Italian Journey. Oct 5, at night, 1786. 26, 89

We talk far too much. We should talk less and draw more. I personally should like to renounce speech altogether and, like organic nature, communicate everything I have to say in sketches. That fig tree, this little snake, the cocoon on my window sill quietly awaiting its future— all these are momentous signatures. Indeed, a person able to decipher their meaning properly would soon be able to dispense with the written and the spoken word altogether. The more I think of it, there is something futile, mediocre, even foppish (I am tempted to say) about speech. How the quiet gravity of Nature and her silence by contrast startles you when you face her collected, before a barren ledge or in the desolate solitude of an old mountain.

Falk, June 14, 1809. *Biedermann* 1185

The impact of an uttered word is terrific when, in a flash, it brings into the open daydreams that the heart has long been accustomed to indulge in.

Elective Affinities I, 16 (1809); 21, 124

A word once uttered becomes part of the unbroken chain of natural forces. Its effectiveness is all the greater because of the closely circumscribed sphere in which mankind moves. The same needs and the same demands occur over and over again.

And yet all transmission via the word is so questionable. One should not cling to the latter but rather to the spirit, they say. But as a rule the spirit destroys the word or at least transforms it in such manner as to leave little of its former flavor and meaning.

On Theory of Color. Historical Part. Third Division.
Interim (1810); 40, 150

I must tell you in confidence . . . I have found more than once that these very zealous purists in language are really not intelligent. Since they do not know how to appreciate the value of an expression, they have little trouble in finding a substitute which to them seems equally meaningful. This crotchet affords them an opportunity, moreover, to show themselves as people of judgment and to criticize the best authors, after the manner of half-baked art connoisseurs who look at paintings of merit only for the chance it gives them to point, rightly or wrongly, to some distortion, some flaw in perspective, whereas they would not know how to make the slightest positive observation on the work's merit.

Generally speaking, here is an instance (and there are others) of people being so bent on producing something good in a negative way that it makes them overlook the good that they could and should promote by affirmation.

To Riemer, June 30, 1813

The eye may well be called the clearest sense organ and the easiest means of transmitting data. But the inner sense is still clearer, and the highest and speediest way of transmission is via the word. For the word is essentially fruitful, whereas what we perceive by the eye is foreign to us as such and need not impress us deeply.

Shakespeare and No End (1813); 37, 38

251

Even though, in keeping with my innate faulty disposition, I have never been able to exert myself sufficiently toward the achievement of correctness and purity of diction, I have, on the other hand, become most intensely aware of the fact that language is only a substitute for expression; and this holds equally true for our innermost interests and for the stimulation we derive from without.

To Schultz, March 11, 1816

He who knows no foreign language knows nothing of his own. *Maxims and Reflections* 91 (1821)

Everyone, knowing how to speak, thinks he knows how to speak about language.

Maxims and Reflections 239 (1824)

The power of a language does not show in rejecting what is foreign, but rather in swallowing it up.

Maxims and Reflections 979 (posthumous)

I cultivate an affirmative purism that is productive and has just this criterion: Where do we have to resort to circumlocution, whereas a neighboring language has a word that hits the nail on the head?

Maxims and Reflections 981 (posthumous)

TRANSLATION

There are two ways of translating, it seems to me. If the intention is to transmit to one's nation the pure concept of a foreign author and to give a vivid awareness of foreign conditions, one must stick close to the original. We can, on the other hand, treat a foreign work as a sort of raw material and transform it in keeping with our own sentiments and convictions, to make of it something more familiar, something that can be appreciated like an original, as it were, by our nation.

To Holcroft, May 29, 1801

Translators are like matchmakers who solicitously praise the charms of a half-veiled beauty. They arouse an irresistible desire for the original.

Maxims and Reflections 299 (1826)

In translating one must venture to the edge of what is untranslatable. It is only then that one becomes aware of the foreign nation and the foreign language.

Maxims and Reflections 1056 (posthumous)

LITERATURE: LITERARY ART FORMS

It takes a nation to produce a national author of excellence. *Literary Sansculottism* (1795); 36, 141

In the novel and the drama alike we see human nature and action. Their difference is not simply a matter of form, not simply the fact that the characters talk in the one genre and are usually told about in the other. Many dramas, unfortunately, are nothing but novels in dialogue form; it would not be impossible, on the other hand, to compose a real drama in the form of letters. In the novel it is primarily *sentiment* and *incidents* that are to be depicted; in the drama it is *characters* and *actions*. The novel must proceed at a leisurely pace, and the sentiments of the chief figure must, in one way or another, retard the development of the whole. The drama has an impetuous tempo, and the character of the protagonist must be impatient for the dénouement while other forces apply the brakes to him. The hero of the novel must be passive, at any rate not active to a pronounced degree.

Of the dramatic hero we expect effective action. Grandison, Clarissa, Pamela, the Vicar of Wakefield, Tom Jones —they are all either passive or tend to slow up the development, and all incidents are assimilated as it were to their sentiments. In the drama the hero assimilates nothing to himself; everything challenges him, and he either clears the obstacles out of his way or succumbs to them.

Wilhelm Meister's Apprenticeship V, 7 (1795); 18, 33-4

I endeavored to conceive the Law of Retardation in terms of a more inclusive principle, and I think I have found this in the over-all precept that a good poetic design permits or rather requires us to anticipate the outcome of the action, and that only the manner, not the matter, must engage our interest. Such a work does not in any way cater to ordinary curiosity, and it corresponds to your formulation that every point of its development has the aspect of an end as well as a means.

To Schiller, April 22, 1797

In tragedy the dominating factor can and must be fate or, what amounts to the same thing, a fixed disposition which carries a man headlong in this or that direction, always at cross-purposes to the goal toward which he is tending. The hero must not be governed by reason. Reason should have no place in tragedy except as regards secondary characters working to the disadvantage of the hero.

In the epic the reverse holds true. Only reason, as in the *Odyssey*, or a purposive passion, as in the *Iliad*, are epic agencies. The expedition of the Argonauts, being in the nature of an adventure, is not epic.

To Schiller, April 26, 1797

It is true that the Greeks—and some Romans as well— had a highly developed taste in differentiating and delimiting the varieties of poetry, but we Nordics cannot follow the exclusive guidance of these models. We have a different ancestry and other models to emulate. If the romantic turn of rude centuries had not produced an interaction of the colossal with the trite, how could there have been a *Hamlet,* a *Lear,* an *Adoration of the Cross,* a *Steadfast Prince?*

Rameau's Nephew [Diderot]. Translation with Notes
(1805); 34, 166

Took down these words of Goethe: Poetic justice is an absurdity. Only what is unjust and fails of fruition is tragic. Napoleon realizes this and the fact that he is the agency of Fate.

Riemer, March 11, 1809 *Biedermann* 1162

The dramatic unities are nothing but a way of demanding that a significant content of large scope be plausibly distributed for representation among a small group of characters. In this way Racine brought the significant scope of Tacitus into the concise compass of Greek form.

Riemer, June, 1811. *Biedermann* 1411

Classic - Romantic

Ancient	Modern
Simple	Complex (Sentimental)
Pagan	Christian
Heroic	Romantic
Real	Ideal
Necessity	Freedom
Obligation	Will ...

In the poetry of the ancients it was the disproportion between obligation and achievement that was pronounced; in that of the moderns it is that between willing and achieving. . . .

In the tragedy of the ancients there is a sense of inescapable obligation bearing down on the individual, and the fact that the will tends in the opposite direction makes the pressure only so much the more acute. Here we are in the fearsome domain of oracle, with *Oedipus* as the unchallenged exemplar of its sinister power. In *Antigone* the pressure appears under the softer guise of duty, and it shows up in many other respects. But all obligation has a despotic quality. . . . The will, by contrast, is free, or seems free and gives leeway to the individual. There is something flattering about the assertion of will, and men were bound to come under its sway once they had become aware of this power. Will is the god of the modern age. Surrendering to it, we fear its opposite, and this disposition sharply divides our art and our outlook from those of the ancients. Through the pressure of obligation tragedy waxes great and strong, whereas the assertion of will makes it weak and small.

Shakespeare and No End (1813); 37, 41-3

The novel is a subjective epic composition in which the author begs leave to treat the world according to his point of view. It is only a question, therefore, whether he has a point of view. The rest will take care of itself.

Maxims and Reflections 133 (1821)

Every tragic situation presupposes an opposition that cannot be resolved by compromise. The moment a compromise takes place or appears possible, the tragic situation has ceased to exist.

von Müller, June 6, 1824. *Biedermann* 2266

It amused Goethe to recall that Lord Byron, who never conformed and never had any regard for law in his own life, ended up by submitting to that most stupid law of the three unities. He was as far from understanding the basis of this law, Goethe said, as the rest of the world. Its basis is ready comprehension, and the three unities are valuable only in so far as they serve this purpose. If they hinder comprehension, on the other hand, it is unreasonable to think of them as a law to be observed. Even the Greeks, who originated the rule, did not always observe it. In the *Phaeton* of Euripides and in other plays there are changes of scene, and this shows that they attached more value to effective presentation of the subject than to the blind observance of a law which never carried any great weight as such. The plays of Shakespeare violate the unities of time and of place to the greatest possible degree; but they are readily comprehensible—they are unsurpassed in this regard—and the Greeks would have found them unobjectionable, therefore. The French poets have attempted to conform to the law of the three unities in the most rigorous way; but they sin against ready comprehension in that they resolve a dramatic situation not dramatically, but through narration.

Eckermann, Feb. 24, 1825. *Biedermann* 2310

What is a *novelle* if not simply the account of an incident of unheard-of novelty? This is the basic criterion of the genre, and a great deal of what goes under the label of *novelle* in Germany is not *novelle* at all but simply narrative or whatever you choose to call it.

Eckermann, Jan. 29, 1827. *Biedermann* 2471

I do not object to a dramatic poet's aiming at a moral effect, but for the task of presenting his subject clearly and effectively to the eyes of his audience moral intention will avail him little. What he needs in order to know what to do and what to avoid is a great gift of projection and knowledge of the stage. If a moral effect is implicit in the theme it will automatically assert itself, even if the poet's exclusive concern is the effective artistic presentation of his subject. If a poet has the lofty soul of a Sophocles, he will produce a moral effect no matter what his attitude may be. He, by the way, was an unrivaled master of stagecraft.

Eckermann, March 28, 1827. *Biedermann* 2481

What is sound I call classical, and what is morbid I call romantic. And from this angle the *Nibelungs* are as classical as *Homer,* for both are sound and doughty. Most recent productions are romantic not because they are modern but because they are weak, sickly, and diseased; and the productions of older times are classical not because they are old but because they are strong, fresh, tonic, and sound. If we differentiate between classic and romantic on this basis, we shall avoid confusion.

Eckermann, April 2, 1829. *Biedermann* 2672

Dream of Leda, Helena [Faust, Part Two, Act II]. You will find that in these earlier acts classical as well as romantic notes are sounded in order to lead, as on rising ground, to the Helena act, where both of these poetical modes assert their specific character and achieve a sort of synthesis. *Eckermann,* Dec. 16, 1829. *Biedermann* 2749

The distinction of classical and romantic poetry, which now provokes so much discussion and dissension all the world over, originated with myself and Schiller. I held to the maxim of objective procedure in poetry and refused to admit of any other; Schiller, on the other hand, with his wholly subjective approach, regarded his way as the right one, and to defend himself against me he wrote *On Naïve and Sentimental Poetry.* He proved to me that I am romantic despite myself and that my *Iphigenie* is, by its preponderance of sentiment, not nearly so classical and in keeping with the ancients as you might be inclined to think. The Schlegels seized upon the idea and developed it further, so that now the world over everybody talks of *classicism* and *romanticism*, whereas nobody thought of doing so fifty years ago.

Eckermann, March 21, 1830. *Biedermann* 2806

[Vampirism] The English and French have outdone us in the presentation of bodies that rot while still alive and derive edification from a detailed contemplation of the process of decomposition; and of corpses that remain alive and sap the life of the living on whom they batten. Our own writers have caught up with them.

Maxims and Reflections 1034 (posthumous)

SYMBOL: ABSTRACTION

True symbolism is present where the specific represents the more general, not as a dream and shadow, but as a living momentary revelation of the inscrutable.

Maxims and Reflections 314 (1826)

When all is said and done, nothing suits the theater except what also makes a symbolic appeal to the eyes—a significant action suggesting an even more significant one.

Shakespeare and No End (1816); 37, 47

The symbol. It is the thing without being the thing, and yet the thing: an image concentrated in the mirror of the mind and yet identical with the object. How inferior is allegory by comparison. Though it may have wit and subtle conceit, it is for the most part rhetorical and conventional. It always improves in proportion to its approach to what we call symbol.

Addenda on the Paintings of Philostratus (1820)
W. A. Werke, 49 (I), 142

259

The treatment [in the second part of *Faust*] had to be general rather than specific; for specification and variety belong to youth.

Titian, too, the great master of color, in his old age painted only in the abstract those materials that in his early days he had imitated so concretely. As to velvet, for example, he painted only the idea of velvet.

Riemer [undated]. *Biedermann* 3012

Symbolism transforms the phenomenon into the idea, and the idea into an image in such a fashion that in the image the idea remains infinitely active and incommensurable, and if all languages were used to express it, it would still remain inexpressible.

Maxims and Reflections 1113 (posthumous)

MUSIC

[Goethe's operetta text *Prank, Stratagem, Revenge*] All our efforts to move in a simple and confined sphere were lost with Mozart's appearance. His *Abduction from the Seraglio* killed all competition.

Italian Journey. Nov. 1787 (1829); 27, 158

[Beethoven] I have never seen an artist more collected, energetic, and *innig* [inward]. I readily understand how he must be on an odd footing with the world.

To Christiane von Goethe, July 19, 1812

I made the acquaintance of Beethoven in Teplitz. His talent astonished me, but unfortunately he is quite unmanageable. He is not to be blamed in the slightest for finding the world detestable, but it does not thereby become any more enjoyable for himself or for the rest of us.

To Zelter, Sept. 2, 1812

After lunch Schütz played several fugues of Sebastian Bach. Goethe admired them greatly, comparing them to illustrated mathematical problems. He remarked on the fact that the themes are so simple and yet achieve such sublime poetic results.

Genast, June 6, 1814. *Biedermann* 1562

. . . My conception of your Grand Master [Sebastian Bach]. I put it to myself thus: As though the eternal harmony were conversing with itself, as it might have done in the bosom of God on the eve of the world's creation.   *To Zelter,* June 21, 1827. "Fortsetzung . . . durch La Roche"

[News of the performance of Bach's St. Matthew's Passion] I feel as though I were hearing the roar of the sea from afar.   *To Zelter,* March 28, 1829

In truth, there is nothing like music to fill the moment with substance, whether it attune the quiet mind to reverence and worship, or whether it make the mobile senses dance in exultation. . . .   *To Zelter,* Oct. 19, 1829

So I have heard Paganini too. . . . Enjoyment is with me always something between sensuous excitation and comprehension, and this pillar of flame and cloud left me somehow up in the air.

If I were in Berlin, I should rarely miss the Möser Quartet performances. Of all types of instrumental music, I have always been able to follow these best. You listen to four sensible persons conversing, you profit from their discourse, and you get to know the individual character of the instruments.   *To Zelter,* Nov. 9, 1829

Music in the best sense does not require the appeal of

novelty. As a matter of fact, the older and the more familiar it is, the more it affects us.

Maxims and Reflections 485 (1829)

In music the dignity of art seems to find supreme expression. There is no subject matter to be discounted. It is all form and significant content. It elevates and ennobles whatever it expresses.

Maxims and Reflections 486 (1829)

The sacred character of church music, the cheerful and inspired quality of folk-melodies are the two poles around which genuine music turns. At these two points it never fails of its effect. The two mixed produce a confusing result, and when music attempts to combine with didactic or descriptive poetry the effect is chilling.

Maxims and Reflections 489 (1829)

The Body Politic

GOVERNMENT

It is a maxim of wise government to deal with men not as they ought to be but as they really are.

Stephani, June, 1792. *Biedermann* 379

The old man stepped between the youth and the maiden and cried with a loud voice: There are three who rule upon earth: wisdom, appearances, and violence.

The Fairy-Tale (1795); 16, 298

In a state everything depends on the executive power. Let the legislative power be ever so enlightened, it avails the state nothing if the executive power is not effective.

Entertainments of German Emigrants (1795); 16, 264

One day the baroness remarked that there is no more striking opportunity to observe how *ungebildet* in every sense people are, than such moments of general confusion and distress. The framework of civic life, she said, seems like a ship that transports a great number of people, old and young, sick and healthy, over a dangerous water, even in times of storm. Only at the moment when the ship founders does one see who can swim, and even good swimmers perish under such conditions.

Entertainments of German Emigrants (1795); 16, 169

The influence of physical climate on the human form is denied by no one, but people are apt to forget that similarly the form of government brings about a moral climate that influences the development of character in a variety of ways. We are speaking not of the multitude but of significant, outstanding men.

A republic gives rise to great, integrated characters of an active disposition that is steady and clear. When it gathers itself into the form of an aristocracy, there develops a strain of dignified, consistent, able men, admirable in command and obedience. If a state lapses into anarchy, straightway there come to the fore bold and reckless men, scorners of custom, with a violent impact upon the moment, men who cast aside all moderation with terrible effect. Despotism on the other hand produces great characters. A wise, tranquil grasp of affairs, strict administration, firmness, determination—all qualities required to serve the despots—develop in able individuals and procure for them commanding positions in the state where they learn to become rulers.

Divan. Notes. Caliphs. Transition (1819); 5, 173

Goethe repeatedly came back to his pet idea, that every individual should be only concerned with being active in his own special sphere, be it great or small, as faithfully and lovingly as possible. Given this attitude, the commonwealth would prosper, no matter what the form of the government.

Prince von Pückler, Sept. 15, 1826. *Biedermann* 2439

What government is the best? That which teaches us to govern ourselves. *Maxims and Reflections* 353 (1826)

To be popular a great ruler requires no other means than his greatness. If he has striven and worked in such a way that his state is happy within and respected without, then he may ride bedecked with all his insignia in a state chariot or wrapped in a bearskin, a cigar in his mouth, in a common cab—it is all the same, he has the love of his people and enjoys the same respect in all circumstances. If, however, a prince lacks personal greatness and does not know how to win the love of his people by good deeds, then he must think of other ways of securing the bond. In that case there is no better and more effective means than religion and joint participation in the same ceremonies by ruler and subject. To appear in church on Sunday, to survey the congregation and have it gaze at him for an hour is the most effective means of achieving popularity, and every young ruler might be advised to practice it. It is a means that even Napoleon, for all his greatness, did not disdain to use.

Eckermann, April 3, 1829. *Biedermann* 2673

The moment tyranny has been ended the conflict between aristocracy and democracy becomes acute.

Maxims and Reflections 956 (posthumous)

Ruling is easily learned; governing, with difficulty.

Maxims and Reflections 967 (posthumous)

PATRIOTISM

I can assure you, said Werner, that I have never in my life thought of the state. My taxes, tolls, and dues I have simply paid because it happens to be customary.

Well, said Lothario, I still hope to make a good patriot of you. For just as he only is a good father who at table serves his children first, so he alone is a good citizen who first lays aside what he owes to the state before he takes up the rest of his budget.

Wilhelm Meister's Apprenticeship VIII, 2 (1796); 18, 274

The sense of liberty and love of country, which is supposed to have its source in the ancients, turns to caricature in most people. What resulted originally from the whole state of the nation, its youth, its relation to other states, its cultural institutions, becomes with us an awkward imitation. Our life leads us not to rigid separation from other peoples, but rather to the freest possible interchange. Our civic existence is not that of the ancients. Our life is much more free and unfettered on the one hand without the restrictions of the ancients. On the other hand the demands of the state on us are not such as to make its rewards a coveted prize necessitating the maintenance of a patrician nobility. The whole course of our civilization, including the Christian religion, makes for communication and participation and for all the social virtues of courtesy and accommodation, including the yielding up of feelings and sentiments, even of rights, that are one's prerogative in a primitive state of nature.

Riemer, Nov. 18, 1806. *Biedermann* 905

Patriotism ruins history, Goethe used to say. Jews, Greeks, and Romans have distorted their own history and that of the other nations. They did not leave an impartial record. The Germans are doing the same. . . .

Riemer, July, 1817. *Biedermann* 1800

It has been said and repeated: Where I prosper there is my fatherland. However, this comforting saw could be even more appropriately modified to read: Where I am of use, there is my fatherland. At home one may lead a useless existence without its being noticed at once. Out in the world the good-for-nothing is speedily revealed as such. If I now say, Let each one strive to be of use to himself and others, this is neither preachment nor counsel, but the pronouncement of life itself.

Wilhelm Meister's Journeyings III, 9 (1829); 20, 139

There is no patriotic art and no patriotic science. Like

268

all exalted good things both belong to the whole world, and they can be made to prosper only through a general free interaction of all contemporaries coupled with a steadfast regard for that which is left of the past and known to us.   *Maxims and Reflections* 690 (1829)

As a man and citizen the poet will love his fatherland, but the fatherland of his poetic powers and his poetic activity is the good, the noble, the beautiful, which is the property of no particular province and no particular land. This he seizes upon and forms wherever he finds it. In this he is like the eagle that lets its eye roam freely over the lands and cares not whether the hare upon which it swoops is running in Prussia or in Saxony.

And what does it mean to love one's fatherland, and what does it mean to be patriotically active? If a poet has endeavored all his life to fight harmful prejudices, to eliminate narrowness, to enlighten the spirit of his people, to purify their taste, and to ennoble their sentiments, what is there better for him to do? And how is he to be more patriotically active? To put such improper and thankless demands to a poet is as though one were to require of a general that to be a proper patriot he should get involved in political reforms and neglect his immediate duties. But the fatherland of a general is his regiment, and he will be an excellent patriot if he pays no attention to political matters except in so far as they concern him, rather devoting all his thought and care to the battalions under his command, seeking to drill and train them so well that if someday the fatherland is endangered they will not flinch in the face of the enemy.

I hate all botchwork like sin, but especially botching in affairs of state, which leads to nothing but harm for thousands and millions.

Eckermann, March, 1832. *Biedermann* 3051

PUBLIC AFFAIRS · POLITICAL IDEAS · THE PRESS

Having always been convinced, and increasingly so of late years, that newspapers exist essentially in order to string the multitude along and warp its judgment—be it that outside force prevents the editor from telling the truth, or that obedience to his party line has the same result—I have stopped reading them.

Annals (1808); 30, 235

Never is there more talk of freedom than when one party wants to get the better of the other with nothing more at issue than to have power, influence, and property pass from one hand to another.

Divan. Notes. Supplement (Despotism) (1819); 5, 208

Whenever I hear talk of "liberal" ideas, I always marvel how men like to fool themselves with empty sounds. An idea must not be liberal! Let it be vigorous, positive, and without loose ends, so that it may fulfill its divine mission of being productive. Even less must a concept be "liberal," for it has a totally different function.

It is in the realm of sentiment, rather, that liberality has its place—in a spirit that is flexible and alive.

But sentiments are rarely liberal, because sentiment stems directly from personality and its immediate relations and needs. *Maxims and Reflections* 216-8 (1823)

Public affairs should be administered with detachment, not humanly with likes or dislikes, passion or partiality; then more is accomplished more quickly. Tersely, imperatively, succinctly. And no recriminations, no reproaches concerning what is past and beyond amends. Let a line be drawn after each day. How is it possible to live, with-

out a willingness to call it quits every evening for oneself
and others?   *von Müller*, Dec. 6, 1825. *Biedermann* 2375

We are made free, not by refusing to recognize anything above us, but on the contrary by revering something
that is above us. For by revering it we rise to its level,
and by our recognition we attest the fact that we ourselves bear within us the germ of the higher existence
and are worthy of matching it.
                    Eckermann, Jan. 18, 1827. *Biedermann* 2469

There is always much talk of aristocracy and democracy. The case is very simply this: In our youth, when we
possess nothing or at least do not appreciate quiet possession, we are democrats. If, however, in the course of
a long life we have come to acquire property, we wish this
to be not only secure, but we also wish that our children
and grandchildren may have the undisturbed enjoyment
of what we have acquired. For that reason in old age
we are aristocrats, without exception, even if in our youth
we inclined to other sentiments.
                    Eckermann, July 15, 1827. *Biedermann* 2509

I find more and more that it is well to be on the side of
the minority, since it is always the more intelligent.
                    von Müller, March 6, 1828. *Biedermann* 2577

Everything great and intelligent exists in the minority.
There have been ministers who were opposed by king
and people and carried their great plans through without
support. It is out of the question that reason should ever
become popular. Passions and feelings may become popular, but reason will always be the possession of a few individuals of distinction.
                    Eckermann, Feb. 12, 1829. *Biedermann* 2656

Nothing is more odious than the majority. For it consists of a few vigorous pacemakers, of rascals who accommodate themselves, of weaklings who follow suit, and of the multitude that trots after without knowing in the slightest what it wants.

Maxims and Reflections 604 (1829)

This prompts me to announce and confide to you something queer: In keeping with a sudden strict resolve I have put an end to all newspaper reading, contenting myself with what comes my way through social channels. This is of the greatest importance. For, it is surely a mark of Philistinism when as private citizens we devote too much of our time and sympathies to matters that do not concern us.

To Zelter, April 29, 1830

REVOLUTION

He had come to know the arbitrary acts of the nation that talked only of law, and the intolerance of those who always talked of freedom. He had seen that in this case too the great multitude remained true to itself, acclaiming with violence the word for the deed and appearances for solid achievement.

Entertainments of German Emigrants (1795); 16, 171

I agree entirely with the monarchists in the principle of trying to preserve what is established and to fend off revolutionary change, only not in the means. The fact is that they call stupidity and darkness to their aid, while I look to reason and light.

von Müller, Sept. 18, 1823. *Biedermann* 2149

I was completely convinced that any great revolution is never to be blamed on the people but rather on the government. Revolutions are quite impossible when governments are constantly just and constantly watchful, meeting them halfway by timely reforms instead of resisting until the necessary change is forced from below. But because I hated revolutions people labeled me a friend of the established order. This, however, is a very ambiguous label which I should like to decline. If all that is established were excellent, good, and just, I would not object at all. Since, however, alongside of much that is good there is much of the vicious, unjust, and imperfect in the established state of things, to be called a friend of what is established is often tantamount to being called a friend of what is outmoded and vicious.

Time, however, moves in an eternal progression, and human affairs assume a new guise every fifty years, so that an institution that represented perfection in 1800 has become a flaw by 1850. Moreover, only that is good for a nation which has developed from its own core and its own general need without aping others. What to one people, at a certain stage of development, can be beneficial sustenance, may possibly turn out to be a poison for another. All attempts, therefore, to introduce a foreign innovation the need for which is not rooted in the deep kernel of the nation in question, are foolish, and all attempted revolutions of this sort are bound to fail; for they are undertaken without God, who keeps aloof from such botchwork. If, however, a genuine need for a great reform exists in a people, God is on its side and it succeeds.

Eckermann, Jan. 4, 1824. *Biedermann* 2214

I hate every violent overturn, because such an act destroys as much good as it achieves. I hate those who execute it, as I hate those who give rise to it. But am I not a friend of the people on this account? And does any right-minded man think otherwise?

Eckermann, April 27, 1825. *Biedermann* 2326

In politics as on the sickbed people toss from one side to the other fancying that they will be more comfortable.

von Müller, Dec. 29, 1825. *Biedermann* 2379

The struggle of what is old, established, and set with the forces of development, expansion, and change is always the same. All order finally turns into pedantry. To get rid of the latter, people destroy the former, and some time elapses before the need to re-establish order makes itself felt. Classicism versus romanticism, rigid guild rule versus *laissez faire,* a policy of large estates versus one of small holdings—it is always the same conflict which ultimately generates a new one. The most intelligent policy on the part of those who govern would be, therefore, to moderate this struggle so as to effect a compensating swing without the destruction of the one side. But this is not given to man, and it does not even seem to be the will of God. *Maxims and Reflections* 346 (1826)

Lawgivers or revolutionaries who promise equality and liberty at the same time are visionaries or charlatans.

Maxims and Reflections 953 (posthumous)

Every revolution tends to return to a state of nature, to lawlessness and abandonment of restraint. (Picards, Anabaptists, Sansculottes.)

Maxims and Reflections 955 (posthumous)

THE MIDDLE CLASS

The translation [of *Hermann und Dorothea* into French] . . . deserves comment, because here the French nation appears in a remarkable contrast to the German. By our appreciation of the middle class we give evidence of a truly republican cast of mind, whereas the [French] republicans are impatient of this and prove themselves on the testimony of their own nationals as inveterate aristocrats. *To von Knebel*, Nov. 3, 1800

Goethe remarked that men should be trained with a view to service, women with a view to motherhood. This present misfortune of the world is after all due for the most part to the fact that the idea of mastery has taken hold of all classes. The middle class took the lead in this trend—the merchant wanting wealth, the bourgeois, culture. Only the nobility is rooted in the time-honored idea of service. And as Joseph II had already remarked, the prince is the first servant of the state.

Riemer, Aug. 13, 1809. *Biedermann* 1206

THE PEOPLE

During the night of the 28th or the 29th of May fire broke out in our ghetto and spread quickly and horribly. I joined with the rest in hauling a drop of water to the scene, and the most wonderful deeply moving variety of feelings rewarded me for my trouble on the spot. Here again I came into closer contact with the common people, and again and again I had occasion to confirm my conviction that these are after all the salt of the earth.

To Schönborn, Frankfurt, June, 1774

[Alba:] Believe me, a people does not become mature or wise, a people always remains childish.

Egmont IV (1788); 11, 308

Given a few individuals that boisterously air their opinions, the people for the most part are content to chant these after them just as loudly. This leads to the strangest situations and to no end of presumptuousness.

A sophisticated, rather crude fellow will often in his shallowness mock an object before which men like Jacobi or Kant, properly counted among the first ornaments of the nation, would bow in reverence. It is proper that the results of philosophy, political science, and religion should redound to the benefit of the people, but there is no sense in trying to elevate the people to the rank of philosophers, politicians, and priests. It will not do.

Falk [undated]. *Biedermann* 3097

We need a word in our language which, after the manner of childhood as related to child, expresses the relation of peoplehood to people. The educator must attune his ear to childhood, not to the child; the lawgiver and regent must hear the voice of peoplehood, not of the people. The former expresses what is constant; it is reasonable, pure, and true. The latter wants so many things that it never knows what it wants. And in this sense the law can and shall be the universally expressed will of peoplehood—a will that the multitude never voices but the man of sense perceives, the man of reason knows how to gratify, and the man of worth takes pleasure in gratifying.

Maxims and Reflections 682 (1829)

NATIONS

They charge the English with carrying their teapots wherever they go, even lugging them up Mount Etna. But has not every nation its teapot in which, even while abroad, it steeps its dried bundles of herbs brought from home?

Winckelmann. Foreigners (1805); 34, 44

Never must a man, never must a nation think that the end has come. . . . The loss of material things can be compensated; for other losses time provides consolation.

Only one ill is beyond cure: when man gives himself up for lost.

> *La gloire de Frédéric par Jean de Muller* (Review; 1807);
> **36, 289**

Nowadays the nations are so scrambled up in the world that one becomes a cosmopolitan without leaving one's abode.

> *To Perthes,* April 19, 1812

Great cities always mirror the whole nation. And even granting that they distort by exaggerated emphasis, they nevertheless exhibit a concentrated picture of the nation.

> *To Wilhelm von Humboldt,* Aug. 31, 1812

I suppose all nations are alike in the fact that competitors try to blight each others' days. That is why everyone who plans to achieve something worth while must address himself, if not to posterity, at any rate to the morrow.

> *To Seebeck,* Feb. 23, 1815

To achieve an attitude of broad tolerance the safest thing is to ignore the peculiar features of individuals and nations and to hold rather to the firm conviction that genuine merit has the distinction of appertaining to the human race as a whole. To such an attitude of interchange and mutual recognition the Germans have long since begun to contribute. He who understands and studies the German language moves in the market place where all nations offer their produce. He acts the interpreter at the same time that he enriches himself.

> *Carlyle's German Romance* IV (Review; 1828);
> 38, 141-2

Every nation has peculiarities by which it is distinguished from others, and it is these that bring about a sense of cleavage making for attraction or repulsion. The external earmarks of these inner peculiarities for the most part affect other nationals as strikingly disagreeable, at best as ridiculous. And it is due to these that we always respect a nation less than it deserves. The inner peculiarities, on the other hand, are not known or discussed, either by foreigners or even by the nation to which they are proper. The fact is that, as in individuals, so in whole nations likewise, the inner nature works itself out unconsciously. In the end one is surprised, one is astonished at sight of the manifest product.

Supplementary Remarks on World Literature (1829); 38, 204-5

There is something peculiar about national hatred. You will always find it most extreme and violent on the lowest levels of culture. There is a level, however, where it quite disappears and where one stands above the nations, as it were. At this level one experiences a turn of good fortune or a disaster befalling a neighbor nation as if it had happened to one's own. This level of culture accorded with my nature, and this view of things had become firmly rooted in me long before I reached my sixtieth year.

Eckermann, March 10, 1830. Biedermann 2797

No nation is fit to judge any but its own deeds and literary products. The same applies to every age.

Maxims and Reflections 1024 (posthumous)

THE ROMANS

The Romans had moved from a confined, morally sound, well-adjusted, comfortable civil state of society into a broadly expanded position of world rule without divesting themselves of their provincialism. Even their vaunted love of liberty lacks breadth of outlook. They had become kings; yet they wanted to remain old-style family fathers, husbands, friends. And how little even the best of them realized what it means to govern is shown by the most atrociously absurd deed ever perpetrated—the murder of Caesar.

On Theory of Color. Historical Division. Second Part.
Romans (1810); 40, 145

Goethe aired his predilection for things Roman. He had surely led a previous existence under Hadrian, he maintained; he felt an affinity for all things Roman; this great intelligence, this sense of order in all matters appealed to him in a way that Greece did not.

S. Boisserée, Aug. 11, 1815. *Biedermann* 1691

Roman history is beginning to lose its meaning for our age. We have become too humane to contemplate the triumphs of Caesar without repugnance.

Eckermann, Nov. 24, 1824. *Biedermann* 2299

Before the Roman republic degenerated, Goethe continued, when centuries passed without a single case of adultery, when there seemed to be no need for a law against parricide, etc., life wore so sober and tiresome an aspect that no honest man could wish to have lived there.

von Müller, May 28, 1825. *Biedermann* 2335

THE GERMANS

In our [German] faces the features crisscross each other, often without suggesting any character, or at any rate making the type difficult to discern. One may say, in a German face the hand of God is less legible than in an Italian.   *Falk,* July 17, 1792. *Biedermann* 380

[Reporting on Fichte's quarrel with the Kantians:] I have not much else to say, and you see that the Germans are condemned to dwell, as of old, in the Cimmerian nights of speculation.

To Wilhelm von Humboldt, Sept. 16, 1799

The chief loss, perhaps, which we have reason to regret in this political upheaval is the fact that Germany, and northern Germany especially as formerly constituted, gave the individual full opportunity to develop to his capacity and permitted each one to do the right thing in his own way and according to his own choosing, even though the nation as a whole never seemed to show any particular interest in such effort.

To Zelter, July 27, 1807

Goethe goes so far as to assert that the best way out would be to scatter the Germans like the Jews throughout the world; only abroad can they still be tolerated.

W. von Humboldt to his wife, Nov. 17-18, 1808.
Biedermann 1123

Germany is nothing, but every individual German is much; yet they fancy the reverse of this to be true. Like the Jews, the Germans must be transplanted and scattered all over the world, in order to develop fully and for the benefit of all nations their great native endowment.

von Müller, Dec. 14, 1808. *Biedermann* 1134

It has always been the way of the German to know better than the craftsman, to be wiser than the specialist of a lifetime. *Riemer,* Dec. 12, 1811. *Biedermann* 1485

The Germans have a sort of Sunday poetry that dresses up perfectly humdrum figures with language somewhat better than the ordinary; it is a case of clothes making the man, as it were. *Riemer,* Dec. 21, 1811. *Biedermann* 1452

The Germans have the peculiarity of being unable to receive anything as it is offered. If you offer them the handle of the knife they object to its not being sharp; if you offer them the point they will cry injury. They have read such an infinite amount, yet for new forms they lack receptivity. Only after they have begun to feel intimate with a thing do they show discernment and good and truly amiable qualities.   *To von Woltmann*, Feb. 5, 1813

I envy you your knowledge of all the works of Mme. de Staël. Those portions that I have seen have given me much pleasure. It is very instructive for once to see one's nation presented from a foreign point of view with fairness and good will. The Germans among themselves are as a rule sufficiently carping, and foreigners too are not always inclined to do them justice. It rounds out the picture to see a woman of intelligence respecting us to such a degree as to take such pains with us and on our behalf.
To Graefin O'Donnell, July 24, 1813

Taste is a euphemism. Germans have no taste because they lack euphemism and are too heavy-handed. No language can be euphemistic or develop in that direction except one used for diplomacy.
Riemer, Oct. 26, 1813. *Biedermann* 1514

Do not believe that I am indifferent to the great ideas, liberty, people, country. No, these ideas are in us; they are a part of our being, and no one can cast them aside. Also I have a warm regard for Germany. I have often felt acute pain at the thought of the German people who are so worthy individually and so wretched taken as a whole. Comparing the German people with other nations always stirs up embarrassing feelings that I try to get over in every way possible. In the arts and sciences I have found the wings that can lift one above the plane of wretchedness; for arts and sciences belong to the world and transcend the limits of nationality. But the comfort that these afford is rather cold comfort and does not take the place of the proud feeling of belonging to a great, strong, respected, and feared nation. In the same way only the thought of Germany's future affords consolation. I cling to this faith as firmly as you. The destiny of the Germans, to use Napoleon's words, has not yet been fulfilled. If they had had no other mission than that of breaking up the Roman Empire and of creating a new world order, they would have perished long ago. But since they have survived, and with such vigor and positive energy, it is my faith that a great future must be in store for them. Their destiny must be as much greater than the enormous task of destroying the Roman Empire and shaping the Middle Ages as their development now exceeds what it was then. However, no human eye can sight the time and the opportunity and no human effort can accelerate it or bring it to fruition. For us as individuals—each according to his talents, his inclination, and his position—nothing remains but to further the spiritual development of the people, to consolidate it, to make it pervade the whole body politic down to the bottom and, particularly, up to the top so that our people may not lag behind others at least in this respect, but rather lead them. The spirit must not be stunted; it must remain vigorous and serene in order that the nation may not become dispirited and fainthearted and in order that it may preserve its capacity for whatever great deeds are in store when the day of glory dawns.   *Luden*, Dec. 13, 1813. *Biedermann* 1529

Such a union, including even religion, could easily be achieved—through miracle, to be sure—if it were to please God some night to bestow upon all members of the German nation the gift of appreciating each other the next morning according to their deserts. Since this is not to be expected I have given up all hope, and I fear that they will misjudge, despise, hinder, delay, persecute, and damage each other, after as before.

This fault of the Germans, to stand in each other's way, if it is to be called a fault—this peculiarity stands all the less chance of being overcome because it is rooted in a distinction that is peculiar to the nation and one that it is justly entitled to boast of. In no other nation perhaps are there so many outstanding individuals born and existing side by side. But each man of mark has trouble enough developing himself, and each such member of a younger generation has his development modified by the times in a way to produce a cleavage between himself and the members of middle and older age groups. This, taken together with the fact that the German will acknowledge nothing positive and that he is constantly undergoing metamorphosis (without ever reaching the stage of the butterfly)—this gives rise to such motley varieties of *Bildung* (I would not call them stages) that the most thorough etymologist and the most faithful historian could not trace the origin and course of a development that is in an eternal state of self-contradiction. A German is apt to find himself abandoned by disciples before he grows old, and no crop of kindred spirits follows after. Everyone who is conscious of his energy makes a new start—and who is there without the right to feel so? Thus, through circumstances of age, through rivalry of faculties, through provincialism, through fluctuating interests, each is prevented at every moment from knowing his predecessors, his successors, even his neighbors.

To Buchholz, Feb. 14, 1814

I know my dear Germans all right. First they are silent; then they find fault; then they remove you from circula-

tion; then they filch from you and keep mum about it.
Riemer, Aug. 29, 1816. *Biedermann* 1749

We treat the Dutch as fellow-nationals too. For the patriotic German is so crazy that while insisting on his own complete self-sufficiency he straightway appropriates the merits of all nations and maintains that all nations derive from him, or at any rate are side shoots from his parent stem. An amusing child of Adam!

To Meyer, Jena, April 24, 1817

What God says in the Koran is true: We have sent no prophet to any people except in its own tongue. And thus it is only through Luther that the Germans have become a people.

To Blumenthal, May 28, 1819

The German is really not accustomed to bestow honor on the living or to receive it during his lifetime. There is a certain praiseworthy reticence that he finds difficult to overcome, and we shall not blame him for it.

To von Preen, Oct. 7, 1819

It happens to be the destined lot of the German to emerge as the representative of all the citizens of the world.

To Büchler, June 14, 1820

What the French call *tournure* is arrogance toned down to charm. From this it is evident that the Germans can have no *tournure*. Their arrogance is hard and harsh; their charm is mild and humble. The one excludes the other and they defy combining.

Maxims and Reflections 160 (1821)

The Germans are not interested in remaining together; yet they are interested in keeping aloof from other nationals. Each of them, no matter who he be, has an aloofness all his own that he would hate to be deprived of.

Maxims and Reflections 169 (1823)

In general, philosophical speculation works to the detriment of the Germans. It often imparts an abstract, intangible, verbose, and fussily analytical flavor to their style. The more closely they have become involved with certain philosophical schools, the poorer the quality of their writing. The best writing is done by those Germans who as men of affairs or men of the world are concerned only with practical matters.

Eckermann, April 14, 1824. *Biedermann* 2248

One should wish to see every well-meaning German endowed with a certain portion of poetic talent. This would afford him the true means of draping his condition, whatever it be, with a certain measure of worth and charm.

Maxims and Reflections 288 (1826)

I need only look out of the window in our dear Weimar to see how things stand with us. When there was snow not long ago and my neighbors' children wanted to try their little sleds on the street, at once a policeman appeared, and I saw the poor things take to their heels at top speed. Now when the spring sun lures them out of their houses and they would like to play games with their companions out in front, I always see them embarrassed and ill at ease, as if they were afraid of the approach of some representative of law and order. No boy may crack his whip or sing or shout without the police appearing at once with an order to stop. Everything with us tends to tame youth at an early age, to drive all nature, originality, and all wild impulses out of them, so that in the end nothing is left but the Philistine.

Eckermann, March 12, 1828. *Biedermann* 2579

285

What is it that makes Germany great, if not its admirable folk culture which has pervaded all parts of the realm equally? But is it not the seats of the princes that disseminate, support, and cultivate it? Supposing we had had in Germany for centuries only the two capitals Vienna and Berlin, or only one of them. I should like to see what would be the status of German *Kultur* in that case and of that universal prosperity that goes hand in hand with it.

Eckermann, Oct. 23, 1828. *Biedermann* 2635

The Germans, and not they alone, have a gift for making the sciences inaccessible.

Maxims and Reflections 589 (1829)

There is no greater danger confronting the German than forcing his development in an effort to keep in step with his neighbors. Perhaps no other nation shows so great a natural aptitude for developing from within its own self. It was a circumstance of greatest good fortune, on this account, that the German nation was taken note of at so late a moment of history by the world at large.

Maxims and Reflections 764 (1829)

A German man of letters—a German martyr.

Eckermann, March 10, 1830. *Biedermann* 2797

What a fuss the Germans have made to repudiate that which I may be said to have done and achieved, and are they not doing so still? If they had acknowledged it all and gone beyond me; if they had gone to work compounding my gains, they would be further along than they are.

Maxims and Reflections 872 (posthumous)

Nothing gave pleasure to the Germans of olden times except the fact that no one had to obey anyone's orders.

Maxims and Reflections 974 (posthumous)

Justice: Native endowment and fantastic obsession of the Germans.   *Maxims and Reflections* 975 (posthumous)

A versatile *Bildung* plus an integrated character stamp the true German.
    Maxims and Reflections 976 (posthumous)

The German behaved absurdly even while there still was hope. Now that he was conquered he was quite unfit to live with.   *Maxims and Reflections* 1331 (posthumous)

The Germans know how to point out error, not to mend it.   *Maxims and Reflections* 1408 (posthumous)

THE ENGLISH

Say what you will, the English have known from of old how to appreciate what is good, and they have a lordly way of putting it in circulation.
    Italian Journey. Padua, Sept. 27, 1786. 26, 63

The free Englishman has to watch his step very closely in writing about moral questions.
    Italian Journey. Rome, Sept. 14, 1787. 27, 109

The English are perhaps particularly qualified to impress nationals of other countries as superior. Their personal calm, self-assurance, and energy, their pride in their own ways, the sense of ease and comfort they radiate, present an almost unattainable model of what all people would wish for themselves.
    On Theory of Color. Historical Division. Part Six.
    Anglomania (1810); 40, 278

French pride can be made amenable because it is

linked with vanity. Not so English haughtiness because, mercantile in essence, it rests on the dignity of gold.

To von Knebel, March 9, 1814

We learn of everything that happens in the world, and the how and why of it. Englishmen report it to us with the greatest tranquillity, because they know that the world belongs to them. *To Meyer,* Oct. 28, 1817

All Englishmen as such lack the power of real reflection. Distractions and partisanship prevent any steady development. But in the practical sphere they are great.

Eckermann, Feb. 24, 1825. *Biedermann* 2310

Making tea is a sort of function, a make-believe activity, especially in England. And there the women sit about at their ease, and display their white skin and their tall beauty. And it is surely not for us to importune them about it. *von Müller,* May 1, 1826. *Biedermann* 2400

Walter Scott's admission that the Englishman will not take a step unless he has an *English* object in view is alone worth many volumes. *To Zelter,* Feb. 20, 1828

It is not a matter of birth and of wealth; it is rather a matter of their [the English] having the courage to be that which nature has made them. Nothing in them is twisted and bent, nothing half finished or out of keeping. Regardless of how they happen to be, they are of a piece. Of a piece as men, and as fools at times, I readily admit; but in any case it is something, and always registers a certain weight in the scale of nature.

The good fortune of personal liberty, the consciousness of the English name and the weight it carries among other nations, make their benefits felt even in childhood. Both in the home and in educational institutions they are treated with far greater consideration and enjoy a far more free and happy development than is the case among us Germans.

Eckermann, March 12, 1828 *Biedermann* 2579

But while the Germans labor over the solution of philosophical problems, the English with their great practical intelligence laugh at us and win the world. Everyone knows their declamations against the slave trade, and while they make a great show basing these on humane principles we now discover—what we should have known in the first place—that the true motive is a practical consideration, without which the English are well known never to raise a finger.

Eckermann, Sept. 1, 1829. *Biedermann* 2731

THE FRENCH

The French are pedants, that is to say they cannot break through the shell of form.

Riemer, March 20, 1807. *Biedermann* 972

The Frenchman never acts from a spontaneous impulse, for the sake of the thing as such. He always attaches to it a quirk of ulterior design, to gain some end at court, with the Emperor, with the public, with women, and so forth.

Women taken as a class are French. What Frenchmen are among men, women are among the human race. In this sense one may term the French the women of Europe.

Riemer, July 20, 1809. *Biedermann* 1192

The Frenchman, just as he translates foreign words into his own idiom, proceeds in the same way with feelings, thoughts, even objects. For every foreign fruit he consistently demands a substitute that has grown on his own soil.   *Divan. Notes. Translations* (1819); 5, 304

The French have brains and *Geist* [wit] but no substance and no reverence. That which is of use to them at the moment and benefits their party is what they seize upon. That is why they praise us only when our views can be made to lend weight to their party.

Eckermann, Nov. 24, 1824. *Biedermann* 2299

The French are in a curious position with regard to German literature. Theirs is quite literally the case of the clever fox who cannot get at the contents of the long-necked vessel. With the best will they do not know what to make of our things. They treat all our artistic products as so much raw material, waiting for their hand to shape it.   *To Zelter*, April 11, 1825

The French may someday make a great contribution to philosophy. Once they have mastered this field, their eminent gift of lucid presentation must lead to incalculable results.

Varnhagen von Ense, July 8, 1825. *Biederman* 2346

It is really remarkable what a perspective the Frenchman has attained since he stopped being narrow and exclusive. How well he knows his Germans, his Englishmen, better than these nations know themselves. How precisely he depicts the latter as self-seeking men of the world, the former as good-natured provincials.

To von Reinhard, June 18, 1829

The French *esprit* approaches what we Germans call *Witz*. Our *Geist* the French would perhaps render by *esprit* and *âme*. Our *Geist* involves the idea of productivity. This does not hold for the French *esprit*.

Eckermann, March 21, 1831. *Biedermann* 2941

The French always remain a curious and remarkable lot. But the Germans must be under no delusion about ever doing anything thoroughly to their satisfaction. Whatever it be, they have to dress it in their peculiar way before they can assimilate it. Their deplorable respect for calculation limits them in all things artistic, aesthetic, literary, philosophical, historical, moral, and religious, as if all these matters could be reduced to mathematical terms. They are quite unaware of the fact that this holds them fettered in a most wretched way. In all other matters, where they let themselves go and apply their gifts spontaneously, they are most charming and unique and one cannot take one's eyes off them.

Diary, June 7, 1831

THE FRENCH LANGUAGE

How can one feel hostile toward a language, Wilhelm exclaimed, to which one owes the greatest part of one's *Bildung* and to which we shall have to owe a great deal more before the contours of our national character can become defined.

It is not a prejudice, Aurelia replied. An unhappy experience has spoiled my pleasure in this beautiful and cultivated language as a hateful reminder of my faithless lover. How I now hate it with all my heart! As long as we were close to one another he used to write in German, and how it came from the heart, and what a genuine vigorous German it was! But now when he wanted to be rid of me he began to write in French as he had occasionally done before only in fun. I sensed, I noticed what it meant to convey. What he blushed to say in his mother tongue, he could now set down with a good conscience. For reservations, ambiguities, and lies it is a first-rate language. It is a perfidious language. I find no German word, thank God, to render "perfidious" in its full extent. Our poor word "faithless" is an innocent child by comparison. "Perfidious" is faithless with a relish, with exultation and *Schadenfreude* [delight in the ill-fortune of others]. Oh, the development of a nation is to be envied that knows how to express such fine shadings in a single word! French is quite properly the language of the world, worthy to be the universal language, so that they can lie and deceive each other to their hearts' content.

Wilhelm Meister's Apprenticeship V, 16 (1795); 18, 75

The French language is quite the appropriate medium to express the specious film of appearance.

To Schiller, March 14, 1798

[A reading of Racine's *Phèdre* by Madame de Staël.] It became clear once more that the German has probably turned his back for good on this confined form, this calculated and tumid declamation. As for the pretty kernel of sentiment hidden under all this verbiage, he would do without it rather than good-naturedly husk it out of all its many gradually contrived layers of artificiality.

Biographical Jottings for the year 1804. 30, 399

Through the introduction of misunderstood ancient doctrines and through precise conventions the French have circumscribed their poetry to such a degree that in the end it must cease to exist altogether, since it can no longer even be resolved into prose.

Value Terms of French Criticism (1817); 37, 99

THE JEWS

The Jewish people . . .
Even to this day, having lost all its ancient virtues while

retaining all its former faults, it exhibits a definite character and a decided talent.

Outline for a Popular History (1808).
W. A. Werke, 40 (II), 422

The impression I received in my native town as a small child was rather frightening. The figures of the dark and narrow ghetto were outside the ken of my experience and they exerted a strange fascination upon my imagination. I just could not understand how this people had brought forth the most remarkable book in the world. What I felt in the way of active aversion to the Jews in my younger days was rather a sense of embarrassment in the presence of the mysterious and unaesthetic. The contempt which I felt at times was largely a reflection of the attitude of the Christian men and women of my environment. Only later, as I came to know many highly gifted and sensitive men of this race, did a sense of esteem begin to mingle with the admiration which I feel for the people who created the Bible and for the poet who sang the *Song of Songs*.

A. Frankl, June, 1811. *Biedermann* 1415

Old Testament themes in modern treatment evoke a peculiar response. I reflected on this apropos of Robert's *Jephtha* and Alfieri's *Saul*. It is not antipathy that is aroused, but rather a lack of response; not aversion, but rather disinclination. Those myths, of true grandeur, present a respectable aspect at a sober distance, and the devoutness of our youth remains attached to them. As soon, however, as these heroes enter the present it occurs to us that they are Jews, and we feel a contrast between ancestors and descendants that confuses and irritates.

To Zelter, May 19, 1812

Parodies of classical plays were an abomination to him. At Wurm's attempt to expose the Jews to ridicule on the stage he flew into a rage, saying: It is shameful thus to pillory a nation that contributes so outstandingly to the arts and sciences. As long as I am directing the theater, such plays must not be given.

Source unknown. Biedermann 1776

Not altogether out of place here may be the observation that the value of every religion can only be calculated from its results after a lapse of centuries. The Jewish religion will always give currency to a certain rigid obstinacy coupled, however, with unfettered alertness and vital activity.

Divan. Notes. Mahmud of Gasna (1819); 5, 175

The Israelite people has never amounted to much, as it was told a thousand times to its face by its leaders, judges, overseers, and prophets. It possesses few virtues and most of the faults of other peoples. However, in independence, firmness, courage, and—when all this no longer avails—in tenacity it has no equal. In ability to survive it exceeds all other peoples on earth. It is, it was, it shall be, in order to glorify the name of Jehovah through all the ages.

Wilhelm Meister's Journeyings II, 2 (1829); 19, 186

Energy the basis of everything. Immediate ends. No one, not even the paltriest, most insignificant Jew who is not marked by a determined drive, a drive focused on earthly, temporal, momentary ends.

The speech of the Jew has a declamatory emotional flavor. *Maxims and Reflections* 1330 (posthumous)

WAR AND PEACE

Our modern wars make many miserable while they last and nobody happy when they are over.

Italian Journey. Rome, Sept. 6, 1787. 27, 108

I am a child of peace and am resolved to keep the peace for ever and ever, with the whole world, inasmuch as I have concluded it at last with my own self.

Italian Journey. Castel Gandolfo, Oct. 12, 1787. 27, 133

Thus our daily living was a constant seesaw between order and disorder, between efforts to destroy and to preserve, between forced exaction and payment, and perhaps it is this primarily that makes war so demoralizing for the heart. You play now the role of the reckless destroyer, now that of the gentle friend of life. You get into the habit of mouthing phrases in order to fan and encourage hope in the midst of most desperate conditions. And this leads to a kind of hypocrisy that has a character all of its own quite distinct from that of priests, courtiers, and all the other brands of hypocrisy.

Campaign in France. Sept. 3, 1792. 28, 34

Having returned to our quarters, we encountered a high-ranking émigré of our acquaintance. . . . He expatiated on the cruelty to which the King of Prussia was subjecting the French princes. Astonished, startled by this, we asked for an explanation. So we were told that in setting out from Glorieux the King had put on no coat, no cover, despite the most terrible downpour—and what was there for our royal princes to do but to follow suit? Our marquis had been moved to the greatest commiseration at the sight of these persons of the very highest rank, lightly dressed, wet through and through, dripping with moisture. In fact, he would have given his life, had it availed, to see them proceed in a dry carriage—these princes, the hope of the whole fatherland and so unaccustomed to this mode of life!

We had no answer to make, for he would have derived no comfort from the reflection that war, as a form of death before the fact, makes all persons equal, commandeers all private property, and threatens even the highest personage with privations and danger.

Campaign in France. Sept. 11, 1792. 28, 39

War is in truth a disease in which the juices of the body that serve health and preservation are used to nourish an intruder at odds with the organism.

Riemer, Dec. 13, 1806. *Biedermann* 927

You gentlemen are warriors or you occupy an even higher place in public life, and the world takes shape according to the results of your deeds. But as for me, when I wake up in the morning and see the sun through the steaming vapors as I walk to the top of my lovely Schlossberg, from which I have just come, and when I think that in this blessed quiet valley it is now only the hearts of the children that continue to beat tranquilly, whereas the orderly growth of centuries and the quiet of all the other inhabitants are already imperiled and disturbed—then I wish I could instill into the colossus of our age [Napoleon], in order to incline his thoughts to peace, even the one-hundredth part of the sentiments that I feel every morning for the dwellers of this paradise.

Freiherr von Hess, May 27, 1813. *Biedermann* 1503

To heal the many wounds of the fatherland and to make new life spring from the ruin wrought, there is no more effective way for the Germans than to practice mutual esteem and recognition—not just tacitly here and there but lovingly and confidentially expressed and uttered. For, in truth, the mutual distrust and impatience of our people; the points of friction which so many have made it their business to raise and to sharpen (because that is easy), with only a few to urge the cause of moderation and fairness (because that is difficult); the engendered conflicts between personalities and points of view that could well exist side by side; and whatever else might be enumerated in this sad litany—all this has done more damage than the foreign influx, for it has destroyed mutual faith and dissolved familiar ties of affection.

If the present great epoch can attune the German spirits to a sense of mutual esteem, the nation will scarcely need a further stimulus to extricate itself from the present and face the future with confidence.

To Caroline von Woltmann, Nov., 1813

NAPOLEON

Extraordinary men, like Napoleon, transcend the pale of morality. In the end they behave like physical causes, like fire and water.

Riemer, Feb. 3, 1807. *Biedermann* 957

Napoleon had the greatest intelligence that the world has ever seen.

S. Boisserée, Aug. 8, 1815. *Biedermann* 1690

We touched upon Napoleon and I expressed my regret that I never got to see him. Right, said Goethe, there was something worth opening your eyes to. This Compendium of the World!

Eckermann, Feb. 16, 1816. *Biedermann* 2391

Napoleon, though he moved entirely in the realm of the idea, yet lacked the conscious grasp of this his essence. He pooh-poohs everything ideal emphatically and denies its validity, while he tries his best to give it reality. Such a perpetual contradiction, however, is too much for his clear and unswerving intelligence to support, and it is highly significant to see him comment on the matter, despite himself, as it were, archly and with a very personal touch.

Maxims and Reflections 263 (1825)

According to him the idea is a spiritual essence devoid of reality, yet leaving behind as it evaporates a *caput mortuum* [residue], to which reality cannot wholly be denied. If this appears to us a rigid and materialistic view, we find him expressing himself very differently when he discourses with faith and confidence to the circle of the faithful on the inevitable consequences of his life and activity. There he is ready to admit that life brings forth life, and that a thoroughgoing fertilization leaves its mark on all subsequent ages. He takes pleasure in confirming that he has given the movement of the world a new impulse, a new direction.

Maxims and Reflections 264 (1827)

His personality certainly was superior, but the main thing was that men were sure of attaining their aims under him. That is why they flocked to him, as they do to everyone who instills in them a similar assurance. . . . Napoleon knew human nature too well, and he knew how to make proper use of men's foibles.

Eckermann, April 6, 1829. *Biedermann* 2675

Is it not moving to see the arbiter of kings reduced in the end to wearing a turned uniform? And yet, considering that this was the end of a man who had trampled underfoot the lives and happiness of millions, the fate meted out to him appears very gentle. Even Nemesis, dwelling on the grandeur of the hero, cannot refrain from a touch of gallantry. Napoleon affords an instance of the danger of invading the realm of the absolute and sacrificing everything to the execution of an idea.

Eckermann, Feb. 10, 1830. *Biedermann* 2772

And you are quite right to hold on to your *concept* of Napoleon. To arrive at it has cost us too much for us to let go of it again at the bidding of noisy demagogues.

To Zelter, March 7, 1830

THE CONTEMPORARY SCENE

[Cannonade of Valmy.] From here and from today a new epoch of world history takes its start, and you can say that you were there to witness it.

Campaign in France. Sept. 19, 1792 (1822); 28, 60

Whoever can contrive to do so should escape from the present because with some of the events going on about us it is impossible to lead a merely passive existence without eventually going insane from worry, confusion, and bitterness.

To Meyer, July 21, 1813

For the sake of the world the northern Protestant states should remain closely allied against northeastern barbarians. Prussia and England above all should participate in this alliance.

Wagner, summer, 1824. *Biedermann* 2271

Young people are exposed to excitement much too early and then caught up in the whirl of time. Wealth and speed is what the world admires and everyone strives for. Railroads, fast mails, steamships, and all other facilities of communication are the aim of the civilized world. It wants to outdo itself, to force its development and thereby abide in mediocrity. And all this common endeavor leads, of course, to the result that a certain middle range of civilization comes to prevail everywhere. . . .

This is just the century for men of brains, men of quick

299

and practical disposition, men gifted with a range of adaptability that makes them feel superior to the multitude even if their talents stop short of the highest.

To Zelter, June 6, 1825

We moderns now do better to say with Napoleon: Politics is fate. Let us guard, however, against joining our latest writers in saying politics is poetry or that it is a fitting subject for the poet. . . .

The moment a poet tries to exert a political effect, he must yield himself to a party, and the moment he does this, he is lost as a poet. He must say farewell to his freedom of spirit, to his untrammeled view, and draw the cap of narrowness and blind hatred over his ears.

Eckermann, March, 1832. *Biedermann* 3051